The Essential Guide To

MOTORCYCLE TRAVEL

Tips, technology, advanced techniques

Dale Coyner

Whitehorse Press
Center Conway, New Hampshire

This book is dedicated to my love and my lifetime touring companion.
Sandy, this one's for you.

All illustrations are provided by the author unless otherwise noted:
Ayres Adventures 1, 7 TR, 9 BR, 13, 16 T, 20 BL, 25, 34 TL, 100 MR, 164; Andy Bajka 102 TR; Dan Bard 16 B, 17, 27, 37, 80 T, 95, 100 BL, 105, 138 T, 144, 150 B, 162, 163 TR, 176; Patricia Breed 161; Carl Coyner 99, 101 L; Nick Diaz 126 B; Francois Dumas 29, 94 BL; Jamie Edmonds 20 T, 26 TL, 79, 150 T, 163 BL, 166 L, 166 R; Etymotic Research 92; Tim Gales 140 R; Garmin 83 T; Doug Gilmer 7 BL, 18, 24 L, 24 R, 117 TR; Vicky Harding 138 B; Heli Modified 111; HelmetCamera.com 104; Jerry Hihn 141 BR, 141 TL; Mark Holt 116 BL; Jim Lehr 142 ML, 142 MR, 142 T; Mixit Products 89 BL; Jerry Molaver 42; Ed Morrison 6 MR, 89 TR, 129 BL; Motorola, Inc. 91 R, 98; Nikwax North America 49; Outlast Technologies 40 B; Bill Perry 139 B, 139 T; Allan Pratt 23, 32 BL, 34 BR, 157; David Propst 147; Roll a HOME 142 B, 143 L, 143 R; Susan Spittle, Shade Tree Graphics 137 TR; Total Control Advanced Riding Clinic 33 B; Whitehorse Press 6 T, 8 TL, 8 TR, 9 BL, 10 BL, 10 BR, 10 ML, 11, 12, 20 BR, 21 L, 33 T, 35, 36 R, 38 BL, 39, 40 T, 41, 41, 44, 45 L, 45 R, 46 L, 46 R, 47, 50 Inset, 50 M, 50 R, 51 L, 51 R, 52, 53, 54, 55 L, 55 R, 60 B, 61, 64, 65 R, 69, 70 B, 71 R, 72, 74 B, 75 R, 76 TL, 77 B, 79 BL, 80 MR, 81 B, 81 T, 87, 88 B, 90, 91 L, 96, 97, 102 BL, 110, 112, 113, 115, 116 MR, 118 R, 119 B, 121, 122 BR, 128 BL, 130 BL, 131 BL, 132, 133 TR, 134 R, 135 BL, 135 TR, 136, 145, 151, 155, 158 B, 160 BR, 167, 168; Dale Wilson 66 TL, 71 L, 73 B, 74 T, 76 MR, 153 BR, 153 TL

Front cover photo courtesy of David Hough and Ayres Adventures

Whitehorse Press books are also available at discounts in bulk quantity for sales and promotional use. For details about special sales or for a catalog of Whitehorse Press motorcycling books, write to the publisher:

Whitehorse Press
107 East Conway Road
Center Conway, New Hampshire 03813
Phone: 603-356-6556 or 800-531-1133
E-mail: CustomerService@WhitehorsePress.com
Internet: www.WhitehorsePress.com

ISBN-10: 1-884313-59-0
ISBN-13: 978-1-884313-59-2

7 6 5 4 3 2

Printed in China

Acknowledgements

What you draw from this book about motorcycle travel is based on many opinions, not just mine. This book contains the collective wisdom of dozens of riders gathered over many years and thousands of miles. Thank you for your insights.

I am particularly indebted to the LD Riders, an Internet-based consortium of long-distance motorcyclists. Members of this group ride tens of thousands of miles each year and many responded in great detail to my questions about their experiences with a particular piece of gear or how they would respond to a given situation.

Members from the LD list and my Appalachian Highways subscribers who contributed advice, pictures, feedback, and encouragement include Richard Antoine, Peter Bansen, Gary Batten, Michael Boge, Jackie Brunken, Louis Caplan, Paul Cassel, Catfish, Bob Collin, Bob Colvin, Erin Darling, Tony Delorenzo, Bob Durrstein, Ray Fagan, Harold Haldeman, Joseph T. Hammond, Mark "Onethumb" Johnson, Michael Jordan, Jonathan "smthng" Kalmes, Dennis Kesseler, John O'Keefe, Mary Luet, Waldo Meeks, Rick Moffett, Adam Molaver, Bob Naumann, Jim Nyffeler, Frank L. "Cranky Franky" Palmeri, Jim and Donna Phillips, Kevin Powers, Allan Pratt, Phil Tarman, Ben Timms, Mike Traynor, David Vaughan, George Wacaser, Timothy Weltz, Allen Wilson, and Joseph Zulaski.

When I was assembling pictures for this book, I wanted to get as many as possible from riders like you and me. The riders on this list, many from BMWSportTouring.com, were good enough to send me pictures from their adventures around the world. I regret we couldn't print them all, but I appreciate their submissions nonetheless. My thanks for pictures go to Gary Archer, Patricia Breed, Guy "Bamarider" Boutin, Alex Clanner, Carl Coyner, Joe Drummond, Francois "Navman" Dumas, Jamie Edmonds, Tim Gales, Doug Gilmer, Ken Gregg, Vicky Harding, Jerry Hihn, Mark Holt, John Jambor, Mike Jones, Jim Key, Jim Lehr, Barry Lockyer, Jerry Molaver, Ed Morrison, Bill Perry, John Papovich, Nat Papovich, David Propst, Roger Riley, Allen Short, Susan Spittle, and Iron Butt tech guru Dale "Warchild" Wilson.

A number of vendors responded to my request for specific pictures or product information. I would like to thank Ayres Adventures, Escapade Trailers, Roll A Home, Kennedy Technologies, Mixit Products, Mortons BMW, Powerlet Products, Sportbikecam, Helmetcamera, Larry Grodsky's Stayin' Safe Motorcycle Training, and Lee Parks' Total Control Advanced Riding Clinic for their help.

A final group of riders deserve special thanks for several reasons. Some took extra time to offer thoughtful advice and encouragement. Others have been faithful friends and riding companions for years. My thanks to Jeff Adams, Steve Anderson, Ron Ayres, Dan Bard, Jon Conti, Nick Diaz, Red Fehrle, Rich and Linda Holman, Dave Morton, David Paul, Allan Pratt, Jon Spittle, John Weinstein, and veteran camper and gypsy Jim Wilson.

Thank you, Dan and Judy Kennedy and everyone at Whitehorse Press. I am grateful for the opportunity you gave me and appreciate your help putting this together.

Introduction 6

SECTION I: PLANNING YOUR TRIP 14

1 Three Questions 16

2 Rounding Out Your Plan 20

SECTION II   PREPARING YOURSELF 30

3 Mind Powers 32

4 The Right Stuff 38

SECTION III   OUTFITTING YOUR BIKE 56

5 Modification Techniques 60

6 Lighting and Conspicuity 70

7 Cockpit Instruments 80

8 Entertainment and Communication 88

9 Cameras and Camcorders 100

10 Ride in Comfort 106

11 Underpinnings 116

12 Storage Solutions 126

13 Trailer Life 138

SECTION IV   ON THE ROAD 148

14 Putting It All Together 150

15 Managing Contingencies 158

1

2

3

4

5

6

7

8

9

10

11

12

13

14

15

Introduction

"You're going to do what? Are you nuts?" If you haven't heard those questions yet, you will sometime during your motorcycling career. To everyone else, the thought of hopping on a bike and riding for days on end, through foul weather, dodging traffic, encountering who knows what—why, that sounds like crazy talk.

They don't know what we know. What fun is travel by any means other than a motorcycle? Trains were once the height of travel. Now, if your coach is better than a bus it's a novelty. Car travelers are too distracted by cell phones and DVD players to pay attention to what passes by outside their window. Air travel? Please. Here's what I remember from my most recent flight. "Take your shoes off, sir. And your belt. Step over here sir. I'm going to have to ask you to open . . . " Yeah, that's romantic.

Motorcycling and camping, both minimalist pursuits, were made to go together.

Riders are fortunate. Motorcycle technology has evolved dramatically and yet the essence of two-wheel travel remains unchanged. Toss some gear on the bike, throw your leg over the seat and hit the road. That's what I'm talking about. That's traveling.

What you may not realize is that traveling easily and confidently comes with experience. In fact, as I began outlining this book, I started thinking about my early motorcycle travels. What I *didn't* know about traveling by motorcycle could have filled a book.

TOURING SCHOOL

Fifty miles into my trip, four-fifty to go, I had just started my first long motorcycle trip with a friend when I realized I was in over my head. It was winter and we were heading south, but the temperature was dropping, not rising. We had optimistically planned to cover five hundred miles per day when the most I had ever ridden in a day was less than half that. So it was at about

Riders seem to have an inner sense that directs them to scenic vistas.

that fifty-mile mark that the cold air found an opening between my helmet and overstuffed rain suit. I shivered involuntarily, not from the cold, but because I knew that lessons to be learned lay ahead of me. Many lessons.

We made the trip down without incident but it was a real eye opener. My bike, a 600cc Yamaha Radian, was a fine little ride, but sure enough, at about 250 miles my butt ached like my first grade teacher had just whupped me (again). It didn't help that I was wrapped in six layers of clothes.

The trip back, from warm to cold was complicated by a large cold front sweeping across the mid-Atlantic. Weather radar blossomed with yellows, oranges and reds. We were about to enter a two-hundred-mile car wash and I'd never ridden in serious rain. Those storm clouds on the horizon contained yet more lessons. I just hoped the test wouldn't involve dropped bikes or broken bones.

Sure enough, at Fayetteville, North Carolina, we met rain head-on. Heavy, soaking, cold rain. My rain suit proved adequate for a while, but it was so watertight, the effect was like sitting in a cold sauna. At Smithfield, I could feel the rain trickling in under my collar. By Rocky Mount, it was working down my back. Finally, at Roanoke Rapids, my underwear got wet. That was enough. We stopped, rented a truck, and hauled the bikes home.

Crossing the Andes at Mendoza pass. Now those are some Latin curves.

That ended my first motorcycle trip, but it turned out to be a good decision. It wasn't long after we departed Roanoke Rapids that the rain turned to ice, then to snow.

I learned many valuable lessons on that first tour. A few of the more memorable:

► Five hundred miles a day makes a small bike feel smaller.

► Air temperature doesn't necessarily rise as you ride south.

► It's good to have a Plan B prepared before you need it.

► "Waterproof" is a relative term.

► Wet underwear sucks.

Thankfully, the lessons I learned on that first long ride didn't discourage me from further travels. In fact, what we encountered made me hungry to try it again, but with better preparation. It wasn't long before I found better gear. I bought a larger bike for longer trips. Over the years I've continued to refine my approach to touring, I've learned what style works for me, and I've learned how to change my approach according to the type of ride I'm planning.

Motorcycle travel isn't exclusively about chasing curves. Sometimes it's about overcoming obstacles.

Listen to the experiences of other riders. You will move up the learning curve faster than trying to learn it all yourself.

You can also learn from the many riders who now document their tours on websites, whether they are weekend trips or epic journeys like Chris and Erin Ratay's record-setting ride.

I certainly haven't done this alone. In addition to my experience, this book encapsulates the wisdom of a large group of folks from the motorcycling community who took the time to review this text and contribute their best ideas. This book and the other resources I'll suggest, together with miles and miles of your own on-road practice, will help you develop a touring style that works well for you.

So the next time you explain to a friend that you're planning to take a cross-country motorcycle trip and you hear the familiar "Are you crazy?" you can honestly answer "Absolutely. Crazy like a fox."

ABOUT THIS BOOK

The book you're holding is a shortcut to touring success that I would love to have had when I got started. *The Essential Guide to Motorcycle Travel* is a compendium of information, tips, checklists, guidelines, evaluations, and opinions on motorcycle tour planning, preparation, gear, and trip management.

If you're new to motorcycling or returning after a long absence (welcome back!), this book will offer you the advice you need to avoid many of the problems I faced when I first started out.

For example, when I first started traveling by motorcycle, I didn't know how far I could ride in a day and I didn't know how to plan a trip in segments to match my abilities. I would have been far more comfortable with riding apparel having less bulk and better warming capabilities. A range of simple accessories could have made touring more comfortable, but I didn't know about them.

If you have more than a few miles under your belt, I hope to offer *you* something, too. Motorcycle touring technology has advanced on many fronts, making it easier than ever to find great roads by design rather than by accident, uncover new things to see and do, and travel in added comfort, style, and security. We'll cover the things you need to know to make better buying decisions, the best methods for adding them to your bike, and how to make practical use of these accessories in your travels.

The Essential Guide to Motorcycle Travel is divided into four sections that correspond with the same general steps you'd follow in putting together a tour: Planning Your Trip, Preparing Yourself, Outfitting Your Bike, and On the Road. Here's an overview of what you'll find in each section.

Section I: Planning Your Trip

The idea of motorcycle travel seems simple at first–strap some clothes onto your bike, jump on and start riding. Sure, that's one way to go at it, but motorcycle travel is broader than that. Touring can include solo riding or group riding. Spur-of-the-moment road trips or highly planned and precisely executed tours. Themed rides such as "Four Corners" or "Three Flags." A dash around the state or an odyssey around the world.

The purpose of the first section, Planning Your Trip, is to help you lay a foundation for your tour by thinking through the main components of a tour.

Chapter 1 leads off with a discussion about the three questions you'll ask yourself about every tour: Where to? How far? How much? You'll be encouraged to set touring goals and you'll learn how to put together a basic plan and budget.

In Chapter 2 we'll lay out a route using a combination of tools—maps, trip planning software, and the Internet—and we'll consider elements that may influence your plan such as highway selection, camping or motelling, or deciding whether to ride solo or with friends.

Proper riding gear is essential to safe touring.

Section II: Preparing Yourself

Someone took a picture of me and my buddy Dave before we headed off on our first motorcycle adventure. I was wearing a half-dozen layers of clothes, covered with an oversized blue and white rain suit that made me look strikingly like Bibendum, the Michelin tire man. The caption would have read, "Man Without a Clue." Read the section Preparing Yourself to avoid a similar fate.

Chapter 3 begins with matters of the mind and body that will improve your touring comfort and safety, including a discussion about mental preparation and how physical conditioning increases your endurance.

Clothing technology has advanced rapidly over the last few years with innovative fabrics and gear that have extended riding comfort from a few months to year-round. Chapter 4 covers each layer; what materials work best to keep you dry, at a comfortable temperature, and well-protected.

Will you ride alone or with friends? Riding to the ends of the earth with friends is a story you'll enjoy retelling for the rest of your lives.

Auxiliary lighting makes it easier to see at night. It also makes you more conspicuous to car drivers.

You'll always know where you are on the map with a GPS.

Luggage designed specifically for motorcycles will keep your gear secure and dry.

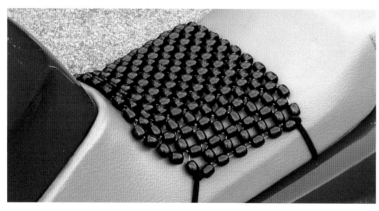

Comfort accessories help you enjoy longer days in the saddle.

Electrical problems are the most common source of trouble on the road. Chapter 5 tells you how to avoid these troubles.

Section III: Outfitting Your Bike

I'm an advocate for touring on any bike that runs reliably, but whether you're riding a modestly-equipped standard bike or a decked-out full dresser, chances are there's something you can do to enhance your bike's touring capabilities.

In Section III, we'll focus on just those things—enhancements you can make to your ride that will improve your touring range, comfort, safety, and enjoyment.

Chapter 5 discusses the right way to add accessories to your bike: mounting systems that eliminate the "press and pray" system of attaching devices, estimating power loads, and properly wiring devices so they'll work when you need them and won't compromise your bike's electrical system.

Normally in matters of touring "less is more," but not when it comes to lighting. Chapter 6 covers enhancements from a simple bulb change to add-on systems that improve your ability to see at night and in less favorable driving conditions such as fog. We'll look at reflective materials that can be added to increase your conspicuity, as well as headlight and tail light modulators and high intensity brake lights.

Chapters 7, 8, and 9 focus on electronic devices. Just a few years ago riders had to choose from only a handful devices, and those usually had some type of improvised mounting. Miniaturization, new technologies, and improved mounting have opened up a whole new world of possibilities for gadgets you can add to your bike.

We'll discuss GPS in depth, including what features are most important for motorcycle use. We'll cover many communication and entertainment options with a focus on how to integrate them on your bike. We'll also talk about cameras and recorders, emphasizing how to mount them for best results.

It's possible that the most important modifications you can make to your bike for extended travel are described in Chapter 10, Ride in Comfort. A great deal of attention is given there to the business end of touring: your butt. We'll also cover other mods like windscreens, highway pegs, and heated grips and seats.

What do you really need to bring when you travel? We'll discuss the essential items that every rider should carry.

Carrying heavy loads by riding two-up with luggage or pulling a trailer will likely require different choices in tires and suspension. We'll talk about that in Chapter 11, Underpinnings.

You shouldn't feel the need to take everything with you when you tour by bike, but for the things you do need to take, you'll need somewhere to put them, secured and dry. In Chapter 12, Storage Solutions, we will review methods and equipment for putting everything on the bike.

You don't need a 1000cc+ bike to tour, not even in the famed Iron Butt Rally.

While we're on the topic of storage solutions, we'll cover what you should know about purchasing a trailer for your bike in Chapter 13. Properly installed, a trailer will add enjoyment to your touring. Poorly installed, a trailer can kill you. We'll help you do it right.

Section IV: On the Road

Going back to my first touring experiences I realize the greatest lessons I learned in those early days related to knowing what to expect and how to handle situations on the road. For that reason, the section On the Road will cover many things you'll want to keep in mind during the planning stages and on your tour.

Chapter 14, Putting It All Together, is organized by timeline. In that chapter we'll detail what you need to do and how far in advance you need to do it to fully prepare for your tour.

Chapter 15 concludes the book with thoughts about how to handle matters that arise during your tour: weather conditions, security, night riding, emergencies, and more. And just before we conclude, I'll share with you two ideas I believe are the key to a great touring experience.

GENERAL WISDOM

As you can tell from this Introduction, motorcycle touring is a broad subject. For that reason, there are a few topics we can't cover and a few assumptions we'll make.

We'll assume that you already own a motorcycle or know what you want to buy. You can take a motorcycle trip on any bike, and unless your bike is a beater, the best one to travel on is the one you have right now. If I still had my old Yamaha Radian, nothing would stop me from hopping on it tomorrow for a nice long trip—250 miles at a time.

Some of the techniques we discuss will involve modifications to your motorcycle, particularly its electrical system. We'll describe techniques that are generally non-invasive, but it is still possible that modifications improperly made may affect your motorcycle's ability to operate properly or void your motorcycle warranty. It is imperative that you fully understand the implications of what you're planning to do.

Frequently I'll refer to a specific product that enjoys widespread use in the motorcycling community or that I believe is a good value relative to its features and price. Don't count on my opinion exclusively. Do your homework to make sure the product's features and performance will meet your needs before you buy something.

Motorcycle safety is an important topic. We will discuss some safety tips throughout the book as they relate specifically to touring, but our discussion won't cover fundamental riding strategies. For a more complete discussion on safety, pick up a copy of *Motorcycling Exellence* by the Motorcycle Safety Foundation.

Throughout this book, I use the terms "tour" and "trip" interchangeably. To some, the idea of a tour is a highly-structured, regimented ride from Point A to Point B with chase vehicles, sherpas, etc. That's not what this book is about. When I say "tour," I'm talking about you, and maybe your friends, riding for a weekend, a week, or a month or more. Your plan might be a fixed route or maybe you're just chasing the horizon. Whether you prefer to call it a tour or a trip, the important thing is you're out on the open road.

LAST THOUGHTS

Lying in bed at night, I go to sleep thinking about the trips I plan to take. I'll bet you do the same. I've had a lot of fun and have learned a lot putting together this book. I hope you have as much fun reading it. Even more, I hope you'll use this information to ride more.

Books like this benefit greatly from the availability of updates via the Internet. For that reason, please join me at my personal site (dalecoyner.com). You'll find my contact info there as well as new information, corrections, updates, and discussion about motorcycle travel.

Whether we catch up online or on the road, I look forward to meeting you. But first, let's start laying some plans for a great motorcycle tour!

Adventure is calling. Will you answer? These riders are visiting the Torres del Paine (Towers of Pain), a famous national landmark in Chile.

Section I:

PLANNING YOUR TRIP

Tour planning. Motorcycling is such a free-spirited pursuit of independent-minded people, do the words "tour" and "planning" even belong together? I think they do. Most of the time.

About the time I started writing this book, I was chatting with a fellow rider and as I explained the book idea, he got that grin on his face that told me he was thinking, "This guy is a truckload of crap." After another minute or so he broke me off in mid-sentence and said, "Man, spare me. I don't need a book to tell me how to ride. I just hop on and lay down some rubber!"

But wait! I wasn't finished explaining yet!Motorcycling crosses so many lines, everyone has a different idea about what motorcycling means. When I asked a few riders about planning, one would answer "Yes, I plan everything in advance in detail." Another would say "If I had to 'plan' a tour, I'd rather be at work." Different riders, different rides.

I'm sure you've heard that old business cliché, "You can have it good, fast or cheap; pick any two." Motorcycle touring is like that,

too. When riding, you are balancing forces like acceleration, momentum, gravity, and friction to produce a pleasant and safe outcome. The same thing happens with trip planning. You're juggling time, money, weather, abilities, interests, and more to accomplish a specific riding goal and have an enjoyable time of it.

Personally, I like the idea of planning because it gives me an excuse to ponder the possibilities. I see myself riding the roads I'm browsing on paper or tracing on the computer. Beyond that, it gives me a chance to identify things along the way that sound interesting. I have the opportunity to prepare the bike, myself, and my gear so I'll be equipped to manage the conditions I'll encounter on the road.

Maybe I like planning because I love looking at maps, but I find that tour planning lets me spend more time enjoying what's best about motorcycling—riding enjoyable roads, visiting interesting places, and meeting new people.

1 Three Questions **16**
Where To?. 16
How Long? 17
How Much? 18
Summary 19

2 Rounding Out Your Plan **20**
Route Mapping 20
What's Your Preference? 22
Time of Year 23
Camping 24
Moteling 25
Solo or Group Ride?. 26
Touring with Passengers. 27
International Touring 27
Visit the Neighbors 28
Guided Tours. 28
Resources 28
Summary 29

Three Questions

Planning is at the heart of motorcycle touring, whether you plan a little for a weekend jaunt or extensively for an around-the-world trek.

As we talk more about planning, I'll take you through an example to show you how a little extra thought can add a lot to a trip without overdoing it. I believe even skeptics will see the value in this approach.

The process starts by finding answers to the three primary questions that define any tour: Where to? How long? How much?

WHERE TO?

Where are you itching to ride? Without even trying hard, you could make a list of a dozen regions or roads you'd like to visit right now. Some are routes you're familiar with that you'd like to visit again. Others are bolder visions, journeys that you know will require bigger thinking, more planning and larger budgets. Whatever they are, take a few minutes to write some of them down right here. Yeah, go ahead. Write in the book!

I'd really like to ride . . .

1. _____

2. _____

3. _____

4. _____

5. _____

Just like having a set of life goals, it's a great idea to create a list of personal riding goals. I've ridden a fair share of miles, but I still have a long list of items remaining on my Riding To Do list. I revisit that list every six months or so, revising it as I complete some rides and think of others. I rarely subtract anything. Here's a sample of what's on my list right now.

Short Term

▶ Re-ride Skyline Drive and the Blue Ridge Parkway from start to finish

▶ Do an Ironbutt Saddlesore 1000 run to New Orleans with riding buddy

▶ Ride the Natchez Trace

▶ Motorcycle camping in West Virginia

Sometimes the destination is the reward.

Table 1.1 New Orleans Iron Butt Run – First Pass

DAY	ORIGIN	DESTINATION	MILES	HOURS	NOTES
1	Herndon	New Orleans	1076	17	Saddlesore 1000 run via interstate
2	New Orleans	N/A	N/A	N/A	Layover in New Orleans Eat way through French Quarter
3	New Orleans	Nashville	542	14	Via I-55 and Natchez Trace Parkway
4	Nashville	Herndon	667	12.5	Via I-40, I-81 and I-66

Long Term

▶ Follow Appalachian mountain range from Alabama to Gaspé Peninsula

▶ Ride the Black Hills region of South Dakota

▶ Touch the "Four Corners" of the United States

▶ Ride the Alps

I divided my list into short term and long term to separate the rides I could do on short notice from those that require more planning.

Did you finish your list? Check it once in a while and you'll be surprised how many of your riding goals you've met. You may also find that your list has gotten longer instead of shorter. It's strangely comforting to know that for every journey you undertake, you'll get ideas for a dozen more along the way.

HOW LONG?

Next question, will the trip fit your allotted time budget and personal riding range? After you get the idea for a journey, I'll bet the first thing you do is start the math in your head to figure out if your idea is feasible. If you're like me, you'll do this whether you are serious about the tour or not. It's fun to play the "What If?" game. In any case, this step in planning sets the pace for the entire tour, so consider the answer to this question carefully.

As an example, let's look at the New Orleans Ironbutt run from my short term goal list. The plan, as my neighbor and I discussed, was to ride to New Orleans in less than twenty four hours, thus earning an Iron Butt Association Saddlesore 1000 ride certificate. Here's a rough itinerary:

A riding group reviews the day's agenda before heading out.

Mapping this out revealed some interesting points (see Table 1.1). At first glance, it appears that the trip we have in mind is do-able, but this specific plan could use some improvement. Riding the Natchez Trace would be scenic, but at a distance of 542 miles and an estimated riding time of fourteen hours, the first return day looks like a long haul. Day number two looks like an unappealing blast up truck-choked I-40 and I-81. Those roads are included in the first day of our run to qualify for the Saddlesore, so it would be nice to avoid them on the return trip if possible.

Canada is a spectacular touring destination for Americans and riders from around the world.

Another study of the map reveals that we could pick up the Natchez Trace Parkway near Jackson, Mississippi. A good part of our first return day would be spent riding from New Orleans to Jackson before getting on the Parkway. What would the trip look like if we left New Orleans on Day 2 and rode just a couple of hours to overnight near Jackson, and then added one more day to the return trip? (See Table 1.2)

This plan isn't perfect, but it's better than the first cut. By adding just one extra day we can spend a lot less time on the interstate and reduce the length of our daily runs to a more manageable mileage. (In Chapter 3, Mind Powers, we'll talk more about what "manageable mileage" means by talking about your personal riding range.)

HOW MUCH?

Sooner or later, any trip must deal with the matter of money. Still, I prefer to answer this question last because I figure that when I plan out a trip that I really want to ride, I'm going to find a way to afford it.

With that, let's discuss finances briefly in two segments: first, pre-trip purchases, then travel budgeting.

Motorcycling is either an inexpensive way of traveling or an easy way to make a small fortune out of a large one. If you were to buy every accessory discussed in this book, you would likely spend more for extras than you paid for your bike. And you haven't even traveled a mile yet! How do you decide what comes first?

Custom seats and show chrome are not prerequisites for touring. Strictly speaking, you don't need headlight modulators, GPS navigation systems, or electrically heated clothing for touring either (though we'll discuss why these are worth considering). You must have a good helmet, abrasion resistant outerwear, gloves, and sturdy boots. Any other add-on you might consider is a bonus. When you are budgeting for things you need to purchase for touring, high quality protective gear is your top priority.

Budgeting for your expenses on the road is easy. Table 1.3 represents a simple worksheet I created to help me estimate expenses for longer trips. This sheet projects per-mile and total costs for a trip based on whether I'm riding solo or two-up, and how many miles I plan to cover.

Let's take the New Orleans trip as an example: five days and four nights, sharing a room.

Table 1.2 New Orleans Iron Butt Run – Second Pass

DAY	ORIGIN	DESTINATION	MILES	HOURS	NOTES
1	Herndon	New Orleans	1076	17	Saddlesore 1000 run via interstate
2	New Orleans	Jackson	185	3	Visit New Orleans, departing at 6 p.m. for Jackson via I-10
3	Jackson	Nashville	357	10	Natchez Trace Parkway to Nashville
4	Nashville	Blowing Rock	449	11	Via I-40, Cherohala Skyway, US 221
5	Blowing Rock	Herndon	395	11	Via Blue Ridge Parkway to Roanoke, then I-81, I-66

Freshly prepared home-cooked meals can be just as quick and nearly as inexpensive as fast food.

What a person plans to spend on food, lodging and extras (gifts, park admissions, Elvis sheet sets, etc.) is highly variable from one rider to the next, but this worksheet sample will give you a good framework in which to make your own estimate.

After figuring the total cost of gas, food and lodging, I add approximately one-third more and distribute that amount over the length of the trip. This represents "extras" for maintenance and small purchases like souvenirs, batteries, film, etc.

SUMMARY

Trip planning offers you a way to sketch out your riding ideas before you hit the road. Planning is beneficial in helping you make sure the trip you plan is within your riding comfort zone. This means you'll come back from your trip hungry for more rather than exhausted and ready for a vacation. You'll also have the opportunity to examine your expenses to make sure you're staying within your budget. Ultimately, the extent of your planning is a personal choice.

Now that we've talked about some general trip planning concepts, let's dig a little deeper into the planning process and cover a few additional topics that will round out your touring plan.

Table 1.3 Budgeting Worksheet
New Orleans Trip Expenses

Travelers	2 (on two bikes)	
Gas mileage	40 mpg	
Gas price	$4.00 per gallon	
Est. total trip	2500 miles	
Duration	5 days, 4 nights	
Miles per day	500	
Gas	2500 miles / 40 mpg = 62.5 gallons	$250
Food	5 days @ $30 per day	$150
Lodging (budget motel)	4 nights @ $49 per night for 2 people	$98
Extras	5 days @ $30 per day	$150
TOTAL COST		$648
AVERAGE COST PER MILE		$0.26

Rounding Out Your Plan

The plan we laid out in Chapter 1 is a good template for a short trip, but there are things beyond time and money that will affect your plan. The list of considerations gets longer depending on the type of trip you're planning. Answering the questions raised by these options puts meat on the bones of your plan.

▶ What time of year do you plan to ride? Your choice will influence your route and what you pack.

▶ Will you ride alone, with a friend, or with several? Will you have a co-rider? Group dynamics have an important effect on your plans.

▶ How will you shelter and feed yourself? Will you camp exclusively along your route? Will you just pack a credit card and a toothbrush and "motel it" along the way? Some of both? What you decide will change your gear list significantly.

▶ Will you cross international boundaries on your tour? Touring countries outside the U.S. will require even more contingency planning.

Let's look at what it takes to create a well-rounded touring plan, starting with more detail on the planning process.

Got your paperwork ready? You never know when you may need it. This checkpoint is in the Kalahari Desert, Botswana.

Google is a powerful web-based search engine that makes tour planning fun.

ROUTE MAPPING

Route mapping is the first thing that I do whenever a trip idea occurs to me. With a few clicks, I quickly sketch a route to see if it fits my available time and budget. I've become comfortable with DeLorme's Street Atlas (delorme.com), but the approach I use works with most mapping software. For example, one of my dream trips is to ride the entire length of the Appalachians. If I were to map that route, here's how I'd do it.

Step 1: Map the start and end points. Using a paper map and a Google search, I can see that the Appalachian range runs from about Birmingham, Alabama to the Gaspé Peninsula in Quebec province. Those become the start and end points in my plan.

Step 2: Adjust routing preferences. Mapping programs like Street Atlas are pre-wired to suggest the fastest or shortest route between two points. For a motorcycle trip, you often care about neither. To help the mapping program make better choices, I'll adjust my routing preferences. A program setting allows me to avoid interstates and toll roads and favor primary and state highways.

Step 3: Insert manual waypoints to follow desired route. Routing preferences give the program some guidance, but routing software will still fall back to its "prime directive," calculating the shortest or fastest time between the start and end of a route. Waypoints, also referred to as "vias," will force the routing software to include these points in its calculations. I set waypoints liberally along scenic highways or specific places I want to visit on the trip.

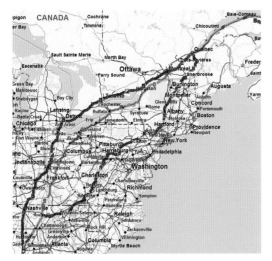

Using default route settings (red), the mapping software suggest a fast but unattractive route along major highways. Changing route settings yields better results (blue), but more tweaking is needed. Adding extra waypoints forces the map to choose more of the roads you want. The purple route looks pretty good.

Tracing the Appalachian mountain chain would make a great trip, taking you from Birmingham Alabama to the far reaches of Canada's Quebec province.

Step 4: Adjust trip planning settings. Trip planners predict gas stops and daily stopping points based on the route length and an average speed along the type of road you selected. I change these settings to reflect a moderate pace of about 350 miles per day. I like to explore things I find along the way and I like to shoot a lot of pictures. I can do that and cover around 350 miles comfortably. I'm not wedded to the daily stopping points the program suggests, but it does tell me what towns I'll be near at day's end.

Step 5: Sanity check and clean-up. I'm just about done with most of the route planning at this point. I'll go over the trip like I did in the previous chapter to make sure there are no surprises like back-to-back 700 mile days. Maybe I'll add a day or two of rest along the way or mark specific places where I know I want to stop. I'll continue to play around with the route as I think of new possibilities, but I now have a good idea where I'll be riding.

Not all Interstate is boring as demonstrated by this cut through Sideling Hill along I-68 in western Maryland.

WHAT'S YOUR PREFERENCE?

Interstates. Interstate highways allow you to cover the greatest distance in the shortest amount of time. Some interstate highways have a well-deserved reputation for high speed and volume, rough pavement, and uninspiring scenery. Other sections of the superslab are wide open smooth lanes through vast expanses of countryside. I've been on sections of I-25, I-55, I-68, I-70 and I-90 through pretty country and practically alone. These are worth considering for the initial push to get started on your trip or for the final days of a tour when you have the itch to get back home.

Mile-for-mile the best riding action will be on the old US federal highways.

US Highways. Once known as "federal highways," US highways are now state maintained. These highways offer the longest memorable stretches for motorcycle travel in the US. With the advent of the interstate system, long-distance traffic was taken off the US highways, opening them up for scenic travel. These highways are Main Street for most towns and cities across the country, so expect slow going in populated areas. Planning will help you avoid densely populated areas while enjoying the best of these varied and vital American byways. These are the foundation for good motorcycle trips.

State Primary Roads. State primary routes fill in where the federal routes leave off. These mostly rural roads often connect smaller population centers such as county seats. State primary routes are good for getting farther off the beaten path and for working around large population centers.

State secondary roads run the gamut of pavement condition but offer an intimate look at the heart of the country.

State Secondary Roads. Typically maintained by the county or parish they run through, state secondary roads are the true back roads of America. Conditions vary widely from well engineered, glass smooth, properly banked stretches of paved bliss to dirt roads. Don't hesitate to investigate an interesting secondary road, but don't use these as the primary basis for your tour unless you're specifically seeking out an adventure touring experience.

Forest Roads. There are 380,000 miles of Forest Service roads in the US, most built in the last fifty years for logging. Today their predominant use is recreational. While some Forest Service roads are passable by even the largest bikes, they are best suited for dual-purpose bikes.

Tour planning includes accounting for wild swings in weather conditions.

TIME OF YEAR

The time of the year you plan to travel will affect your route, daily mileage, the sites you plan to visit and what you need to pack, in other words, every aspect of your tour.

For example, northerly routes may have numerous high-elevation passes that are open only in limited times during the year. The famous Beartooth Pass out of Yellowstone doesn't open until the end of May and closes in mid-October. In summer months, the sweltering heat of the southern US won't prevent you from riding, but it does mean you need to pay extra attention to hydration and make sure you have a cooling system.

If your plans take you on routes with significant changes in elevation, you'll need to be equipped for both warm- and cold-weather riding. Once, on a mid-summer cross-country trip, I rolled into Las Vegas at midnight when the temperature was 98 degrees. A couple days later, I was passing areas where the snow hadn't melted and riders I met were wearing an extra layer.

As you formulate your route then, consider the range of temperatures you'll encounter. If you're covering a lot of territory, you will experience a wide swing in temperatures.

Doug Gilmer (left) and his son Greg enjoy quality father-son time on their motorcycle trips.

CAMPING

It's an appealing picture, riding into the sunset with nothing but a sleeping bag tied to the bike. At day's end, roll the bag out under the stars. Cook some beans and coffee over a campfire. Tell stories about ropin' dogies and dodgin' bullets . . . Wait a minute. That's cowboying. Well no doubt it's that association between horses and motorcycles that has created such a strong link between motorcycling and camping. All I know is that some of the best times I've had motorcycling have involved sitting around a campfire with other riders, telling stories about crazy drivers, stupid dogs, and great curves. Pavement, that is.

There are many tangible and intangible benefits to camping. If you enjoy motorcycling because you're riding in the great outdoors, sleeping in it seems to follow naturally. Camping is a viable way to stretch your travel budget. Within National Forests, camping is free outside of developed areas. Camping allows you to achieve a greater sense of escape than you'll feel when throwing your bags on the bed in your motel room.

Based on my experience, motorcycle camping is divided into two levels. Following the light camping philosophy, you camp only as a means of lodging, but forgo cooking, taking your meals in restaurants. You enjoy some of the greatest joys of camping—the camaraderie, the restfulness and beauty—without the extra time and preparation that cooking involves.

If you can't bear to miss cooking out, then you fall into the category of the complete camper, whereby you are a fully self-sustaining traveling unit on the road. If you plan to visit remote areas, you'll have to be self-sustaining anyway. Today's cooking gear is light and small enough that it won't occupy too much space. If equipped, you'll have the option to cook if you want, or not.

There are, I think, a few keys to successful motorcycle camping. First, you need a sense of adventure and a willingness to ignore minor inconveniences such as the occasional pit toilet or a day without a shower. Second, you need to equip yourself with the right gear, designed for advanced campers. Equipment found at RV stores and Wal-Mart's is designed for casual campers and will be bulkier and heavier than optimal bike camping gear should be. Third, you need to develop a systematic method of organizing, packing and deploying your gear and a willingness to experiment and refine your methods of campcraft.

While space doesn't permit me to go into greater detail about motorcycle camping, I do want to offer a few thoughts to help you explore this area of touring if you like. First, I would

Camping on the road is a popular way to stretch travel dollars.

encourage you to "just do it," as a famous Nike advertisement once encouraged. If you're totally new to the concept, why not pack up and camp out just a few miles down the road? Chances are there is a suitable camping location not far from where you live. Take notes on what you should have done differently, and if you forget something really critical, you're just a few miles from home.

Second, there are some great resources available for authoritative information on two-wheel camping. Bob Woofter's *Motorcycle Camping Made Easy* is the definitive book devoted exclusively to this topic. Finally, there's no more timely and complete resource for advice than motorcyclists who practice motorcycle camping on a regular basis, like the International Brotherhood of Motorcycle Campers (ibmc.org). Members of the IBMC organize campouts around the country every year and they welcome motorcycle campers of all skill levels. In just one weekend at an IBMC campout, you can elevate your camping knowledge and skills dramatically.

MOTELING

When I first started riding a motorcycle, I felt like I wasn't really touring unless I was also camping. That attitude began to change as I planned longer rides during the colder months, when I often encountered less than ideal weather conditions. As much as I like it, camping isn't always the most convenient or desirable choice. Moteling may not be the purist's choice for lodging, but the benefits of time saved, convenience, and comfort are enough to tip the scales when you're sticking to a tight time schedule, riding in consistently bad weather, or traveling with a co-rider who doesn't care for camping.

Are you the kind of moteler who figures you'll find something at the end of the day or the type of person who prefers to have everything nailed down in advance? I go back and forth on this question, and my approach hinges on whether I'm traveling alone or not. If I'm riding with someone else, I prefer to have accommodations arranged in advance. Yes, this does put a fixed destination on the end of the day, but I prefer that to thinking all day about where we'll find accommodations. If I'm by myself, no sweat. I'll

Tour companies like Ayres Adventures manage the logistics of foreign motorcycle tours so you can enjoy the ride. They arrange options you might not think about such as safari tent accommodations, enjoyed here by travelers Jeff and Ann Roberg.

ride till I get tired and then stop at the first acceptable place I find.

Small independent motels have developed an undeservedly bad reputation, largely because they're operated by folks who've migrated to the U.S. Here are the facts. A room in an independent motel is about one-third to one-half the price of a chain hotel. No one is offended if you ask to inspect the room first. You can often park the bike right at your door or up front where it will be watched. Accommodations are often minimal but adequate. You just need a clean, warm bed and hot shower. As a motorcyclist, you're familiar with undeservedly bad reputations, aren't you?

Wherever you end up, either pre-arranged or not, when you're staying in a large metro area, don't stop at the first place you come to on the edge of town. Ride through the urban area and position yourself on the other side of town. That means you'll be riding against the flow of traffic the following morning.

Meeting members of an online community is a great reason to go traveling, as members of the BMWSportTouring.com forum will attest.

SOLO OR GROUP RIDE?

Did you know motorcycling is like dating? It is when you think about who you'll ride with. As the length of a trip increases, so do the complexities of managing group dynamics. Everyone has different preferences, attitudes, and riding styles. Maybe you're an assertive rider. Maybe you are the epitome of the laid-back cruiser. Or maybe, like myself, you like to mix it up—casual riding along some stretches punctuated with spirited riding through an inviting set of curves. That's what makes motorcycling so interesting! Given our variations in temperament, experience, and riding preferences, the longer and farther you plan to ride, the more carefully you need to think about who you ride with.

Here's what I've come to think—and my conversations with other riders echo my thinking. Unless I've found myself in a pack of riders hell-bent on riding as fast as possible, I know I can enjoy a ride with anyone in any size group for a day. For a weekend, I look forward to riding with a smaller group of people, principally those who share my riding style. For a high-mileage endurance run or a long cross-country trip, that list would dwindle to a handful of names. Around the world? I would go it alone.

The advantages of riding solo are three-fold. First, you have complete freedom. It's easy for you to manage a comfortable timetable. You rise and leave when you want and stop for the day when you're ready. Just passed an interesting looking road? Turn around and check it out. You don't have to clear it with anyone.

Secondly, when you travel alone you're responsible for no one but yourself. When riding with a friend or in a group, what happens to the ride when someone breaks down? On a day ride, this is an easy contingency to manage but if you're half-way across the country, or in a different country for that matter, decisions become more difficult to make and have more significant ramifications.

Lastly, travelers say they find it easier to meet people when traveling alone. People are less intimidated by solo riders and are more willing to offer them assistance.

Riding in a group has its good points, too. Riding together means security. You'll always have someone ready to come to your aid should you find yourself in a jam not of your own making or if a mishap should occur. When camping, you can eliminate redundant gear like stoves and cooking supplies. Your buddy can carry a spare key to your bike and you can do the same for

You'll need to either prepare yourself to ride in the rain or bring a deck of cards for solitaire to wait it out. Properly equipped, you can handle rain with no problem.

them. Should you fall, someone is there to go for help immediately. If you're not the outgoing type, riding buddies are a source of companionship and comfort. Shared travel experiences create lifelong bonds.

Let's Stay Friends

It is possible to manage some of the issues of group travel and help ensure that everyone on the trip will have a good time and still be friends at the end of the trip. With adequate planning, good communication, and setting realistic expectations, you can have a great group ride.

Date before you marry. This is akin to the idea of a "shakedown run" when you're trying new gear. If you're considering riding together with a casual acquaintance, try a long day run or a weekend trip together first. Maybe you'll be compatible on the road, but it's better to identify conflicts on a three-day weekend than three days into a two-week cross-country trip.

Decide ahead of time what happens if contingencies arise. Four days into your ten-day trip, your riding partner falls off their bike and sustains a non-life threatening injury. Their trip is over, but what about yours? Discuss your expectations and theirs before you set off.

Occasionally during your trip, ride separately during the day and meet up at pre-appointed times. Even though you're riding with others, you don't have to stay within five seconds of each other for the entire trip. Arrange a meeting time and place for lunch or even dinner, then ride your own ride throughout the day.

TOURING WITH PASSENGERS

I have always enjoyed motorcycle trips more when my wife Sandy comes along for the ride, because I like sharing the experience with someone else. However, traveling with a co-rider requires the same kind of consideration as with a riding buddy. If your passenger is having a good time, you will too.

I have found that it's a good policy to see that my co-rider is at least as well equipped, if not better, than I am for the ride. If you're wearing electric heating gear, they should, too. Your co-rider should have the same or better quality protective gear.

Members of the "Between the Sheetz" gang have ridden together long enough to be very comfortable riding as a group.

Has it been a while since your co-rider has ridden with you? If that's the case, adjust your plan to start out with a reasonable daily mileage. They will need to build up their riding muscles just like you have. Give your co-rider some input into your agenda and let them name a few stops along the way. When they have something personal invested in the ride, they'll have a better time.

Riding with children is a touchy subject. Legally, kids can ride in most states when their feet touch the floorboards or footpegs of your bike. Realistically though, you wouldn't want to take a seven-year-old on a cross-country tour, even if they fit on the bike. Riding with children is a personal decision, but one of the best guidelines I've heard is that the child should be old enough to understand the consequences of their decision. An eight-year-old child will gladly hop on your bike with no reservations, just because you asked them to ride. An eleven- or twelve-year-old is better able to weigh the risks and rewards.

INTERNATIONAL TOURING

As beautiful and varied as the United States is, there's also spectacular riding to be had in other parts of the world. How about those crazy switchbacks in the Alps or the Andes? They're just begging you to come scrape your pegs. Do you hear whispers in the wind? Those are urgings of China's ancient Silk Road. How about the hemisphere-spanning Pan American High-

Paper maps are still the best way to explore large areas with a quick scan.

way and roads that lead to Tierra del Fuego and the Artic Circle?

International travel is enticing for more reasons than great roads and spectacular scenery. If you've ever thought there must be more to traveling than cookie-cutter motel rooms and blue-plate specials, plotting a journey through regions with different cultures and languages is in your future. Exhaustive resources exist for planning and executing tours that will take you around the world, but I would like to offer a few thoughts on strategies for getting started with international travel.

VISIT THE NEIGHBORS

Develop your foreign touring chops by exploring Canada and Mexico. Canada is an especially good choice for a first-time tour. Cultural and language differences are minimal (well, language anyway) and you don't need special paperwork for your bike. Road standards and signage are familiar and travel facilities are excellent. If you plan to tour Canada, you will want to do the following:

▶ Confirm that your health insurance is applicable to facilities in Canada, including medical evacuation.

▶ You don't need a special vehicle permit for Canada, but you will want to make sure your motorcycle insurance covers you.

▶ Does your road service cover you in Canada? A program like AMA's Mo-Tow

service does but you'll need to check with others.

▶ Get your passport if you don't already have one. Visit the State Department website (travel.state.gov) or visit your local post office for the necessary forms.

▶ While you are there read the State Department's Consular Information Sheet on Canada to familiarize yourself with differences you can expect. The section on traffic safety and road conditions is especially useful. It also contains a summary of requirements unique to motorcycles.

GUIDED TOURS

There are many approaches to world travel including those arrangements in which the traveler is surrounded by an entire contingent of guides, chase vehicles, etc. That type of traveling caravan is out of reach for many of us, but tour companies offer most of the benefits.

A good motorcycle touring company takes the guesswork out of travel to a foreign country without imposing an activity-filled agenda on you. Companies like Ayres Adventures (ayresadventures.com) prepare a bike for you to ride, arrange accommodations and meals between travel points, provide maps and guides, and offer emergency support services, but the pace and the exact route that you take from point A to B each day is up to you.

A guided tour sounds expensive until you compare the cost of the tour with what you would spend in time researching requirements, making arrangements, etc. Then add to that what it would cost if a mistake in paperwork delayed the arrival of your bike by two weeks (or two months). By taking a guided tour, you'll have the benefit of learning from the tour operator what it takes to travel on a foreign continent. Next time, you'll be in a better position to plan your own tour.

RESOURCES

If you think world touring is something you'd like to try or you just enjoy reading about it, let

Once you've tackled domestic riding, the world is at your doorstep.

me suggest a few resources for furthering your education.

Horizons Unlimited (horizonsunlimited.com) contains so much good information about world travel, it's a bit daunting at first. The advantage of this site, hosted by world motorcycle travelers Grant and Susan Johnson, is the free exchange of information between like-minded motorcyclists who plan to or are actively engaged in international travel on two wheels.

Riding The World by Dr. Gregory Frazier is an informative and entertaining book that outlines the author's experiences and approach to world touring. Greg Frazier is Mr. Been There Done That. In particular he discusses the pros and cons of specific bikes favored by adventure riders. He also presents common sense strategies for preparation, packing lists, how to choose routes, and the best ways to get your bike from one location to another when you're not riding it.

One of the best documented early round-the-world tours is recounted in *One Man Caravan* by Robert Fulton, Jr. The origin of his odyssey and the subsequent journey that unfolds is a two-wheel version of Jules Verne's *Around the World in 80 Days*.

After Canada, touring Mexico is a good next step for developing your own international travel skills. Recommended books from the Whitehorse Press Motorcycle Journeys series include *Motorcycle Journeys Through California and Baja* by Clement Salvadori and *Motorcycle Journeys Through Southern Mexico,* written by Neal Davis.

SUMMARY

Whether the trip you plan is for a long weekend or a month-long journey, just remember that the success of a motorcycle tour does not depend on whether your GPS is the latest model, your riding suit matches your bike, or you have electrically heated socks. Instead, a great trip depends on how well prepared you are before you head out in your travels. Thorough research and planning is the foundation of preparedness and, except for the cost of your time, it's nearly free. For what you will save later in aggravation and possibly real money, spend generously now.

Section II

PREPARING YOURSELF

In Chapter 1 I mentioned that the only absolute requirements for motorcycle touring were a well-maintained bike and a rider who is properly trained and equipped. You can determine whether a bike is fit for travel by fairly objective measurements and observations. But what exactly is a "properly trained and equipped rider?"

It means more than just having a motorcycle endorsement on your driving license. As we all learn sooner or later, extended motorcycle travel requires us to develop a frame of mind that is unique from casual cruising down the boulevard at the beach. Traveling long distances by motorcycle is serious business and we need to think about it that way.

The next two chapters will explore what it means to be fully prepared in all personal aspects of riding. We'll cover topics that will enhance your enjoyment of motorcycling and lessen your risk of injury as you do so.

3 Mind Powers **32**
   Mental Preparation 32
   Rider Training 33
   Your Personal Riding Range 34
   The Iron Butt Association Says 35
   Expanding Your Range 35
   The Other Half: Physical Preparation . . 36
   Summary 37

4 The Right Stuff **38**
   Layers of Gear. 39
   Base Layer 39
   Streetwear 41
   Electric Gear 43
   Cooling Gear 44
   Outerwear. 46
   Body Armor 53
   Rain Gear 53
   Summary 55

3

Mind Powers

MENTAL PREPARATION

Yogi Berra once famously said that baseball is ninety percent mental and the other half is physical. The same can be said about motorcycle touring.

Nearly everyone recognizes that motorcycle travel requires a great deal of physical preparation. But riding a motorcycle requires a heck of a lot more mental acuity than driving a car. You are exposed to a wider array of elements, which take a toll physically and mentally. Every corner you encounter requires an instant, sophisticated analysis of curve geometry, bike position, speed, lean angle, pavement condition, and a dozen other factors. You repeat this process over and over every single mile.

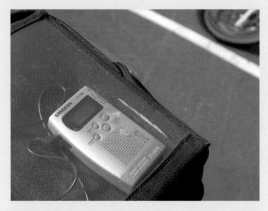

Simple accessories like a radio or MP3 player can help you fight mental fatigue on long days or monotonous stretches of road.

Each judgment you make about accelerating, turning, leaning, and braking has a potentially significant effect on your well being. When you've been riding many miles for several days and you feel like slowing down or stopping for a few days, that fatigue is as much mental as physical.

We can learn a lot about mental preparation from the long-distance riding community. These folks know about the mental aspects of riding. They are the Zen Masters. Where it might take you or me a week or more to make a cross-country trip, long-distance riders have conditioned themselves to ride coast to coast in as little forty-eight hours. Some airline flights seem longer than that. When you're riding a bike for thousands of miles at a clip, you have to become expert at managing your frame of mind. Here are a just a few nuggets of invaluable wisdom long-distance riders have contributed to our sport.

Know your limits and plan your trip around them. Of the many suggestions offered by members of the Iron Butt Association (ironbutt.com),

It's important to be fresh before you start a trip, not worn and frazzled attending to last-minute details. Allan Pratt looks well-rested, properly-attired, and ready to begin a new motorcycle adventure.

the first tip on their list is the same concept we discussed in detail in Chapter 1. Knowing your limits is the most important. If you adhere to this rule, you'll avoid having to deal with other issues.

Learn how to avoid boredom. Not every mile or every hundred miles will capture your imagination, so you'll need to develop some techniques to keep your brain engaged when it might otherwise drop into neutral. Accessories like a satellite radio or an MP3 player can help you avoid zoning out (We'll discuss these later in the section Outfitting Your Bike).

Know when to stop. You don't always need a fixed plan with designated layovers, but you do need to recognize when mental fatigue is setting in. As your attention level drops, your riding skills decline across the board. It's time to take a break and stretch, get a bite to eat, or if you're near the end of the day, find a place to hole up for the night.

Maintain a good mental attitude. You don't realize it, but all those little things you didn't deal with before you left will continue to bug you as you travel. You meant to send in your credit card payment before you left. Will your card work at the next ATM? You intended to replace your cell phone, it's been acting up. Will it work when you need it? You'll find yourself turning those nuisances over in your mind again and again and after a while, they contribute to mental fatigue. So as you prepare for your trip, refer to your "To Do" list and take care of those details before you hit the road.

Whether you plan to cover 250 or 1,250 miles in a day, properly managing your mental state will help you cover more miles.

RIDER TRAINING

Although this book doesn't focus on motorcycle safety issues, I do want to touch on rider training as it relates to being a "properly trained" rider. Research shows that riders who complete a basic riding skills course are involved in fewer accidents than those who don't. That should be enough to motivate you to take a basic riding course if you haven't already.

Once you've completed a basic course, you shouldn't stop there. Several riding schools in

▶ ENDURANCE RIDING

Endurance riding gives its participants a whole new perspective on motorcycle travel. After you've ridden 2,200 miles and crossed a dozen state lines in a weekend, those little four- and five-hundred-mile trips will seem shorter than your morning commute. It makes great water cooler conversation on Monday morning.

For a complete picture of long-distance riding, check out Ron Ayres' book *Going the Extra Mile*. It's a highly detailed examination of the techniques riders use to cover long stretches on a bike. While you're waiting for that to arrive, visit the Iron Butt website (ironbutt.com) to view their list of riding tips and the entertaining travel narratives that riders post as they attempt various endurance runs. For insightful opinions and nearly instant answers to your questions, visit the LD Riders mailing list. Instructions for joining can be found at micapeak.com/ mailinglistroundup. ■

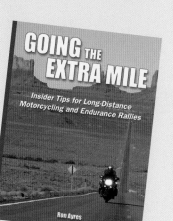

Lee Parks' Total Control riding program goes several steps beyond a basic riding course.

Desert riding requires attention to proper hydration as well as vigilance against unexpected obstacles that are difficult to spot.

the U.S. will help you improve your riding skills. At the high end are track schools run by Reg Pridmore (CLASS) and Keith Code. These schools focus on helping riders achieve their maximum performance. In recent years, a new category of skills classes has evolved that fills the gap between beginner riding courses and track schools. Lee Parks (leeparksdesign.com), a well-known racer and motojournalist, offers an advanced riding clinic, based on his book *Total Control*. Parks' clinic is offered on a closed range and focuses on three elements: braking, lean, and acceleration.

YOUR PERSONAL RIDING RANGE

Do you know how far you can comfortably ride in a day's time? Do you know what your outer limit is? Can you ride in variable weather conditions like cold, rain, or heat? Are you new to motorcycling or have you been riding for years? Do you ride a sport bike with a lean-forward seating position, a full dress touring bike, or a cruiser? What about your riding style? Are you a ten-tenths rider, always riding at or near the edge of your abilities, or do you ride at a relaxed pace, well within your limits? Which do you ride more often—solo or two-up?

These factors and others add or subtract from a value you might call your personal riding range. It's a distance that, on average, you can ride comfortably every day for a number of consecutive days. As a rider, it's an important number to know for planning, safety, and comfort.

Knowing your range and setting a realistic daily mileage for your trip means you won't repeat my early touring mistake, cramming too much mileage into too little time. As I mentioned in the introduction, my first serious trip covered 500 miles a day when my previous best was 250 miles. In fact, I was comfortable at only 200 miles per day. Riding more than double the mileage you're comfortable with or equipped for, several days in a row, is not fun. It isn't safe either.

So, how do you know what your riding range is? Determining your range comes with riding experience. Ask anyone who's ridden for a few years and they'll recite a number instantly.

If you're just starting out and you don't know, use 150 to 200 miles as a baseline for maximum daily mileage. If you're an old-timer and your first reaction to 200-mile days is "Pffff, I could ride that with no hands," then fine. Double it.

Bad weather conditions require an extra measure of concentration. Even if it isn't raining, the extra attention you must give to hazards will cause mental fatigue.

I'm still fresh at the end of 350 miles or more, but many of my routes end at less than 300 miles for a day's ride because I like to get off the bike and explore. After stopping to take pictures, a leisurely lunch, a park visit, and a conversation or two along the way, even 250 miles of riding adds up to a full day. If you're still developing your riding muscles, keeping your planned daily mileage to a modest number means you'll have some energy left to enjoy your time at the end of the day when you climb off the bike.

THE IRON BUTT ASSOCIATION SAYS

Folks at the Iron Butt Association have recognized a definite trend in daily mileage among long-distance riders. Take a look at Figure 3.1. A rider who covers long distances will generally ride their maximum mileage for only the first couple of days on the road. In days three through seven, their average daily mileage drops off significantly until they are averaging about 65% of the daily mileage they achieved in the first two days.

You can use the same graph to estimate how many miles you can ride consistently. For example, if your maximum daily mileage is 500 miles, your ten-day average and total mileage would look something like Table 3.2.

EXPANDING YOUR RANGE

As you grow in experience as a motorcyclist, there's a good chance you'll want to increase your personal riding range. Adding mileage to your range gives you more options when planning a trip. Adding just 50 miles a day to your average means that on the same ten-day tour, you could cover an extra 500 miles.

Or look at it this way. Adding to your range doesn't mean you have to ride those extra miles each day. Greater range adds a safety margin to your trip. Riding 300 miles when your comfort range is 400 miles means you'll be fully refreshed the next day.

Extra range is also useful for managing contingencies. Should you encounter adverse weather or unexpected repairs you can still complete your original tour by riding to the outside of your range for a couple of days to make up the miles.

When you're really tired, find a spot to drop and snooze. A twenty-minute nap will do wonders.

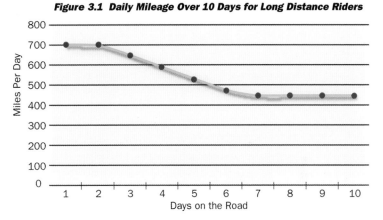

Figure 3.1 Daily Mileage Over 10 Days for Long Distance Riders

Table 3.2 Miles Each Day of a Long Trip

Day 1	500 miles
Day 2	500 miles
Day 3	460 miles
Day 4	420 miles
Day 5	380 miles
Day 6	340 miles
Day 7	300 miles
Day 8	300 miles
Day 9	300 miles
Day 10	300 miles
10 DAY TOTAL	**3800 MILES**

Here's a path that begs to be explored on foot. Varying your activity on the road will improve your stamina.

Maintaining a comfortable temperature with fleece will allow you to ride extra miles.

Many of the items and techniques we'll discuss later in this book are aimed at helping you cover more miles in safety and comfort. Some will yield larger gains than others. In my experience there are four elements that offer the biggest return on investment.

Better nutrition. We could stand to improve our diet and we often use travel as an excuse to enjoy larger meals than what we would fix at home. Lighter and more frequent meals will significantly improve your ability to cover miles as you deliver a steady, manageable stream of energy-boosting calories to your system.

Proper dress. You are stressing your body and increasing fatigue when you ride without proper gear. A riding suit protects you from wind and sunburn and decreases your rate of dehydration. Ear plugs have a major positive impact not only for preserving your hearing, but reducing the fatigue your brain develops from processing wind noise for long periods of time.

Temperature management. Basic gear like an electric vest for heat or a wet towel for cooling will help you manage temperature extremes with ease. Keeping your temperature in check will go a long way toward helping you stay alert and focused.

Improved seating. This doesn't necessarily mean a custom seat. I've found great comfort by wearing bicycle pants on both short and long rides. The extra padding in the crotch improves comfort and the Lycra material promotes breathability. Plus, I never feel like my pants are bunching up inside my riding suit because the slick material moves with me, not against me.

THE OTHER HALF: PHYSICAL PREPARATION

You hear enough about this already from your doctor, your spouse, and others, so I won't belabor the point. We don't get enough exercise. We could get into great shape by riding bicycles instead of motorcycles for all our two-thousand-mile trips, but then you'd be reading a book about bicycling instead of motorcycle touring, wouldn't you?

Frankly, our sport does not demand a high level of physical performance, but regular exercise will enhance your riding experience. If you've put in a long day in the saddle and you're out of shape, you're shot at the end of the day. If you've been riding in excessive heat or cold and you're out of shape, you'll also be ready to flop at the end of the day. Your body is better equipped to cope with the demands of the saddle when you exercise regularly.

Maybe the biggest motivator is that by keeping yourself in good shape through good nutrition and regular exercise, you can extend your riding career by a number of years. Anything that can reward you with more and healthier years in the saddle is worth considering.

Here's a thought. If you're part of a riding group, ask others in your circle if they'd like to put some miles on a treadmill with you sometime. There might be exercise buddies in your group just waiting for someone to ask.

SUMMARY

Proper mental preparation is one key to motorcycle touring. The longer you can focus on the task of riding, the safer you'll be, regardless of how far you ride.

Drilling on safe riding techniques is one way to get there. The more you practice your riding skills, the more likely you'll be able to anticipate and handle hazards before they become full blown emergencies.

Mental preparation also comes from knowing and planning around your limits. Again, with practice, it's possible to increase how far you can safely ride. You can use that extra range to travel farther or to make up for time lost due to problems encountered along the way. Physical preparation is inseparable from mental preparation. Good physical conditioning improves your ability to manage stress and fatigue, which helps you stay sharper, longer.

Sunny days, clear roads, and scenic byways are motorcycle touring bliss.

The Right Stuff

Riding gear is more than just a series of stylish layers to preserve your hide in a get-off; the right gear also helps you ride farther. It took me a while to make that connection, but experience brought it to my attention. Even in my early riding days, I recognized the safety benefits of protective gear so I bought a full riding suit. It didn't occur to me that I could ride longer because of it. Sometimes I would take a long ride with no gear; other times I wore the full suit. One day after a particularly long ride it dawned on me. It was already hot and humid in the early morning as I prepared to roll out of the driveway for a long head-clearing day ride. I debated whether to ride with the suit or not, but eventually decided to put it on. The first thing I noticed that day was how hot I felt when I stopped and took off the suit. I realized what protection the covering gave me from direct sunlight. Without it, standing still was like bathing under a heat lamp. With the suit on, that direct heat was baking the suit, not my skin. As the day wore on, the heat became even more intense. My energy level was dropping through the bottom of my shoes and I was becoming less focused on riding. I was well hydrated, but the air temperature had climbed past 100. I bought two bottles of water at my next break, drank one and, despite the odd looks from the clerk behind the counter, I poured the other over my head and into my suit. Then I soaked a towel in cold water and wrapped it around my neck and shoulders. Tucked into the riding suit, that brought me relief for the remainder of my ride.

No doubt, wearing that suit kept me cooler and more comfortable on the ride, but the biggest difference was how I felt the next day. For a day or two after riding "naked," I felt washed out. My skin was crackly with sun or wind burn and I was dehydrated. I was happy to be off the bike or a couple of days. By contrast, the next day after this ride in full coverage gear, I felt completely rested and ready to hop on the bike again.

That experience and subsequent ones have convinced me. It may look hot and stuffy, but a riding suit contributes noticeably to your ability to log miles. Anyone can cover a lot of miles in one day. The rider who suits up can do it day after day after day.

A fleece jacket adds considerable warmth with little bulk. Get one with a full zipper for greatest utility.

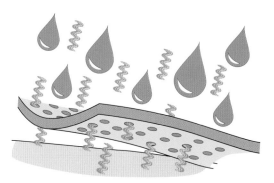 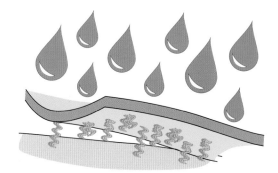

Breathable fabrics (left) are multi-layered. The middle layer typically consists of a thin, tough membrane that contains microscopic perforations. These perforations are small enough to allow water vapor from the skin to pass through, but too small to allow water drops to penetrate the fabric. Breathable fabrics aren't as completely waterproof as vapor barrier fabrics, but are close in performance and more comfortable to wear.

Vapor barrier fabrics, (right) like those used in rain gear, have a coated interior layer that prevents all moisture movement in either direction. Skin moisture is trapped inside the garment, which can make you feel clammy over time. These fabrics are fully waterproof and are a good choice if you frequently travel long distances in wet weather.39

LAYERS OF GEAR

We'll talk more about riding suits when we get to the discussion of outerwear, but suits are just the visible part of the riding gear picture. The complete touring ensemble includes multiple layers.

The *base layer*—underwear (T-shirt, briefs, socks) and head wear—is responsible for perspiration management and long-distance comfort.

Streetwear is your street clothing, which helps to regulate your temperature under normal riding conditions.

Thermal extenders help you ride comfortably under more extreme hot and cold conditions. This might include passive gear such as cooling vests and fleece jackets, or active gear like electric vests.

Outerwear is the protective layer that serves as your first line of defense against the elements and the pavement.

Footwear and *helmets* round out the full riding wardrobe. We'll work our way from the inside out, starting with the base layer.

BASE LAYER

While each layer of clothing plays a distinct role in helping you cover miles with ease, none does more for managing comfort than the layer closest to you. For example, how often have you ridden some distance and begun to notice an uncomfortable itching, burning sensation in the posterior region of your person? At the end of the day, your butt is so sore you can barely sit down. This condition, referred to as "monkey butt" or "saddle soreness" is caused by those cotton briefs and cotton denim jeans you're wearing.

Cotton is a versatile and comfortable fabric until you're seated on a motorcycle. Then it's a butt killer. Friction between your skin and underwear generates heat and moisture. Cotton absorbs moisture until it reaches a saturation point. With nowhere to go, the humidity in your pants rises to jungle levels. Soon, the heat, moisture and continuing friction produce skin irritation which creates this uncomfortable situation. Monkey butt can be eliminated with a few simple changes in the first layer of gear.

Briefs

Briefs made of stretchable polyester have several advantages over those made from cotton. For one, they're cooler in the summer and warmer in the winter. Polyester fibers don't absorb and hold water the way cotton does, so moisture is wicked away from the skin to the exterior of the garment, helping keep your skin dry and comfortable. Polyester is a slick fabric that reduces friction.

Here's another method for managing saddle soreness. Developed by veteran rider Andy Thomson of Buda, Texas, Anti Monkey Butt Powder (antimonkeybutt.com) has become a popular product for diminishing the effects of frictional skin irritation. His unique formulation is an improvement over regular baby powder. By adding calamine powder to traditional talcum-based powders, this formula absorbs perspiration and eliminates the itch associated with long rides in a hot saddle. This results in less friction, which in turn prevents skin irritation. No monkeys were injured during the testing of this product, Thomson claims. He tried out all the product formulations on himself. ■

Outlast is the brand name of a new class of temperature-regulating textiles which was originally developed to help astronauts maintain their body temperature in extreme environments. (Chalk up another one for the space program.) Outlast is unique because the fabric physically changes depending whether it needs to keep the wearer warm or cool. Outlast is embedded with millions of microcapsules tuned to manage the temperature at the surface of your skin. When you are active and generating heat, the microcapsules absorb and hold the heat. When you stop moving, the microcapsules release the stored heat back to your skin. This cycle can repeat itself over and over, meaning that you never feel too hot nor too cold. You always feel just right. ■

Polyester has another significant advantage: it dries quickly. Some products, like Tilley Endurables Quick Dry, guarantee their garments will dry overnight. Rinse your drawers in the sink, wring them out and hang them to dry and they're ready to go the next day. That means two pairs of underwear will last you for an entire trip, no matter how long you're riding.

Riding Shorts

There's a reason why you see so many bicyclists in skin-tight biking shorts. Worn as a substitute for underwear, riding shorts handily improve your riding comfort over any distance, even in hot weather. Riding shorts are made of a nylon/Lycra fabric designed to fit close to your skin. Just like polyester shorts, this material removes moisture from your skin. The close fit means this layer of clothing moves with your skin, not against it, again reducing friction. Riding shorts have flat seams that reduce chafing. Most shorts include a padded crotch area. A few riders advocate shorts that are unpadded, but that's just a personal preference. I like the extra padding.

In hot conditions, riding shorts are an acceptable outer layer of clothing when you're off the bike. As long as you're covered by a riding suit, you don't need anything more in the region below the belt unless you don't care for the form-fitting look. For an investment of $25 to $40, this is the best value in base layer purchases you can make that will boost your riding range.

Tees

In normal riding conditions (neither too hot nor too cold), there's nothing wrong with a cotton T-shirt as both a base layer and street layer. For long trips and more adverse conditions, you might want to think about tees made from a higher performance fabric.

Shirts made from Coolmax material are popular for shedding heat and perspiration effectively in high-temperature environments. Coolmax is polyester fabric using specially-engineered fibers with embedded channels and a weave that enhance the movement of moisture. Some fabrics have to be chemically treated to wick moisture; as a result, they tend to lose their effectiveness over time. Coolmax maintains its performance after repeated washings because its moisture-wicking and cooling properties are built-in rather than sprayed-on.

Shirts constructed of Outlast fabric outperform cotton in both hot and cool temperatures because Outlast is designed to manage moisture and temperature. Outlast is a new breed of fabric that uses "phase change" technology to regulate the wearer's body temperature. Shirts made from both Coolmax and Outlast are designed to fit close to the body while cotton tees are often worn with a loose fit.

Socks

Next to wet underwear, damp socks are close on the misery scale. Wet socks make your feet feel cold, clammy, and uncomfortable. They also promote bacterial growth which makes your boots ripen—and not in a good way.

Here again, skip cotton for best performance. Socks in synthetic and wool blends are designed to transport moisture more effectively, reducing skin irritation and the likelihood of blistering. Full synthetics are preferable for summer wear. Tilley's synthetic socks are designed to be treated just like their underwear. Wash in the sink and dry overnight for a fresh pair of socks every day.

Like synthetics, wool blends manage perspiration effectively, but in cooler riding conditions they are better able to retain heat. Look for socks that use Merino wool. This premium variety of wool is the softest and finest available. It has superior thermal retention properties and is very comfortable. Unlike lesser wool, products made from Merino wool don't itch.

STREETWEAR

Wouldn't it be great if we had perfect weather for every trip we took? It would make packing simpler. Since that won't happen, you need to be prepared for wild swings in weather conditions from cloudy, cold, and wet to sunny, hot, and humid. The layer of clothes you wear between the base layer and outwear, composed of your street clothes and thermal extenders, will help you manage these departures from perfect riding weather—dry weather, low humidity, 60 to 85 degrees Fahrenheit.

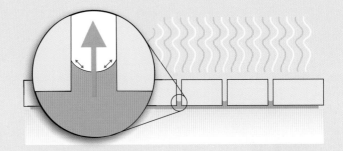

HOW WICKING WORKS

Wicking works by a principle called capillary action. Fibers destined to become fabric—cotton, wool, or synthetic—are spun into threads. These threads are bundled and then braided together. You can't see it, but there are microscopic spaces between the fibers which cause liquids to be drawn into them. A paper towel exhibits this action when you place it over a water spill.

Cotton fibers absorb and hold on to moisture in the same way as the paper towel. Synthetic fibers can't absorb the moisture, so water vapor is drawn along the threads of synthetic fabric to the exterior of the fabric where it evaporates. This evaporation process "pulls" moisture along the path from your skin to the exterior of the fabric. Some materials, like polyester, require a chemical treatment to create this effect.

Yet another method of wicking involves multi-layered fabrics that draw moisture from inside to outside by means of temperature differences. ■

Wrist warmers make a big contribution to cold weather riding comfort by sealing out chilly drafts that sneak up your sleeves.

With a neck warmer and head band, this rider doesn't seem bothered by chilly temperatures.

Beyond this narrow range of perfect conditions, you'll need something extra to keep your body warm or to cool it more aggressively. Thermal extenders like fleece jackets, turtlenecks, and cooling vests perform this function, making it possible to ride comfortably in a wider range of weather conditions.

Temperature management is something you think about every time you get on the bike. Should I wear the lined jeans or just my regular denim? Will I need that fleece jacket or not? Do I want to bother bringing along the electric jacket? Will it be hot enough to require the cooling vest?

Just remember this: if you get too warm, it's simple to shed a layer or soak your T-shirt with water to cool off. But if you're chilly and you've run out of things to put on, your options are limited. I have one fleece jacket that stays with the bike, so I always have one more layer than I think I'll need. I use it often.

Shirts and Jackets

What you wear in this category really is a matter of personal taste and convenience. When it's

warm, you can skip this layer altogether (as long as you're wearing a protective outer jacket). A T-shirt under your riding suit or jacket is just fine in warm weather. In cooler riding conditions, you might go straight to a fleece jacket first. When it gets cold, backfill with a shirt (I'm partial to flannel-lined shirts). If you like them, turtlenecks are a good choice in cold weather because they protect your neck area from chilly drafts. As all skiers know, if you keep your neck warm, you'll be a lot more comfortable. That's because the large blood vessels in your neck play an important part in managing your body's temperature. Keep this area insulated to slow heat transfer and you'll notice the difference.

Pants

Denim jeans are popular among riders as streetwear and for riding. Denim is comfortable but it has about as much abrasion resistance as wet toilet paper. If you plan to wear jeans, check out the suggestions in the section on Outerwear.

Besides lack of protection, there are a few other problems with jeans on motorcycles. If you're riding in warmer weather with a suit over jeans, you'll be uncomfortable as the temperature climbs. When it's really hot, you'll want to wear just riding shorts under your suit. Cotton jeans hold moisture close to your skin which leads to chafing. Jeans aren't waterproof, so if you see rain coming, you'll need to suit up. Finally, if you need to wash them, jeans are slow to dry so you'll have to find a coin laundry.

Synthetic pants sound like a throwback to the days of disco, but they serve a practical purpose on trips. Polyester pants work better under a suit and some have unique features like zippered legs that let you convert shorts to long pants when temperatures begin to drop in the evening. REI's Sahara pants and L.L. Bean's Timberledge convertible pants are both popular options. Ex Officio "Buzz Off" pants, also available from the REI catalog, are not only convertible, they're also treated to repel insects. The pants in this category are made from synthetic materials so they are light, pack small, don't wrinkle. They dry quickly enough that you can rinse them in the sink and have fresh pants after drying overnight.

Table 4.1 Gear by Degrees

TEMPERATURE	BASE	THERMAL EXTENDERS	OUTER	ANCILLARY
Below 30	Top and bottom long johns, riding shorts, wool socks	Electric jacket, fleece jacket, lined jeans	Full length riding suit, insulated winter weight gloves, full-face helmet, riding boots	Balaclava, neck scarf
30 to 50	Long john bottoms, riding shorts, long sleeve T-shirt, wool socks	Electric jacket, fleece jacket, regular jeans	Full length riding suit, insulated winter weight gloves, full-face helmet, riding boots	Balaclava up to about forty
50 to 70	Regular briefs, riding shorts, cotton tee, cotton socks	Fleece jacket, regular jeans.	Full length riding suit, regular "summer weight" gloves, full-face helmet, riding boots	None
70 to 90	Synthetic briefs, riding shorts, cotton tee, synthetic socks	Regular denim jeans. If shorts are desired, substitute convertible pants for jeans	Full length riding suit, regular "summer weight" gloves, open-face helmet, riding boots	None
Above 90	Synthetic briefs, riding shorts, Coolmax or Outlast tee, synthetic socks	None (riding shorts are my "street layer") or convertible pants.	Full length riding suit, regular "summer weight" gloves, open-face helmet, riding boots	Cooling vest or wet towel

ELECTRIC GEAR

I love my electric jacket and apparently a lot of my fellow riders do as well. As I was doing research for this book, I threw out the following question to a group of veteran riders: "What two or three touring accessories have you gotten the greatest value from over the years." While nearly everyone suggested one or two items that they alone considered valuable, nearly everyone who responded said "electric apparel." Why is electric gear so popular? If we have all these layers of space age fabrics, wind-proof suits, itch-free wools, and fuzzy fleece, who needs to be plugged in?

Layers of thermal clothes are great and they can extend your riding season, but you won't feel especially warm when riding unless you have a bunch of layers on. As a passive system, thermal clothing is designed only to retain the body heat you generate. Motorcycling doesn't require the same level of physical activity as, say, cross-country skiing, so you aren't generating as much heat to be retained. What you need in order to

▶ FABRIC CARE

High performance underwear and phase-change T-shirts are great gear that need to be cleaned properly to maintain best performance. With many advanced materials this means less work, not more. You don't always need to seek out a laundromat to clean your clothes, and sometimes you should specifically avoid it.

Some garments, like synthetic socks and underwear, are designed for ultimate convenience in travel. Rinse them in the sink and hang them to dry. They'll be ready to pack tomorrow. Cold water is just as effective as warm for cleaning and will help maintain special fabric treatments longer. Mild soap should be used on fabrics rather than detergents and you can use half the recommended amount and still get clothes clean.

When washing a large garment like a riding suit, I use a front-loading washing machine because it contains no agitator that may inadvertently twist and stretch fabrics. ■

▶ ELECTRIC CLOTHING: HOW IT WORKS

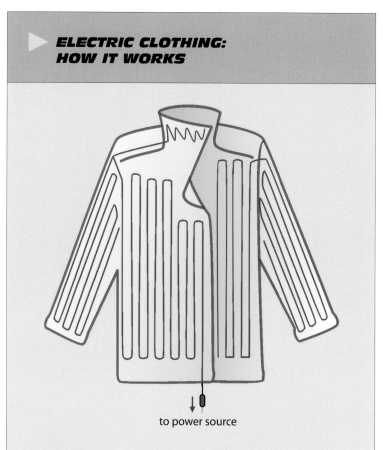

to power source

Electrically-heated clothing works on the same principle that dries your hair and toasts your bread: electrical resistance. The electric vest you put on is wired with long loops of nickel-chromium (nichrome) wire. This type of wire conducts electricity but presents resistance to the flow. As electrons in the flow work their way through the wire, the electrical power expended is given off as heat. Despite the fact that you're wrapped in an electrically-charged blanket, there is no danger of being electrocuted. There isn't enough voltage to harm you. An electric jacket consumes 70 to 80 watts of power, a figure that all but the smallest of bikes can handle. ■

feel warmth on a motorcycle at 60 mph is an active heat-generating system. That's what electric apparel is designed to provide.

You can buy entire suits of electric gear—jacket with sleeves, gloves, pants, and socks—the whole shebang (my wife loves that idea). But do you really need to buy the entire package? Probably not. If you just have trouble keeping your hands and feet warm, start first with an electric vest or jacket. Your fingers and toes function like

a thermometer that gives you a reading on your core body temperature. When your core temperature begins to drop, blood circulation to the outer limbs declines in order to keep warm blood near the vital organs. This decrease in flow to your hands and feet make them feel cold. An electric vest keeps your chest warm, which in turn allows increased circulation of warm blood to your fingers and toes. If the vest alone produces enough satisfying warmth, you won't need to deal with the increased bulk and complexity of the other components. Design of electric gear is pretty stable so if you find later you want to add more electric apparel, you'll be able to add components compatible with the system you buy today.

Electric vests and jackets should fit snugly to ensure the greatest degree of heat transfer. Underneath you can wear just a long sleeve T-shirt. Over top of the vest, a fleece jacket holds in the warmth generated by the vest.

Power consumption is an important factor you'll need to consider. Your bike likely produces enough power to handle a jacket and other accessories to boot. Still, it's good to know just what load you're adding to the system. In the section on outfitting your bike, we'll discuss the full implications of electrical power management.

There are three primary manufacturers of electric gear for motorcyclists. George Widder, a WWII bomber pilot, pioneered the development of the product based on his experience with electrically heated flight suits. He turned out the first motorcycle-specific gear in 1971. A few years later, Gordon Gerbing began producing heated clothing. Widder and Gerbing, along with Aerostich Manufacturing and Heat Troller are primary manufacturers of heated gear for riders today. Harley-Davidson's line of gear is manufactured by Gerbing.

COOLING GEAR

Let's consider the opposite case now. It's summertime in the South and you're riding in ninety-six degree heat and eighty-five percent humidity. When you pull over for a break, it's so hot and humid that sound you hear is the kudzu growing near the pullout. Better make sure it doesn't wrap around your bike. Is this any time to be out riding? At one time, I would have said "heck no." In

Wet down a cap like this on a hot day and it will suck the heat out of your body.

Caps

You've heard that over half your body's heat is lost through the head, so it stands to reason that the head is a good place to apply a cooling solution. The simple act of wetting down your hair will help you cool off fast. Doo-rags or skull caps provide the same cooling effect and will hold moisture longer, which means they'll cool longer. This is strictly a matter of personal preference, but I've also found that a "high and tight" haircut is comfortable in hot weather riding. A short cut, wetted down, generates about the same cooling effect as any other application.

Cooling Vests

When it is really hot and you want long-term cooling, a vest made of Hydroweave is the easiest cooling solution to handle on a bike. Hydroweave requires that you soak the material in water for a few minutes. The fabric absorbs and holds the liquid, then uses evaporative cooling to remove heat from your body as air flows over. It's sort of like wearing a swamp cooler around your chest. You can achieve the same effect by soaking your T-shirt in water, but the Hydroweave fabric will accomplish the same level of cooling without leaving you feeling drenched. It holds water longer, keeping you cool for longer runs.

fact, my wife and I once left on a superheated Friday afternoon for a weekend trip and came back and hour later totally exhausted. We didn't know a thing about staying cool on a bike. Since that time I've been introduced to a number of products that will make riding tolerable on hot days. When you get too hot, your reflexes and judgment decline. Staying cool will help you stay sharp and focused.

Wraps

One of the simplest ways to keep yourself cool is with a wrap soaked in water, draped around your neck and chest. Tucked under your partially-opened riding suit or mesh riding jacket, a wrap made from water-activated materials like Hydroweave or even a simple terrycloth towel make all the difference.

How does it work? As with heating, it's all about managing your body's core temperature and the temperature of your blood. As blood flows through the big vessels in your neck, heat is transferred through the skin. A cool wrap makes this process more effective, allowing heat to transfer out of the body faster. As the cooler blood circulates through your system, you'll begin to feel refreshed.

Cooling vests absorb and hold water. As the water evaporates it reduces your body's core temperature so you will stay sharp, even on the hottest days.

► LEATHER OR SYNTHETIC?

Listening to arguments about buying gear made from traditional leather or new-fangled synthetic materials will remind you of other classic discussions like "best motor oil" or "Japanese vs. American made" discussions. A lot of heat is generated, but not a lot of light.

A well-cut leather jacket is classically stylish. Made from high quality materials, leather offers good abrasion protection in an accident. Newer designs have incorporated mesh ventilation in areas not likely to contact the ground, to improve air flow in hot weather. However, you'll still need to carry a separate rain suit to cover up; leather is not waterproof and riding in wet leather is not fun.

Serious long-distance riders have shed leather in favor of synthetic materials. One and two-piece suits made from a combination of Cordura, Gore-Tex, Temperfoam, and similar materials provide superior abrasion resistance, are cooler, waterproof, windproof, better ventilated, contain many pockets, and are more visible than their leather counterparts. When it's hot, open a few zippers. When it gets chilly or begins to rain, zip them up. No need to get off the bike and don a separate rain suit. When they're dirty, throw them in the wash. ■

OUTERWEAR

The clothes we wear when riding have evolved greatly over the years. Nowhere is that change more evident than with the protective gear we wear. Compared to even twenty years ago, today's gear is lighter, more abrasion-resistant, faster-drying, more waterproof and windproof, with better protective padding, more reflective strips, and plenty of pockets.

Still, the number one job of protective gear is to be your first line of defense when something other than rubber meets the road. More than any other motorcycle equipment, good quality riding gear is your first purchasing priority. We'll start from the top and work our way down.

Half helmets or shorties are comfortable, ventilate well, and allow good peripheral vision. They offer no protection if you fall and take it on the chin.

Helmets

Whether you wear a helmet or not is a point we won't debate. Motorcyclists who take their well-being seriously wear good quality helmets. They don't ride without a lid and they don't wear plastic caps with fake DOT stickers. There are four types of helmets worth consideration: half-helmets, three-quarter, full-face, and flip-up.

Half-helmets

Half-helmets (shorties) are the style favored by motorcycle police because they do not compromise peripheral vision and are comfortable for long stretches at idle. I like the open, airy feel of a half-helmet but I only use one for riding around town in summer at low speeds. For any longer ride or touring at highway speeds, you'll want more protection, not only from possible accidents, but from weather conditions as well. A zippered flap is available on most models to provide more coverage in cold weather riding conditions, but when it gets cold enough to need that, you'll be ready to switch helmets anyway.

When you're wearing a half helmet or open-face helmet without a face shield you need additional eye protection. Those shades you're wearing are not shatterproof to the same degree as a face shield on a full-face helmet. Goggles are cool. They give you that hard-core old-school "motorcyclist" look.

Three-Quarter Helmets

Three-quarter helmets provide a little more protection around the back of your head compared to half-helmets. Like half-helmets, they do not protect your face or chin. Three-quarter helmets are popular with touring riders because they're easy to get on and off and are often accessorized with headsets and boom mics. Three-quarter helmets can be fitted with face shields for good eye protection. Their open nature however means that they won't protect you from cold weather. Three-quarter helmets give you the same unrestricted peripheral vision as half-helmets.

Full-Face Helmets

Structurally, full-face helmets offer you the best protection in a get-off, including scenarios where you "take it on the chin." Full-face lids provide excellent weather and eye protection. Interchangeable tinted face shields eliminate the need for sunglasses during daylight hours. At dusk, you can switch to the clear shield. Using cooling techniques we discussed earlier, a full-face helmet doesn't feel any hotter than the alternatives.

Flip-Up Helmets

A relative newcomer, flip-up helmets are hinged so the face shield and chinbar can be raised above the front of the helmet. A flip-up is a good choice if you want the easy on/off of a three-quarter helmet with the protection of a full-face. Flip-up helmets also have interchangeable,

Riders who wear flip-up helmets enjoy the convenience of an open face and most of the protection of a full-face helmet.

tinted face shields. Rally riders especially favor this type of helmet because they can flip up the front for eating and drinking at a stop, or conversing at filling stations or toll booths, then drop the helmet down and hit the road quickly. Riders who have switched to flip-up helmets rarely go back to another other type of helmet. They like them that much.

Ear protection

Savvy motorcycle travelers wear ear plugs to protect their hearing and reduce fatigue. Long-term exposure to wind noise caused by wind turbulence at highways speeds will lead to profound hearing loss. It seems counterintuitive but it's possible that wearing a helmet can contribute to this problem by generating more turbulence and thus, more noise. Wind turbulence has been measured in some cases to be as loud as 103 decibels. According to OSHA standards, hearing loss can occur after two hours exposure to noise at that level.

Even with a full-face helmet and the full fairing protection of a bike like the Gold Wing, earplugs reduce the fatigue you experience at the end of the riding day. Even though you may have tuned out the sound, your brain is still processing all that sound. That processing uses up mental capacity and will hasten the onset of mental fatigue, cutting your riding day shorter than it could be otherwise.

▶ WHAT'S ALL THIS GEAR GONNA COST?

Do you need to spend a ton of money to get a good set of the essential gear? Not really. What separates "good" gear from "premium" is usually a matter of style, a few extra features and often, brand name. Materials are about the same. ■

CATEGORY/DESCRIPTION	GOOD	PREMIUM	NAMES/NOTES
ESSENTIAL GEAR			
DOT/Snell approved full-face helmet	$250	$600	Arai, Bell, HJC, Nolan, Shoei
Abrasion resistant jacket and pants (synthetic or leather)	$300	$600	Aerostich, Firstgear, Fieldsheer, Joe Rocket, Road Gear, Tour Master
Summer-weight gloves	$40	$110	Jacket makers named above plus Lee Parks Designs
Riding boots	$80	$260	Jacket makers plus Alpinestars, Sidi
Ear plugs	$2	$200	Drug store foam plugs, Westone custom-fitted
Rain suit	$50	$150	Firstgear, Nelson Rigg, Tour Master
Total for essential gear	$572	$1,890	
REALLY-NICE-TO-HAVE GEAR			
Electrically-heated vest	$150	$200	Widder, Gerbing, Warm 'n Safe
Winter-weight gloves	$75	$180	See glove makers above
Full coverage, synthetic all-weather riding suit	$500	$800	Aerostich, Firstgear

Solutions range from simple foam plug-ins available at any drug store for a couple of bucks to custom-fitted earplugs that include high-fidelity in-ear speakers (also known as "monitors"). I've always felt like the foam plugs that attenuate 25 to 30 decibels do a fine job. If I lose them, it's no big deal. Some riders favor musicians' ear plugs which also attenuate noise to safer levels but do a better job of preserving sound fidelity. That's useful if you happen to have helmet speakers. The top-shelf solution is a pair of custom-fitted plugs that contain personal monitors like musicians use on stage. In some states, in-ear plugs are not legal.

Whatever solution you decide on, proper placement is the key. To get the best performance from foam plugs, roll them between your fingers until they're a fraction of their normal size. If you're putting in the right side plug, reach over your head with your left hand and pull your ear up a little bit. This makes it easier to insert the plug. You should be able to insert the plug nearly all the way in, then back it out just a bit before you let go. You'll know you've done it right when you hear the plug expanding in your ear while outside noises slowly die away.

What's great about earplugs is that even though they do reduce the amount of sound you can hear from outside, the reduction of ambient noise (specifically wind turbulence) makes it easier to hear your audio system, car horns and sirens than if you weren't wearing them.

The difference is startling, especially when you've been wearing plugs for a while, then take them out. You'll realize the benefit you're getting. When you get older, you might have false teeth, artificial knees, and Coke-bottle glasses, but you'll be able to hear a pin drop without any dang hearing aid.

Riding Suits

Drop into any motorcycle event where long-distance riders are known to gather and you'll find many of them wearing a full-length riding suit loaded with strategically-placed pockets, zippers and reflective strips. Discolored and faded suits, signs of long days in the saddle, are worn with great pride.

Textile riding suits are popular with moto travelers because they combine convenience and safety all rolled into a one-piece garment. Ease of use is a big factor. If a suit is easy to put on, you're more likely to wear it. Maybe Cordura doesn't match leather for abrasion resistance but it's close and it's a heck of a lot more resistant than your skin.

One popular suit is the Aerostich Roadcrafter suit made in the U.S.A. by Aero Design (aerostich.com). Whoever named it the "Swiss Army Knife" of riding gear was right. With its unique zipper design, you can don a Roadcrafter in just a few seconds and shed it just as quickly. It's fully lined with Gore-Tex which makes it windproof and largely waterproof. The 'Stich, as road veterans call it, also has extra thicknesses of heavy Cordura at likely impact spots and is reinforced in key areas with Temperfoam and plastic inserts for extra impact protection.

As good as the Roadcrafter is, it does have a couple of drawbacks. In hot weather, its one-piece design can be stifling. Vents under the arms and in the back provide some airflow, but not enough, particularly on a bike with a big fairing. Your options are to partially unzip the suit, possibly compromising protection, or adding a cooling vest or water-soaked towel.

The zipper design of the Aerostich may contribute to leaks in heavy rain. When water does find a passage through the suit, it's often at an unfortunate spot, the crotch. If you're on a bike with a large fairing, leaking is less likely because you are better protected. Maintaining water repellency of the outer shell minimizes this problem, too.

Some riders prefer the flexibility of a two-piece outfit, finding they like to switch jackets or pants from time-to-time, or just prefer to wear the jacket with a pair of jeans (made with reinforced denim, of course).

► MAINTAINING OPTIMAL WATERPROOFNESS

Textile riding jackets and pants containing a porous membrane material like Gore-Tex or ShelTex are waterproof, but they don't always feel that way. Waterproof garments rely on a two-phase approach to water repellency that diminishes over time. The good news is, it can be restored.

The outer layer of the garment is not waterproof, but is treated with a durable water repellent chemical (Scotchguard, ReviveX, etc.) that causes water to bead on the outer layer and fall off the fabric before it is absorbed. Some amount of water will inevitably make its way through to the next layer, but the membrane can still effectively conduct moisture away from the body, allowing the wearer to remain comfortable and dry.

As the efficacy of the water repellent coating diminishes over time, the outer layer of the garment can become saturated or "wet out" in a heavy or prolonged rain. Even though the inner porous membrane layer prevents water from penetrating to the skin, it is no longer able to "breathe." Condensation from body moisture builds on the inside of the suit, resulting in a cold, clammy feeling. You'd think the suit is leaking, but in reality, it's just trapped body moisture that can no longer escape.

To maintain your garment's maximum waterproofness, keep it clean by closely follow the maker's recommendations. Dirt build-up compromises the garment's ability to shed water and breathe. When you do wash your jacket or pants, use a non-detergent soap like Nikwax Tech Wash to avoid damaging the sensitive porous membrane material.

After cleaning, test your garment's ability to shed water, especially if you're planning a trip. If water does not bead easily on the surface, reapply a recommended durable water repellent like Nikwax TX-Direct, Scotchguard from 3M, or ReviveX from Gore, the maker of Gore-Tex. ■

If you live in a warm climate, consider wearing a mesh jacket. They offer outstanding airflow to keep you cool, but provide rugged construction and armor for crash protection. The innovative Tour Master design pictured here features removable panels to expose or close the mesh areas, to let you adjust to warm or cool weather.

Armored denim riding jackets don't offer quite the same level of abrasion resistance as heavy-weight nylon or leather but they are much better than riding in a T-shirt. Best of all they are very comfortable, with a casual style.

Jackets

Jackets that provide the best protection are made from heavy materials like Cordura or leather. Dress leather jackets are made of leather that is soft and supple, but they aren't cut for comfortable riding and don't protect you any more than denim. Zippers should be heavy-duty with large tabs that are easy to grab with gloved fingers. Extra leather or Cordura at impact points like shoulders and elbows is important. Removable Temperfoam pads for impact protection are a valuable addition.

Textile jacket makers continue to add features that improve a jacket's ability to handle wider swings in temperature and rain. This reduces the number of extras you need to buy and simplifies your packing. Look for a jacket that is waterproof or, in the case of the new mesh "air" jackets, contains a removable waterproof liner. A

waterproof jacket eliminates the need to bring a rainsuit. An insulated liner adds warmth in the chilly morning air but can be easily removed down the road if temperatures begin to rise. Coupled with other high performance fabrics, these two important features not only allow you ride lighter, you can also ride longer into the year without resorting to electric gear.

The fit of a jacket is as important as its features. If a jacket isn't comfortable to wear, you'll be tempted to leave it at home, and that defeats the purpose of having a jacket. Good motorcycle jackets are designed to be comfortable when you are on the bike with your hands in riding position. The cut should be long in the back so the jacket won't ride up over your beltline and expose your backside. Sleeves will be cut so they fit best when you're stretched out. That means they'll be a little long when held at your sides. Check the fit around the shoulders with your hands extended. A jacket that's just a bit too tight across the shoulders and underarms will stay on the hanger in the closet. Roominess in the chest depends on how many months out of the year you plan to wear the jacket. If you're going to wear this jacket with an electric vest or fleece (or both), it must be a little roomier than if you're going to wear it only during warm weather.

For warm weather riding, you can now find protective clothing that won't cook you like a ribeye. A few years ago, Joe Rocket (joerocket .com) delivered an innovative product in this area, a jacket called the Phoenix. Made from a synthetic textile blend, the Phoenix is perforated throughout so that air passes through the entire garment, not just a few out-of-the-way zippered vents. Protective pads are placed at impact points. It won't replace a full riding jacket, but if your hot weather gear is a T-shirt and jeans, you'll want to check out "air" jackets, as they are called. Most of the well-known jacket makers have an air jacket in their line.

Riding Pants

The best protective pants are either leather or textile with reinforced and padded impact points. The reality is that most of us tempt fate and still ride in ordinary jeans. Leather pants and textile overpants heat up quickly at temperatures over 80 degrees and weighing the risk, many riders opt to chance it, figuring that comfort is more important than protection. To give us more choices, gear makers are introducing new types of pants that are as versatile and comfortable as today's new jackets. For example, a textile "air" jacket can be matched with a pair of textile "air" pants for all-over ventilation. Look for pants that are waterproof for the same flexibility in cold, foul weather as an all-weather, three-season jacket.

Don't ride in jeans alone. Get a pair of riding pants with reinforced seams and cushioned impact points.

Jeans aren't being left behind either. New designs include Kevlar inserts and body armor that reduce the safety trade-off while preserving the comfort and looks of denim. Draggin' Jeans are worth checking out if you love wearing denim but feel insecure knowing it won't protect you. Draggin' Jeans are fitted with a layer of Kevlar in the seat and knees. When ordering you can also specify the pants be fitted with extra armor for the knees.

Gloves

It makes sense to own more than one pair of gloves. There are a few broad categories of gloves to choose from but within those broad categories are dozens of choices. For touring, you can exclude high fashion racing gloves. Pass up the bargain basement cheapie gloves, too. They're so thin they'll rip apart at the critical moment they need to perform.

For summer riding you'll want gloves with ventilation on the back of the hand. My personal preference is for a glove that has a leather palm but a textile back. Gloves made like this will dry quickly after you've gotten caught in a shower. On the palm look for an extra thickness of leather. If you do have to break a fall, it will be with the heel of your hands. Gloves should not be loose-fitting, but still comfortable when you

Well-made gloves are important for safe riding. If you happen to fall, you're likely to try to break the fall with the palm of your hands.

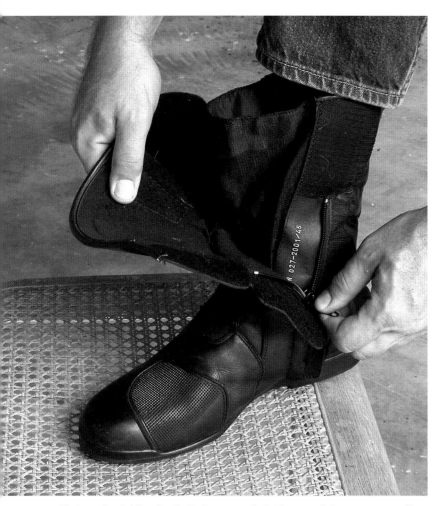

Find a pair of riding boots that are comfortable enough to wear on or off the bike and you'll save yourself some packing space.

close your hand into a fist. Your fingertips should just reach the end of the glove but not push against it. I always check to see what kind of feel I get from the brake and clutch levers and the throttle.

Winter gloves are thicker because they need to provide more insulation from the cold. I dislike thick winter gloves because they reduce the tactile feedback I'm accustomed to. New materials are improving glove design by reducing bulk with materials like Thinsulate. The very latest designs (like those from Road Gear) incorporate Outlast materials in the construction. This is particularly useful if you have heated grips. Thinsulate and other insulators not only insulate you from the cold, they also prevent heat conduction from the grips. Outlast, on the other hand, allows the heat to pass through the gloves

while keeping out the cold. You'll pay a smart premium for gloves of that caliber, but the benefits of reduced bulk and superior thermal comfort make them worth considering. One more thing: your winter glove should have a long gauntlet that fits well over the cuff of your riding jacket to eliminate cold drafts from funneling up your sleeve.

Riding Boots

Another must-have is a pair of sturdy, high-quality motorcycle riding boots. Half-boots with zippers on the side need not apply for this demanding position.

Motorcycle boots have a couple of important tasks to perform. First, they must be constructed to protect your feet when you find them wedged between your bike and the pavement. This won't occur in daily riding, but if you happen to find yourself in this situation, you'll be glad there is something more than sneakers and jeans between your foot and a hot exhaust or, heaven forbid, a motorcycle sliding on its side. Boots are also designed to protect your feet from the elements to keep them dry and comfortable. The only thing as miserable as wet underwear on a long day's ride are cold, wet feet.

There are many styles and models of boots and after a while they all start to look the same. Many of them are good performers, so make a list of the specific features you want in a boot, then shop by fit and feel, then by price.

Look for boots that rise to mid-calf. Boots that just cover the ankle aren't providing enough protection while commando-style boots that rise to the knee are more than you need. Avoid the heaviest boots unless you're planning a demanding trip. Boots with a thick, stiff sole take a long time to break in and make shifting awkward. Like other protective gear, your boots should be comfortable so you'll wear them.

For touring, your boots should be waterproof and include a breathable liner like Gore-Tex or KingTex. Like your hands, when your feet get wet, you feel wet all over. Having waterproof boots means you can leave your rain booties at home, too.

A cleated sole is another important feature. This will give you more reliable traction when you put your foot down at a stoplight or an often treacherous spot—a toll booth.

Cold-weather riders should find a boot that fits just a little looser than normal to give you the flexibility to use a heavier sock or electrics.

Get your boots well before any long trip you might be planning. This will give you a chance to break them in and they'll be more comfortable on long runs. You'll also have time to get a feel for the shift lever. If you're wearing boots for the first time, it's a big change in feel and you'll need some time to practice finding your positions, especially neutral. You'll be better off doing that somewhere comfortable like a parking lot.

Find a set of riding boots you can wear on and off the motorcycle, to save you the space of packing an extra pair of shoes.

BODY ARMOR

An increasing number of riding garments obtain impact protection with Temperfoam and plastic inserts. I feel pretty comfortable with the level of protection these built-in components provide but I understand why some riders prefer to add more.

A popular addition is a back protector. This is a component that fastens around your waist and features a shock absorption system that covers your spine. Most systems are designed to give you freedom of movement bending forwarding but provide less lateral movement. If you are involved in an accident, the shock absorption system will reduce the likelihood of traumatic injury to your spinal column.

Fieldsheer manufactures an add-in protective system designed to fit into popular riding jackets like Joe Rocket, Teknic, and others that have a pocket for holding reinforcements. The dual-density foam will absorb some of the energy your body encounters when you fall, lessening the effect of the fall. You may not escape unharmed, but your injuries will probably be less severe.

One of the most complete systems of body armor is offered by Bohn (bohnarmor.com). Bohn's Bodyguard system includes a set of multi-layered foam pads set into a stretchable Lycra-blend body suit. The suit's snug fit assures the pads will stay in place when called into service.

Modern textile riding jackets offer very high perfomance and plenty of style options. This Firstgear Kilimanjaro jacket is waterproof, breathable, and armored, with lots of convenience features.

RAIN GEAR

When your choice of riding gear is leather or a non-waterproof textile jacket or pants, a good rain suit is necessary. A rainsuit designed specifically for motorcycling will keep you dry under the worst conditions, especially if you're riding a bike with a full fairing.

Pick a rain suit that is brightly colored. You're wearing it when visibility is reduced, so the brighter the color and the more reflective material, the better. Your rain suit should be easy to put on. A one-piece suit is fully waterproof and draftproof, but it can be tricky to get into. A two-piece suit is easier, especially when you wait too long to suit up and you see a wall of rain a quarter-mile down the road. Find a suit that has roomy legs and leg openings. It's not practical to take your boots off to get a suit on and if you're wearing rugged boots, they don't have a lot of flexibility.

You'll also want a roomy suit if you plan to ride in colder weather when you're packing on

▶ MATERIAL CONSIDERATIONS

Leather is still the most durable, abrasion resistant, and stylish material for riding.

There are a number of advanced materials used in today's clothing. Some, like polyester, are used in a wide range of applications while other materials, like Gore-Tex™, are used in very specific applications.

Polypropylene. The lightest and thinnest of wicking synthetic materials. Blended with other materials and offered in products designed for close skin contact (briefs, running pants, close-fitting tops) in temperate weather. Most recognized name is Helly-Hansen's Lifa branded material.

Polyester. New designs have made polyester a versatile fabric that's a good value. Treated polyester is an efficient conductor of moisture. Fabrics like Coolmax and Capilene are good choices for summer weight clothing. Malden Mills' widely-recognized Polartec brand is used in all layers of clothing and is very effective in cooler conditions. Yep, Polartec and other fabrics like it really are made from recycled soda bottles.

Smartwool™. A specific brand of advanced Merino wool from New Zealand with the desirable thermal and comfort properties of wool without the itch normally associated with wool fabrics. A great performer in cool weather riding. Doesn't dry as fast as polyesters.

Outlast™. Proves there are more benefits to the space program than Velcro and Tang. Outlast, a fabric available only in the last ten years, incorporates "phase-change" materials designed to absorb, hold or release heat depending on your skin temperature so that you remain comfortable regardless of your activity level or outdoor temperatures. More expensive than other fabrics, but may eliminate the need for multiple sets of gear for different climates.

Gore-Tex™. A popular brand of waterproof/breathable fabric. Gore-Tex is a membrane attached underneath an outer fabric and protected on the inside by a nylon or mesh liner. Its pores are 700 times smaller than a water drop, but still large enough for perspiration vapor to pass through. Thus after several hours of wear you don't become damp from your own perspiration. It's also windproof. This fabric and others like ShelTex™are important components in waterproof garments.

Thinsulate™. This material developed by 3M contains microfibers that capture and hold body heat, even when wet. Its fibers are about one-tenth the size of other insulating materials, so it packs down smaller and yet provides the same degree of insulating

protection. You'll find Thinsulate in active outdoor winter gear.

Cotton. Cotton is widely appreciated for comfort and it's likely that cotton garments make up a large part of your wardrobe. Too bad it isn't more functional in riding conditions. Cotton absorbs up to 30% of its weight in moisture and it doesn't wick very effectively, so when cotton gets wet, it feels wet and stays wet. Off the bike, cotton shirts and denim jeans are fine for campsite and around town.

Cordura™. This abrasion-resistant material comprises the outer layer of most non-leather riding suits and gear like tang bags and saddlebags. Cordura is available in a range of weights which make it usable as a fabric for lighter weight garments like jackets and even summer shirts and shorts. As a synthetic, is can also be dyed to nearly any color. As an example, for the ultimate in personal conspicuity, check out textile riding jackets and suits in hi-viz yellow.

Leather. Nothing says "bad to the bone" like a leather-clad motorcyclist. Leather looks tough because it is tough. Heavy leather is the best abrasion resistant material available. On the downside, leather is heavy, doesn't ventilate well, and can't be made waterproof. Synthetic fabrics sport all these features with ever-improving protection against pavement surfing.

Kevlar™. This fabric earned its reputation as a lifesaver among law enforcement officers for its ability to stop bullets. Now Kevlar's properties are being extended to other applications where extreme durability is required. Sounds like a good fit for motorcycling. Blended materials containing Lycra and Kevlar are finding their way into the top-end clothing lines. Kevlar's primary drawback is expense. ■

If you don't wear waterproof riding boots, consider rain gators to keep your feet dry. Nothing makes you quite as miserable as wet feet.

Motorcycle-specific rain suits have important features that set them apart from ordinary rain gear: zippers and pockets with storm flaps to fight high wind, neck closures with high collars, and even hoods to keep rain from seeping down your neck.

layers. A rain jacket with high collar and long cut will reduce drafts above and below. Tuck that collar underneath your helmet and you'll eliminate an entry point for rain. It doesn't feel good when rain starts trickling down your back. It pools under your butt. You know how I feel about wet underwear.

Rain suits across the price spectrum have similar construction: a vinyl or nylon outer shell backed with a thin polyurethane coating on the inside. No water gets in and no perspiration gets out. Some suits provide zippered vents which help circulate air and present a path for moisture to escape. Suits lined with a mesh material are easier to get on and provide more layers to capture moisture inside before it starts building up on the layers closest to you.

SUMMARY

There are lots of clothing options available to today's rider to fit nearly any type of riding style for any type of weather.

What's most important is to have a quality set of basic protective gear: helmet, gloves, jacket, pants, and boots. For less than $600, you can get all the essentials. You don't have to spend a fortune to equip yourself with the right stuff.

Special purpose gear, such as quick-dry underwear and socks, is helpful when you're traveling because it can significantly reduce the amount you need to pack for a trip of any length. Products such as riding shorts make long days in the saddle seem shorter by helping you stay comfortable.

Section III

OUTFITTING YOUR BIKE

Motorcycles were invented by tinkers who thought engines and cycles went together like peanut butter and chocolate. Their spirit of better motorcycling through experimentation is part of the genetic code among riders today. In this section, we're going to continue that tradition by highlighting popular touring accessories and mods for your bike.

Before we start, let's separate what you need from what you want. In the past, preparing a bike for long-distance travel might have meant learning how to repair spokes or how to rebuild a carb by flashlight on the side of the road. Making extensive home-built modifications to carry equipment and prepare it for poor road conditions was a given. Today's bikes are highly reliable and include features that make them ready for touring right out of the crate. You don't need to do a thing but get on and ride.

But having a GPS on your bike is a lot of fun. You can explore side roads without worrying about getting lost, and navigating to your overnight stop is a breeze. Cell phones and PDAs can be a pain sometimes, but if having a phone along to keep in touch with the office means you can ride an extra hour or day (or week, maybe?), then it's worth having. Tunes would be nice. Carrying your entire music library in a four-ounce shockproof device is awesome. So is listening to a commercial-free radio station anywhere on the continent via satellite.

A few upgrades deserve special attention and should be higher on your priority list. Lighting improvements, both for improved night vision and conspicuity, should be at the top. Among personal accessories, a custom seat and an electric vest give big returns for your investment. A stable and secure means of carrying gear is a priority for those whose bikes don't have integrated luggage.

Whatever you choose to do, you should approach modifications in a systematic way. By some estimates, eighty percent or more of bike troubles on the road are due to electrical problems. I'll bet most of those troubles could be traced to bad wiring installed by the owner. Wiring and plumbing are both black arts, but with plumbing you can see what's leaking. With electrical wiring, who knows where all those electrons are spilling out? Bad wiring can create problems you know nothing about until you are two hundred miles down a gravel road.

In Chapter 5, I'll describe proper soldering, crimping, and wiring techniques so you can add devices to your bike with confidence. At the end of the chapter, I've included a special project to add a relay-controlled fuse block. This is one project that every rider who adds more than once device should consider.

5 Modification Techniques. 60
Device Mounts 61
Tethering. 62
Scotty, I Need More Power! 63
Wiring Tips 65
Soldering and Crimp Techniques. 67
Adding a Fuse Block 67

6 Lighting and Conspicuity 70
Color Temperature and Intensity 71
Bulb Technology 72
Packaging. 72
Lighting Upgrades 73
Auxiliary Lights 75
HID Lighting 76
About Relays. 77
Becoming More Conspicuous 78
Summary 79

7 Cockpit Instruments. 80
Advantage: Maps. 80
Advantage: GPS. 81
Satellite Tracking. 85
Radar Detectors 86
Summary 87

8 Entertainment and Communication 88

Product Lifecycles 88
On-Bike Audio Options 88
Audio Integration 89
Headset Options 90
Bluetooth Headsets 91
Canalphones 92
Devices à la Carte 92
Satellite Radio 93
MP3 Players 93
Cell Phones 94
Rider-Passenger Intercoms 95
Radio Communication Solutions 96
Battery Technologies 98
Summary 99

9 Cameras and Camcorders 100

Film or Digital? 100
Purchasing Considerations 101
Mounting and Integration 102
Camcorders 103
Lipstick Cameras 104
Summary 105

10 Ride in Comfort 106

Listen to Your Body 107
Improving the Bottom Line 107
Custom Saddles 108
Ordering a Custom Seat 109
Seat Pads 109
Handlebar Improvements 111
Windscreens and Fairings 113
Highway Pegs 114
Footpegs and Floorboards 115
Back Support 115
Summary 115

11 Underpinnings. 116

Tires. 116
Suspension Basics 120
Bike Protection 122
Fuel Cells 124
Summary 124

12 Storage Solutions. 126

Luggage Systems 127
Soft Luggage. 130
Tankbags 132
More Soft Luggage Components. . . . 134
Special-Purpose Solutions 135
Storage Accessories 136
Summary 137

13 Trailer Life 138

Trailer Basics 139
Pop-up Campers 142
Hitches. 143
Proper Trailer Loading 144
Purchasing a Used Trailer. 145
Safe Towing Tips 146
Summary 147

Modification Techniques

When you start adding accessories to your bike, even simple changes require some thought. Take that cup holder you've been thinking about. Sure would be nice to have a mug of hot brew on the road. But wait, if you mount it on the handlebar where you're thinking, will it make contact with the bike anywhere when you turn the handlebars from lock to lock? Does the design of the mug make it possible to easily access it, use it, and put it back while riding? Is it secure enough to stay fixed on washboard pavement at highway speeds? How do you squeeze the mug into your full-face helmet? That's one example. For bigger projects like adding a trailer hitch and wiring harness, or electronic devices, the list of questions is a bit longer.

Reliability. How could this modification compromise the reliability of the bike? Is it of sufficient quality for its intended purpose? Is the device shockproof and weatherproof or will it need special accommodations (like a rain cover)? Will this accessory alter the balance, handling, or braking of the bike? What are the likely ways this item could fail? If it breaks will it be a nuisance or will it render the bike inoperable? What would be needed to repair it?

Mounting. Where and how will I mount this device so that it is easy to use and able to withstand vibration? Can it be easily removed and re-mounted for security? Will it interfere with the bike's normal operation?

Power. For an electrical device, does the bike have sufficient excess generating capacity to power it? What type of wiring is required? Is a special harness available to plug directly into the bike, or does it require modification to the bike's wiring harness? Is a fuse block needed? How will the circuit for this device be fused?

Unlike bolt-on accessories that are specifically designed to fit a particular bike, products like radar detectors, satellite radios, and cell phones have to be adapted for use on motorcycles. Translation: The solution for mounting and wiring will be left up to you.

Considering what a good GPS costs, you want to make sure it doesn't shake loose while you're coaxing the bike up Pike's Peak. If you aren't confident in how it's mounted, it's a distraction even when it doesn't come loose. An electrical short in power to a device that is not properly fused could fry more of the electrical system than that one gadget. Improper wiring or a poor connection won't always fail, but it will rob you of power that could otherwise be put to use in your electric vest.

For these reasons and more, the rest of this chapter will be devoted to properly mounting and powering devices on your bike.

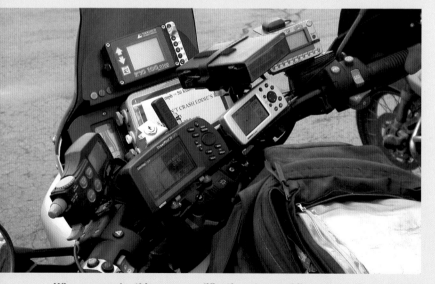

When you make this many modifications to your bike, you really must do it right if you hope to avoid trouble down the road.

The Round A Mount (RAM) ball and socket mounting system needs a base, an arm, and a device mount. This base attaches to the brake or clutch mount on most bikes.

PROJECT SUCCESS TIPS

Start with a clean work area. With plenty of clean, flat surface area, you can lay out parts you pull off the bike in an orderly fashion. It is less likely you'll lose parts and makes the reassembly process go faster.

Don't rush the job. Enjoy the process. You already know that when you do things in a hurry you'll make mistakes. Another reason to slow down is to make your modifications look like they were part of the bike's original design. When someone looks at a change you've made and says "That looks like stock," you'll get some extra satisfaction from that.

If it's complicated, document it. No matter how often you tell yourself "I'm going to remember where every bolt went, no problem," in a project with a lot of steps, you'll forget where at least one bolt or fastener went. As you unbutton your bike, take pictures of fasteners and their locations. A video camera is even better. "I took these three bolts out of here, here and here," you say as you point the camera to each location.

When troubleshooting, change one variable at a time. An item you've added to the bike doesn't seem to be working just right. Check your work starting from Step 1. When you find something you think needs to be changed, stop and retest before changing anything else. If that doesn't solve your problem, decide whether you should keep the change, then continue to step through the installation process and look for other issues to rectify. ■

DEVICE MOUNTS

Motorcycle cockpits have always presented a challenge for adding devices. There just aren't many places to mount a device securely. I've seen a lot of custom mounts created. For better or worse, much has been done with Velcro. That all changed with the introduction of Round-A-Mount systems, better known as "RAM mounts" (rammount.com), a series of more than 800 ball-and-socket components designed to fasten just about any device to your bike anywhere you want. (Browsing the RAM catalog gives me the same feelings the Montgomery Ward holiday catalog once stirred. Oh, the possibilities!)

You begin building your RAM system with a base mount. The base mount attaches to your bike and provides a standard size ball to which you can attach arms for mounting devices. Bikes that have a length of exposed handlebar can use handlebar mounts. Another option is the brake/

clutch reservoir base mount. This replaces the front part of the clamp that holds your brake or clutch reservoir to the bike with a RAM base mount that can include one or two mounting balls. This mount blends so well with the bike, it looks like part of the bike's design.

Other options for base mounts using this system include simple ball mounts with a mounting hole that attach with bolts already present on the bike. Other mounts can be used to hold either a solid or flexible steel rod to which mounting balls can be attached. Using the RAM system, it's possible to mount just about anything to your bike that you might desire.

After you add a base mount, choose an arm to attach to the base. The arm mount slips over the ball of the base to elevate your device to a height comfortable to use. A 3-inch arm is a good

Table 5.1 Peak Electrical Output

MAKE	MODEL	YEAR	FUEL DELIVERY	PEAK OUTPUT
Buell	Blast	2001	Carbureted	297 watts
BMW	R1150RT	2003	Fuel injected	700 watts
BMW	K1200LT	2003	Fuel injected	840 watts
Ducati	996	2000	Fuel injected	520 watts
Ducati	ST2/ST4	2002	Fuel injected	520 watts
Harley	Heritage	1998	Carbureted	360 watts
Harley	Electra Glide	2002	Fuel injected	585 watts
Honda	Shadow 1100	2002	Carbureted	329 watts
Honda	ST1300	2003	Fuel Injected	740 watts
Honda	Valkyrie	2000	Carbureted	546 watts
Honda	GL1800	2003	Fuel Injected	1000 watts
Kawasaki	Vulcan 1500	2000	Carbureted	377 watts
Kawasaki	Vulcan 1500	2001	Fuel Injected	588 watts
Kawasaki	ZX6R	2001	Carbureted	305 watts
Suzuki	Bandit 1200	1999	Carbureted	405 watts
Suzuki	V-Strom DL1000	2002	Fuel Injection	360 watts
Yamaha	FJR1300	2003	Fuel Injected	490 watts

Source: PowerletProducts.com

length to use for mounting in-cockpit devices that you access regularly, such as satellite radios and GPS units. For cameras, a long 5-inch arm might be needed to elevate or move the camera forward.

Next you choose a cradle to attach to your device. Custom-fit cradles are available for popular devices like Garmin GPS units and iPods. Add a ball to the cradle, attach this assembly to the arm, and your device is mounted.

The RAM system is designed to absorb some shock transmitted from the road through your bike's chassis. It won't swallow all of it. When you can, use shorter arms for mounting devices, as they amplify shock to a smaller degree than devices mounted on long arms.

TETHERING

You'll often read that "devices should be tethered for safety" but no one tells you how to do it. Isn't a RAM mount enough? It's a good start, but until I strapped down my XM radio, I narrowly missed propelling it into near-earth orbit after missing a couple of DIP signs in Kentucky. (Unlike other states, when Kentucky DOT posts a DIP, they mean it.)

The simplest way to lasso your valuable gadgets is a long plastic zip tie. You can buy a package of these at Home Depot or Radio Shack in all sizes for a couple of bucks. I carry a few with me for emergency repairs. Some devices, like your GPS, may require more thought. A zip tie across the face would compromise the functionality of the unit so you can cement a cable clamp to the back of the unit with instant glue. Now you have an attachment point for a thin cable.

When you tether a device make sure you plan an easy way to remove it. At overnight stops, you may want to remove XM or GPS units and bring them into the room with you. Takes half a minute. That removes all concern you might have about the security of your devices on the bike.

SCOTTY, I NEED MORE POWER!

Ever notice how the engineers on the Starship Enterprise could always summon power at a mission-critical moment, even when Klingons had punched a few holes in the warp drive? Scotty isn't riding shotgun on your travels, so you'll need to figure out for yourself what your bike is capable of supporting.

Small electronic devices (such as GPS units) that require a power supply aren't a big deal because they consume just a few watts each. You need to pay more attention to power reserves when you add several big-draw items like electrically-heated suits and auxiliary lighting systems. All of today's bikes are capable of supporting at least a heated jacket and most can also handle a set of lights. If you think you'll be adding more than that, you should calculate what your bike's system can manage.

Step 1: Determine total power produced by your bike's electrical system

In your bike's operating manual or service guide, find the power output specs for its alternator. You'll find a value called "peak output" or "alternator output" expressed as watts generated at a minimum rpm. For example, the 2003 Gold Wing's output is rated at "1 kw @ 2400 rpm min." This means the alternator generates 1,000 watts of power when engine speed is 2,400 rpm or higher. If this number isn't available, multiply the alternator's output voltage (we'll use 12 volts) times the number of amps the alternator can generate. Table 5.1 contains peak power output figures from a range of motorcycles.

Step 2: Calculate the operating load of your bike's electrical system.

Core operating components such as lights, fuel pumps, cooling fans, and engine control modules all draw power from your electrical system. This is called the "operating load" because all of these devices are required to run your bike. This figure isn't supplied as a single number on any spec sheet, so you'll have to make this calculation for yourself. Table 5.2 shows approximate numbers for major components. For a more precise figure you'll need to look these up in your

▶ VOLTS, AMPS, AND WATTS

The basic principles of electrical flow can be compared to water flowing through a garden hose. We measure the water output in gallons per minute. The flow of electric charge is measured in amps and represents how much charge moves past a point in one second. Water won't flow through a hose without a pressure exerted on it and neither will electricity. In electrical terms that push is expressed as "volts."

In many cases, you'll be dealing with electrical requirements measured in "watts." Wattage is the amount of power a device consumes. Wattage is the product of voltage multiplied by amperage. For example, if the label on a 12-volt accessory says it requires 3 amps to operate, it draws 36 watts of power (12 volts × 3 amps).

Sometimes you are given the wattage rating of a product and you need to know the amperage to calculate a fuse or decide what gauge of wire you should run. If Power = Volts × Amps, then Amps = Power ÷ Volts.

For example, an electric clothing manufacturer says their jacket consumes seventy watts of power. Your bike is a twelve-volt system. To determine the number of amps this circuit will draw, divide 70 by 12. Your jacket will pull 5.83 amps (actually a little higher, since the bike's voltage is actually a bit more than 12 volts). ■

Table 5.2
Common Operating Loads

High Beam	55 watts
Low Beam	55 watts
Number Plate	5 watts
Brake/Tail	21 watts
Instrument Panel	2 watts
Engine Control Module	25 watts
Fuel Pump	60 watts
Cooling Fan	60 watts
Electronic Ignition	50 watts

Source: PowerletProducts.com

bike's technical data or examine the components themselves for markings. On average, fuel-injected bikes consume about 300–350 watts of

Table 5.3 Available Electrical Power

EXAMPLE	PEAK	OPERATING	AVAILABLE POWER
Buell Blast	297 watts	195 watts	102 watts
Kawasaki ZX6R	305 watts	200 watts	105 watts
Ducati ST2/ST4	520 watts	285 watts	245 watts
Suzuki V-Strom DL1000	360 watts	285 watts	75 watts
Honda Valkyrie	546 watts	250 watts	296 watts
Vulcan 1500 Fl	588 watts	340 watts	248 watts

Source: PowerletProducts.com

When you add more than a couple gadgets to the bike, it's a good idea to include a voltage monitor to make sure you're not overtaxing the charging system.

Table 5.4 Fully Loaded Calculation

BIKE MODEL: 2003 HONDA GOLDWING	
	Power (in watts)
Max Output @ 2400 rpm	1,000
Operating Load (estimated)	350
Available power	650
Accessories	
Electric Jacket	60
XM Radio	2
GPS navigation unit	5
Trailer running lights	30
Heated handgrips	30
Auxiliary driving lights	60 (30 each x 2)
TOTAL DRAW	**187**
EXCESS POWER	**463**

power. Carbureted bikes have fewer electronic management components so they consume about 200–250 watts.

Step 3: Calculate available power

Now for math. Subtract the operating load of your bike from the peak generating ability and you'll find the bike's available power output. Table 5.3 shows the available output from a sampling of small to large bikes. Many bikes are capable of handling several high-draw devices, although this exercise shows us that the V-Strom will support fewer devices simultaneously. Table 5.4 illustrates a quick calculation I did to see how a few typical accessories would tally against the Gold Wing's power output. Even after adding several items, there is an excess capacity of 463 watts. That's enough remaining capacity to power a small town or a couple of head-to-toe heated suits.

If you can find the spec for power output at idle, run through this calculation again (power output − (operating load + accessory load)) to see if you still have a positive available power balance. It's possible the balance is negative, meaning your accessories are drawing more power than the alternator is capable of generating at low rpms. Your accessories will still work but the shortfall will be supplied by the battery. When you resume travel your alternator will once again supply enough power for everything and recharge the battery. This is only a concern if you are idling or riding at low engine speed for a significant distance. If necessary you can turn off a couple of items for a while to avoid drawing the battery down too far.

WIRING TIPS

More and more products are available today with pre-configured wiring harnesses. Use them when you can because they are designed to snap into existing connectors on your bike. This exact fit increases reliability. When you need to do your own wiring, follow these guidelines for the best circuit.

Always use stranded wire for your projects. Pictured are 12, 18, and 22 gauge wire for heavy- to light-current loads. Sparkly nail polish isn't required for wiring jobs.

Start by adding a new fuse block. A fuse block is like a sub-panel to your bike's electrical system. Instead of cutting into existing wires (a bad idea) or running several harnesses to your battery, all auxiliary circuits you add should run to the new block. When a relay is included in the circuit, the block can be wired so your accessories will only run when the key is in the ignition and turned on. Check out the end of this chapter for an easy-to-follow fuse block project.

Select the right wire for the job. Always use multi-strand wire for running circuits on a bike. Solid wire breaks easily with just a few bends. Multi-strand wire won't break when flexed; this is especially important for wiring that might run between a fairing and handlebars that are constantly turning.

Wire is sold in a range of gauges. Gauge is a sizing system that rates the thickness of the wire. The lower the number, the thicker the wire. All wire contains some resistance to electrical flow

▶ POWER OUTLETS

If you don't want to wire a device to your bike permanently you can add a power connector for quick connects and disconnects. These are the most common connector types being used.

Cigarette lighter. In the U.S. the standard auto cigarette lighter has evolved into the role of power outlet. Many accessories come with a lighter adaptor. It's an acceptable design for light duty bike use for low wattage devices that need temporary power. Since there is no physical standard for lighters, variations in size can lead to a sloppy power connection.

SAE/2. You'll find this two-conductor plug on many trailer connections, Battery Tenders, and some electric vest products. It's a sturdy plug that's vibration resistant but requires two hands to unplug.

Powerlet. Known by some as a "BMW type" connector, this connector family looks similar to cigarette lighter connectors, but is made to an industry standard size (unlike cigarette lighters) and is designed to handle high loads (again, unlike cigarette lighters) for products like electric suits. Popular in Europe and gaining traction in the U.S. (powerletproducts.com). ■

and that resistance reduces the amount of power delivered to the device. Heavier gauge wire has lower resistance and delivers power to your device with less loss. In other words, heavier wire is more efficient.

In motorcycle applications, you can use 14 and 18 gauge wire for almost all circuits powering accessory devices. 18 gauge is good for low-load devices like radar detectors and radios. Thicker 14 gauge wire is preferred for high-load products like electrically-heated clothing. The thicker wire delivers more juice to the jacket

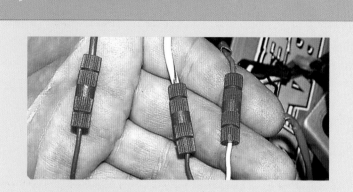

POSI-LOCK CONNECTORS

If you hate soldering, take a look at Posi-Lock connectors (posi-lock.com). These are similar to the ubiquitous wire nuts used in house wiring, but are designed for conditions where vibration and moisture are present. I'll stick with my soldering iron when it's convenient, but a package of these would be useful in the spares kit for emergency repairs. ■

which you will feel as extra warmth. In rare cases where you are running power to multiple circuits, you may need to use a very heavy wire like 10 gauge, as we will in our fuse block project later in this chapter.

Choose the right fuse. Fuses are designed to protect your bike's wiring from short circuts. A "short" occurs when electricity finds an unintended path directly back to its source, resulting in a sudden, large current flow that can damage components connected to that circuit and other circuits on the bike. Fuses prevents this from happening. A fuse is a strip of heat-sensitive metal inserted into a circuit. It is rated to allow a certain amount of current flow through a circuit before melting. When a short occurs and a large current begins to flow, this generates heat causing the fuse to melt or "blow," which opens the circuit, stops the flow of current, and prevents serious damage to the bike.

Since a short circuit draws many times more current than a properly operating device, you don't need to exactly match a fuse to a circuit. You just need to be close. For example, a circuit powering a low-load device, or a couple of small devices, will be fine with a 7.5 amp fuse. An electric jacket drawing 80 watts of power pulls

6.6 amps in a 12 volt circuit (amps = watts ÷ volts) so choose a 10 amp fuse.

Solder splices and crimp connectors. When you want to permanently connect two wires, solder them and insulate the connection with heat shrink tubing. If your practice is to twist wires together and cover them with electrical tape, you're setting the stage for a roadside repair along a rain-slicked Interstate on a foggy night. Get the picture? When you need to connect a wire to a terminal block, the most reliable method is to crimp a spade or ring connector onto the end of the wire.

Secure the wire along its path. Using a wire loom to contain your wire runs protects your work from engine heat and moisture and makes for a neater looking job. A wire loom is a length of plastic tubing designed to encase wires, protecting them from heat and wear. Wire loom is available in rigid or flexible forms; the latter are made by firms such as TechFlex (techflex.com). If you run wires along routes where a wiring harness already runs, you can then use zip ties to attach your loom to the harness. Avoid spots where a wire might rub or is pinched by body work; over time vibration may result in a broken internal wire or worn insulation which could lead to a short circuit.

Where connectors are exposed in the cockpit, find a location where you can secure the wire if the accessory is not in use. I picked up a package of cable clamps and use double-sided tape to create a cord clip. When I don't have the GPS on the bike, the cable tucks neatly and securely into the clip.

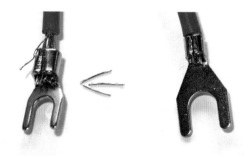

(Left) This is a bad crimp. Too much wire exposed, broken wire strands and a poor crimp. (Right) Just enough wire, no missing wire strands, and a tight crimp make this a good connection.

SOLDERING AND CRIMP TECHNIQUES

Good electrical connections are essential to lasting performance in the harsh environment of your motorcycle. Here are some tips to help you solder and crimp like a pro.

For soldering and crimping, it's important to strip wire properly. Use just enough pressure to remove insulation from the end of a wire. Avoid nicking or cutting wire strands. Strip just enough wire to make a good crimp or solder connection.

For crimps, the end of the connector should butt against the wire insulation. The wire should project just beyond the crimp. If the wire is frayed or has missing strands, cut it clean and re-strip the insulation. The exposed wire should be straight with no nicks or missing strands.

Choose the right size crimp terminal for the gauge of wire. Terminals will list the range of wire gauge they can be used with. Use a crimping tool. The right tool applies pressure to the right point in the crimp and create a superior connection. Using pliers or the old "squeeze in a vise" method will create inferior connections.

When soldering, use a low-wattage pencil-type soldering iron for your work. High-wattage soldering guns produce a lot of heat very quickly and it's too easy to melt the plastic insulation on a wire or a plastic connector if you're soldering wires to connector pins. A 20- to 30-watt iron (Radio Shack 64-2066) works well for motorcycle wiring applications. Keep the tip clean. When the iron is heated, wipe the tip on a sponge, then "tin" the tip by applying a small amount of solder. Repeat this process after each connection you solder.

Fix components in place before soldering. If the connection is moved before it cools, this results in a dull-looking "cold solder" connection, a poor conductor. To remedy this, reheat and remove the old solder, then try again.

Briefly pre-heat the joint. Apply heat to the joint for just two or three seconds, then add solder. Pre-heating the components will help the solder flow smoothly and quickly. Too little heat will also result in a "cold solder" connection.

Finally, don't apply too much solder. Add just enough to make an adequate joint. A lump of solder won't improve the connection and can

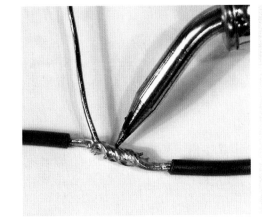

A low-wattage soldering iron and thin solder will help you create effective solder joints with less risk of melting the insulation.

A good solder connection has just enough solder to coat the wires.

After the solder cools, cover the connection with a shrink wrap and heat it to complete the soldering job. In some situations, you'll have to slide the shrink tubing onto the wires near the joint before you solder it, and then move the shrink tubing over the joint.

possibly come in contact with other components and short out.

ADDING A FUSE BLOCK

If you ever plan to add more than one accessory to your bike, I strongly recommend that you add a fuse block to your bike. Most accessories come with a wiring harness that's designed to attach directly to the battery on your bike. Your electric vest (or vests), power outlets, lights, just about everything is set to hook directly to the battery. That's fine if you attach only one accessory, but when you start adding on more items, you soon won't be able to reattach the battery terminals. Having all those connections come to one point is a mess and a likely source of trouble.

A fuse box solves this problem. A fuse box is like an electrical sub-panel you add when you want to run extra circuits in your house. It is an easy project that allows you to neatly add and properly fuse several accessories. You can also

▶ MATERIALS LIST

For less than $50 you can add a fuse block to your bike that will help you avoid common electrical wiring problems and will be the envy of your friends.

MATERIALS

- ▶ Fuse block ($35, Whitehorse)
- ▶ Relay (SPST relay, 12 volt, 30 amp, $6, Radio Shack #275-226)
- ▶ 12 gauge stranded wire ($5, Radio Shack #278-566)
- ▶ Blade-type automotive fuses ($3, Radio Shack #270-1201)
- ▶ 18 gauge stranded wire ($5, Radio Shack #278-1220)
- ▶ Inline fuse (mini-blade, $3, Radioshack, #270-1237)
- ▶ Crimp connectors
- ▶ Heatshrink tubing
- ▶ Tools
- ▶ Wire cutters
- ▶ Wire strippers
- ▶ Low-wattage soldering iron
- ▶ Crimping tool
- ▶ Rosin core solder
- ▶ Wiring diagram for your bike ■

Here's the finished relay-controlled fuse block installed on the bike.

wire the fuse box with a relay so that your accessories are powered only when the bike is running. A fuse block will save you grief down the road by avoiding short circuits and dead batteries.

Following is the outline of a procedure you can follow to add a fuse block to your bike. This describes a general approach but you may need to modify these steps to suit your particular bike. If you aren't comfortable making electrical modifications to your bike, seek help from a knowledgeable friend or have your local shop install this.

Project Overview

This project uses a fuse block with components sourced from Whitehorse Gear and Radio Shack. If you're familiar with fuse blocks, you can make substitutions. We're going to wire the fuse block to the battery by way of a relay switch. The relay will be controlled by a circuit

on your bike that becomes active when you turn on the ignition switch. The accessories you wire to the fuse block will then be powered only when the bike's ignition is keyed to the ON position.

Step 1. First you'll need to locate a spot on your bike where the fuse block will fit. An underseat location is best because you'll have ready access to this location to run new accessory circuits. The particular fuse box specified in this application is a marine-grade box with a weather cover, so it can handle some exposure to moisture. Just don't mount it under the rear fender.

Step 2. Mount the relay and fuse block in close proximity to one another using double-sided tape. Make sure the surface of the components and the bike are clean for the best possible adhesion.

Step 3. Referring to your bike's wiring diagram, locate a circuit that is energized when you turn on the ignition switch. Tap into this circuit to use it as the trigger to power your relay which will in turn power up your fuse block. A good candidate is the circuit for your license plate light or a running light, since those circuits are energized whenever the ignition switch is turned on. Look for the wire running to the tail light bulb that does not run to "ground." Use a Posi-Tap connector to tap into this circuit without cutting the wire.

In my example, the wire running to the Wing's license plate light is Brown and Blue. After I've identified the candidate wire, I trace it to its end and then check it with a voltmeter to make sure it carries positive 12 volts when the key is turned on. If you find a wire is inconvenient to trace to its end, you can insert a sewing pin into the wire. Use this as the point to test with your voltmeter.

Step 4. Find a convenient point and splice into your "trigger" circuit with an 18 gauge stranded wire. This wire will need to run back to pin 86 on the relay.

Step 5. Connect an 18 gauge wire from pin 85 on the relay to a negative terminal on the fuse block.

Step 6. Run a 12 gauge black wire from the negative side of the fuse block to the negative terminal on the battery.

Step 7. Run a 12 gauge wire from pin 30 of the relay to the positive connector on the fuse block. This is the positive 12 volt "hot lead" that is switched by the relay.

Step 8. Run a 12 gauge wire from the positive side of the battery to pin 87 on the relay. Add the inline fuse to this wiring run.

Again, make sure all connections are properly soldered or crimped. Use a voltmeter to test your wiring to make sure the right voltages appear at the expected places. If they don't, switch off the power to your bike immediately and re-check your connections.

Now when you want to add an accessory, you can run its power leads to your fuse block. The block I used has space for up to six accessories and can handle a total of thirty amps of load. That is plenty of capacity to handle all but the most demanding loads.

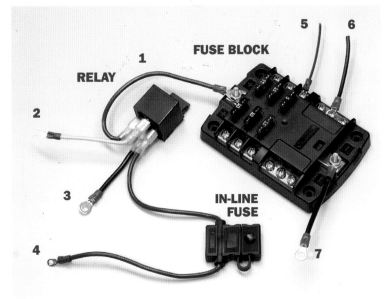

1) Relay-controlled 12 volt positive lead to fuse block. 2) Relay trigger wire to license plate light circuit. 3) Relay ground. 4) To 12 v positive terminal on battery. 5) Attach 12 volt positive lead from accessory here. 6) Attach accessory ground here. 7) Fuse block negative terminal of battery.

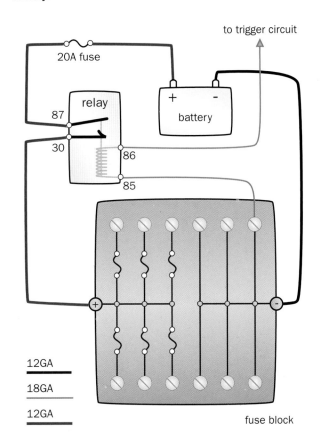

Lighting and Conspicuity

There are two reasons why improved lighting is a priority upgrade for veteran riders. Abundant light makes night riding safer and makes you more conspicuous to other vehicles on the road.

The extra lights on this VFR make it stand out in bad weather.

Compared to a Hummer, Ford Expedition, or even a Mini Cooper for that matter, motorcycles, even big ones, aren't easy to see in traffic. Cars with daytime running lights have further compromised our one advantage of riding with lights on. It's no wonder then, according to the oft-cited Hurt Study on motorcycle accidents, that crashes involving a bike and another vehicle often occur because the other driver "never saw the bike." As eye-popping as your bike may be, other drivers simply aren't looking for you and you don't stand out.

Likewise, it is enjoyable to ride at night, but treacherous. Most of the Roadkill Café's daily specials are created at night. If you aren't dodging skunks, possums, deer, or moose, you have to be concerned about gaps in pavement, potholes, and shredded retreads that are invisible until you come upon them.

Lighting modifications and additions will improve the width and depth of your sight field at night, but adding the right lights for the right circumstance is important. Here's the tricky part. Lighting is a complex blend of physics, design, and packaging. There are dozens of products to choose from. You can choose from upgrade lights, auxiliary lights, low-beam assist lights, fog lights, driving lights, and high-beam assist. You need to consider focal points, color temperatures, lumens per watt, reflector design, lens design, spots, and floods. And then there are modulators, signal, and brake light upgrades.

You get the point. With so many options to choose from, there is a lot to learn. Let's first consider the important factors in lamp technology and lighting design that will influence your choice of lighting system enhancements.

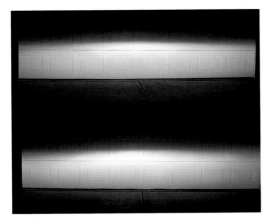

(Top) Low-beam halogen light. (Bottom) Low-beam HID lighting upgrade. The yellow-hued, lower color temperature of the halogen bulb is very apparent when compared to the whiter light from the HID upgrade.

COLOR TEMPERATURE AND INTENSITY

A 60-watt bulb produces more light than a 30-watt bulb, right? That was true when all we had were incandescent bulbs, but with new lighting technologies, more light is produced with less power. A 30-watt halogen bulb, for instance, far outshines a standard 60-watt incandescent bulb. So, judging light output strictly by wattage is no longer sufficient. Instead, we rate lights by intensity and color. These measures can be compared regardless of the technology used to produce the light.

For today's lighting technology, *luminance* is a more objective way to compare the light output of two different bulbs. Luminance is the measure of how much light falls on a square meter of a surface at a prescribed distance. The higher the lumens rating, the more light.

Another critical factor that influences lighting performance is the *color of the light*. Vision is based on how objects reflect light and the human eye perceives objects differently depending on the color of the light source. The color of light is measured on the Kelvin temperature scale. We refer to light color by its "color temperature" but this isn't temperature like we measure heat.

So, by using both luminance and color temperature measures, you can get a pretty good idea of how a light will perform on your bike, on the road.

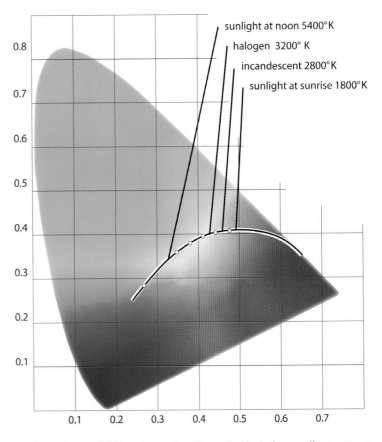

Visible Light Spectrum

sunlight at noon 5400°K
halogen 3200°K
incandescent 2800°K
sunlight at sunrise 1800°K

Light is made up of different wavelengths and affects how well we can see objects, particularly at night. This diagram shows the color temperature of a range of common lighting technologies. Standard incandescent bulbs are near the yellow end of the spectrum. HID bulbs are much further up the scale, emitting light similar to that of sunlight.

Incandescent lights, such as standard household light bulbs, generate light with a color temperature around 2600 degrees K. At this level, the light tends toward the yellow end of the spectrum. Yellow light (like late afternoon sunlight) makes objects look softer. We often refer to this as "warm" lighting.

Halogen bulbs generate light in the range of 3000 to 4000 degrees K. At the higher end of this range, halogens produce light that contains more colors across the spectrum, so they appear whiter and "cooler." High Intensity Discharge (HID) systems generate light in the range of 4300 K to 5000 K, close to the color temperature of noontime sunlight at 5200 to 5500 K. At color

Halogen bulbs use tungsten filaments surrounded by an inert halogen gas.

temperatures above this, light begins to take on a blue hue and perceivable light output drops.

What's important about color temperature is how it interacts with the objects it illuminates. Sunlight contains all the colors in the visible light spectrum so it illuminates the widest range of objects. When the color temperature of a light source approaches that of sunlight, a wider range of objects reflect more of that light and thus, they become more apparent than when illuminated by lower-temperature light. This is especially true for road markings and other reflective surfaces.

BULB TECHNOLOGY

Standard incandescent lighting is relatively unchanged from the days of Thomas Edison. Some of the materials have changed to improve light output and longevity but today's incandescent lights still work by heating a filament until it glows and gives off light. And today's incandescent is still just as inefficient because a large part of the bulb's output is emitted as heat rather than light. On motorcycles, incandescent lights are used for signaling and conspicuity but even that role is being challenged. As a headlight, standard incandescents have been replaced entirely by

more efficient, brighter technologies like the halogen bulb.

Halogen bulbs represent a significant advance over standard incandescents because they produce more light with less power and at a higher color temperature. Like standard incandescent bulbs, halogens heat a tungsten filament to produce light output. The difference lies in the way the bulb is packaged. In halogens, the filament is encased inside a small quartz envelope and sealed at high pressure with halogen gas. As the bulb heats, tungsten vaporizes from the filament, but combined with halogen, it is re-deposited on the filament. This process allows the halogen bulb to operate at higher temperatures with more light output. Since the envelope is so small and close to the filament, halogen bulbs are hot. Halogen lighting is standard equipment on bikes today, including the majority of lighting upgrades.

For something more exotic, how about packing some stadium lighting on your bike? That's the operational theory behind high intensity discharge lighting systems. HID systems generate light from an electric arc that excites a metal vapor inside the envelope. The result is an explosion of light nearly three times brighter than incandescent systems for about the same level of power. Similar to fluorescent lighting, a ballast generates the high voltage needed to start up the lamp without affecting the vehicle system. HID systems are standard on some high-end vehicles and will likely trickle down to more vehicle types, including motorcycles, over the next few years. It's possible to adapt HID lighting for your bike but as we'll see in a minute, it isn't a plug-and-play technology just yet.

Light-emitting diode (LED) technology is rapidly emerging for use as vehicle lighting. LEDs are already generating enough light output to power signals and tail lights. LEDs consume up to 85% less power than incandescents to generate the same light output, and have a service life of up to 100,000 hours.

PACKAGING

An exposed bulb throws light in all directions. That's great for illuminating a campsite. On a dark road, you want that light focused to the

The low beam reflector on this Wing focuses light low and wide. The cap on the front of the bulb controls light dispersion.

By comparison, the high beam reflector is designed to toss as much light forward as possible.

front and sides where it will expose hazards like potholes, tire carcasses, and deer standing on or near the road. For this purpose, bulbs are encased in a system to direct light where it's desired. Standard lights contain three components: bulb, reflector, and lens.

Yesterday's reflectors were a standard parabolic shape that would redirect light from the back of the bulb to the front. Computer-aided design has given us reflectors with complex shapes that do a better job of putting that light to work. The lens complements the work of the reflector to provide additional focus and shape to the light. Projector-style lights contain a mask element between the bulb and the lens. When bounced off the reflector in a particular way, this cuts the light off the top of the beam and produces a squarer and wider beam. You'll find this used in low-beam applications to improve near-distance and side visibility that doesn't blind oncoming vehicles.

The filament's location inside the bulb/reflector package also has a significant influence on how the light performs and where it goes. For example, some bikes have a single headlight unit that contains both low and high beams. A single unit can throw both short and long distances based on where the filaments are located relative to the focal point of the reflector. In this system,

the high beam light is at the focal point of the reflector while the low beam light is shifted away from the focal point.

LIGHTING UPGRADES

There are three distinct levels of lighting upgrade you can make for your bike. The first level is a higher performance halogen bulb. The bulbs your bike runs are probably on the lower end of the color temperature scale, so switching to bulbs with a higher K value is an easy change. The Sylvania SilverStar bulb (sylvania.com)

HID lighting kits include the bulb assembly, a relay, and a ballast. The ballast is required to spark and maintain the arc that produces light.

▶ *HANDLING HALOGEN BULBS*

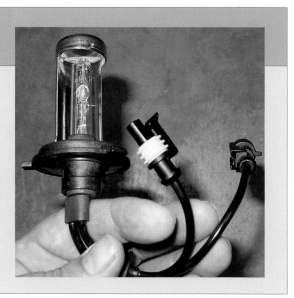

When you replace halogen bulbs, heed the manufacturer's advisory about bulb handling and make sure your fingers don't touch the surface. Why? Oils and other contaminants from your fingers (even clean ones) left on the surface of the bulb will cause uneven heating of the quartz envelope. Uneven heating causes uneven stress on a container that's already under high pressures. The resulting imbalance can cause the envelope to shatter. If you do happen to touch the bulb, no worries. Just wipe the envelope with rubbing alcohol to remove fingerprints and contaminants. ■

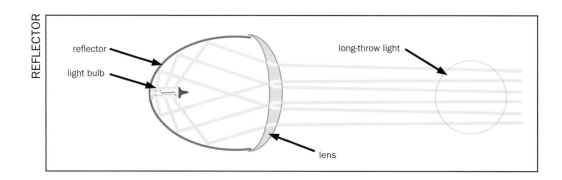

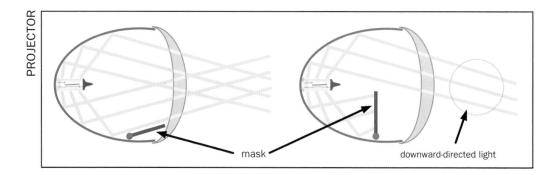

Reflector vs. Projector Designs There are two predominant designs in headlight applications that focus light where it is needed; reflectors and projectors.

Reflectors increase the effective luminance of lamps by directing light through a lens to the front of your bike where it will do the most good. Reflectors are used in "high beam" designs because they are designed to send light long distances ahead of the bike.

Projector lights use a mask and a specially designed lens to create a sharp light cut off. This helps prevent blinding on-coming drivers while producing the maximum amount of forward-directed light. Projectors are used in low beam applications.

emits light at 4000 degrees K, nearly the color temperature of HID lighting. These bulbs and other improved halogens come in the same lamp base as your bike's lights, so this upgrade is a simple swap-out operation.

You may have considered using a higher wattage bulb. The socket and wiring on many bikes will accommodate a higher wattage bulb, but before you do this, check the specs on your bike's headlight circuit. A higher wattage bulb may pull more amps on the circuit than its design allows. You will probably notice a big difference just upgrading your lights with high K value bulbs without having to resort to higher-wattage bulbs.

AUXILIARY LIGHTS

As a second step, auxiliary lighting is an easy upgrade. The only difficulty is deciding which upgrade to choose. Some bikes, such as the Gold Wing, are pre-wired to accept auxiliary lights but for many applications you'll be adding hardware to accommodate the new lights. There are dozen of combinations of lights and reflectors for both driving and fog applications.

If you don't have a spot to mount lights, several companies make light bars and brackets for adding auxiliary lights.

Because Motolights mount low, they'll help your visibility in poor weather.

LET THERE BE LIGHTS

Driving lights. Fog lights. What's the difference? Fog lights project light low and wide to get more light onto the road in front of you. In foggy conditions, this is more effective at lighting the road than light from high beam headlights which is reflected back at you. Driving lights have a narrower, rounder beam pattern and are designed to project far into the distance, supplementing the look-ahead distance of your high beam lights. That's the theory.

In the marketplace what you'll actually find is much confusion. You'll find driving lights mounted high and low, designed to work with low, high, or both beams, and combination lights which purport to handle both fog and driving applications. Before you buy, decide what kind of light you really want. If you drive a lot of narrow country backroads with unpredictable turns and forests close to the road, a low-mounted wide-beam fog light will throw more light to the sides of the road where deer may be waiting to launch into your path. If you frequent higher speed roadways with long straights, that calls for a high-mounted driving light. If your bike's alternator and your budget can handle it, there's nothing stopping you from doing both. ■

▶ **AUTOSWITCH**

The Autoswitch lets you control auxiliary lights with your low/ high beam switch.

Most auxiliary light kits come with an independent switch. If space is limited or you'd simply prefer not to mount another switch, the Autoswitch might be your answer. Autoswitch is a relay designed to control lights without a switch. Instead, you wire the relay sensor to the high beam circuit on your bike's headlights. Flip the high beams on for 1 to 2 seconds and this will energize the Autoswitch relay, turning on your auxiliary lights. You can still flash your lights and use high or low beams as normal. The Autoswitch only responds when it senses that one- to two-second high-beam pulse. (autoswitch.com) ∎

With extra light output comes extra responsibility. Make sure your lights are aimed properly to avoid blinding oncoming drivers.

Among driving lights, there are differences in philosophy and design. Driving lights should be mounted close to the plane of the headlights to throw the extra light ahead of you. PIAA (piaa.com) makes popular lighting systems for this purpose which are often mounted on the underside of the upper cowling near the stock headlights. On the other hand, the Motolight system (motolight.com) is mounted low on the engine guard or front brake calipers. These may not project as far as higher mounted lights, but the separation of light sources may be more noticeable to

Did I say HID lighting was bright? That doesn't look like a bike. It looks like a freight train. If you add HID lights to your bike, make sure they are aimed away from oncoming vehicles.

drivers. Motolights can also be used to assist both high- and low-beam lights where higher mounted lights would blind on-coming vehicles.

HID LIGHTING

Have you ever been on a road so dark that it seems to swallow the light from your bike? If you frequent such roads, you're a candidate for high intensity discharge lighting. For 35 watts of power draw, an HID light can crank out as many lumens as a 120-watt halogen bulb, all at a higher color temperature. There are a few caveats to be aware of. HID lighting systems aren't plug-compatible with your current lighting system. Some retailers claim to offer plug-and-play components and these will become more common as HID systems penetrate the market.

If you decide to purchase an HID upgrade for your existing lights, quiz the vendor very carefully to understand just what is required to install the kit. HID systems require a ballast (that's a unit that generates a high voltage needed to start the lamp without draining your bike), so you'll need to have a place to tuck one ballast for each HID light. Second, if the HID light is designed to fit into the existing reflector on your bike, it's imperative that it be in the same position as the old bulb. As we discussed earlier, the bulb's position relative to the focal point of the reflector affects the amount of light thrown forward. If the new HID bulb is off-axis or too far forward, its output will be significantly diminished.

HIDs have a couple of other trade-offs. HID aftermarket systems haven't been approved yet for use on motorcycles, so you'll have to come to terms with the fact that your lighting system may be illegal and could earn you a ticket.

HID lights require a brief warm-up period before they are at full brightness. For this reason, HID lights are best used in applications where they are not cycled on and off frequently, so they are not a suitable replacement for high-beam lights. They are not compatible with headlight modulators.

HID lights can be used as a replacement for low-beam headlights if the headlight's reflector is designed with a cut-off to keep the intense light from reaching drivers in oncoming vehicles. They are also a good choice for auxilary lighting in isolated riding areas where you don't encounter a lot of traffic and you need as much light as possible to illuminate potential hazards.

If you do elect to pursue HID lights, you're better off with an all-inclusive kit that either replaces your stock headlight or is mounted as an auxiliary light. Kits are on the market now from PIAA and Kuryakyn for BMWs, Harleys, and Gold Wings.

ABOUT RELAYS

A relay is an electrically operated switch that serves two purposes in motorcycle applications. Devices wired directly to a battery can be operated any time, whether the bike's ignition switch is on or off. That may be convenient for the accessory but it's a problem if you forget to turn it

A relay makes it possible for a low-current circuit to control a high-current circuit. This means you can use thinner wires and mount small switches on the handlbars to control the lights. The relay has heavy-duty contacts that switch the higher current required by headlights.

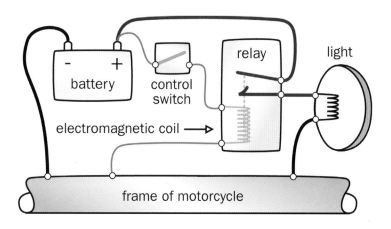

A relay is an electrically-controlled switch. It is made up of two circuits: one that carries the load (red) and the control circuit (blue). The load circuit includes a spring loaded switch positioned over an electromagnet (yellow). When the switch of the control circuit is closed, the electromagnet is energized, which, in turn, attracts the spring-loaded switch, causing it to close. This completes the load circuit, delivering power to the desired device. When the switch of the control circuit is open, the electromagnet becomes de-energized and the spring opens the load contacts. Relays allow low-current circuits to control high-current circuits. On motorcycles, this allows small switches and thinner wire harnesses to be used on the handlebars where space is at a premium. The handlebar switches control relays which can switch the higher currents required by such devices as lights and the electric starting motor.

▶ HOW MODULATORS WORK

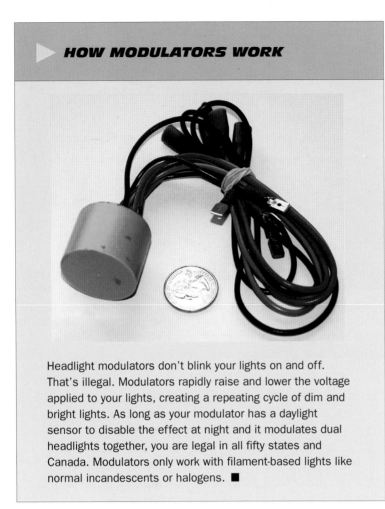

Headlight modulators don't blink your lights on and off. That's illegal. Modulators rapidly raise and lower the voltage applied to your lights, creating a repeating cycle of dim and bright lights. As long as your modulator has a daylight sensor to disable the effect at night and it modulates dual headlights together, you are legal in all fifty states and Canada. Modulators only work with filament-based lights like normal incandescents or halogens. ∎

off. A relay solves this problem. A relay is wired to the ignition. When the key is turned ON and power flows, it activates the relay, which in turn sends power to the circuit it controls.

Relays are also used in high-current applications like lighting systems. If the switch on your handlebar directly controlled the lights on your bike, it would have to be bulkier to handle the heavy gauge wires needed for the high current required by the lights. Instead, the switch activates a relay through its low-current control coil, and that in turn switches the light circuit. The handlebar switch can be made more compact and will last longer because it is controlling a low-current circuit.

BECOMING MORE CONSPICUOUS

Riders are always searching for ways to stand out among vehicles on the road and this section

will explore some of those options. From the front, back, and sides there are several things you can do to make yourself more visible to others.

Headlight Modulators

If you've upgraded or added auxiliary lights to the front of your bike, you've taken a good step toward being more visible to other drivers. Adding a headlight modulator will significantly raise your visibility to all traffic in front of you.

Headlight modulators are legal in all fifty states and Canada when the modulator includes a sensor to turn off modulation at dusk. On dual-headlight bikes, modulators must work in sync on both lights. The ping-pong modulation effect between two lights is reserved for emergency vehicles. No scientific studies have been conducted to prove or disprove the effectiveness of modulators, but there is anecdotal evidence to suggest that they do make motorcycles stand out on the road. I've also noticed that when riding a modulator-equipped bike, vehicles will move out of your way a little faster on the interstate.

Headlight modulators have been around long enough that aftermarket kits are available for many bikes. Compatibility is determined by the type of bulb your bike uses. A modulator fits into your bike's electrical system between the bulb socket and the plug on the wiring harness. The sensor that turns the modulator on and off must be mounted where it can sense available light. When you purchase a modulator, check to make sure the sensitivity of the sensor can be adjusted.

Watch Your Back

So far everything we've discussed has been focused on front-end lighting performance. Improvements to the back side of your bike will make you more visible to people behind you and (again, anecdotally) reduce your chances of taking a shot in the rear end.

What works for the front will work for the back as well. Tail light modulators flash your brake light for a few seconds each time you grab the brake. After blinking for a few seconds they will change to a steady non-blinking state. Tail light modulators usually require some splicing to work for your application. You'll identify the hot lead that runs to your brake lights and insert the headlight modulator into that part of the circuit. Triggering the brake will activate the modulator which then flashes the light.

LED technology is beginning to find its place in motorcycle applications, beginning at the back. LEDs are gaining an edge over standard incandescent bulbs because their design allows them to direct more intense light in the direction where it will be useful: the driver coming up behind you. Nearly every bike uses model 1156 and 1157 bulbs for tail lights and brake lights. LED versions of the 1156 and 1157 bulbs are now available, so upgrading to LED is just a matter of swapping bulbs. Light bars made of rows of LEDs are another easy way to get the attention of drivers when you brake. Light bars can be added to your bike, or even the back of your helmet.

When purchasing LED lights, get good quality LEDs like those from Custom Dynamics (customdynamics.com). You can find cheap LED replacement lights but the low quality of materials and manufacturing produce an LED that isn't very bright, has a limited viewing range, or both. Good quality LEDs look bright from a wide range of viewing angles and project more light than the incandescent bulbs they replace.

Reflective Tape

You can be more conspicuous, especially at night, with a passive system like reflective tape. This is an easy way to add a margin of safety. It's also inexpensive. Reflective tape can be cut to any length or shape and can be applied to any smooth clean surface on your bike or your gear.

When light strikes an ordinary object, the light scatters and only a small portion is reflected back for you to see. Reflective tape is based on 3M's Scotchlite retro-reflective material; when light strikes it, most is reflected back to the source it came from, in this case, headlights. This makes the object stand out from its surroundings.

Retroreflective tape makes bikes and people much more conspicuous at night.

SUMMARY

If you plan to make just one accommodation to your bike for long-distance travel, add auxiliary lights. Being more conspicuous in traffic will reduce your likelihood of playing the bug to someone else's windshield. It doesn't hurt that you'll be able to see farther and better on those occasions when you do find yourself riding at night.

Simple lighting upgrades can be made just by changing your stock head lamps to improved-output halogen bulbs. Long-distance riders who cover a lot of ground at night have begun using high intensity discharge lights that put out extraordinary amounts of light for less power than any other technology. However, HID lights aren't always a practical solution and can't be used with headlight modulators.

Improved lighting extends to the rear of your bike with high-intensity tail lights and directional signals. You can also easily add a universal LED light bar to supplement your turn signals and get the attention of vehicles behind you. Reflective tape added to your saddlebags significantly increases your visibility at night to vehicles behind you.

Cockpit Instruments

Not long ago I hooked up for a ride with a guy I'd recently met and was getting to know. We chatted over breakfast about favorite rides, bikes we'd had—the usual "get to know you" kind of conversation. On the way out the door he paused and asked, "So, have you gone over to the 'Dark Side?'" I wasn't sure what he meant until he added, "You know . . . do you use a GPS?"

To me, that summed up the divided opinion in the motorcycling community about adding electronics to bikes and GPS-enabled navigation systems in particular. Some riders swear by GPS units and rely on them heavily in their travels while other riders don't see the need and may even feel that a GPS compromises some essential element of motorcycle exploration.

Paper maps are still best for seeing the bigger picture.

ADVANTAGE: MAPS

Even with today's abundance of electronic alternatives, a set of good paper maps are valuable. I enjoy hauling out the DeLorme state maps and poring over them. They're still the best for scouting out new riding ideas. In regions where I'm not intimately familiar with the roads, I take paper maps along with me to plan the next day's ride and have them as backup in case the GPS fails. Planning is easier with paper maps because you can see a larger area than on a tiny GPS screen or even a laptop. There will always be a place in my saddlebag for good paper maps.

I've never cared for navigating exclusively by paper maps though. Did I bring the right ones? Should I bring the big comprehensive atlas that shows secondary roads or just the high level state map? Or both? When I need to consult the map, I have to find a safe place to pull over. At night, where's that flashlight? I can't remember what road I passed last, so where am I on the map?

With a GPS, you can aimlessly wander the backroads secure in the knowledge that you can get to your planned destination at day's end.

ADVANTAGE: GPS

GPS units are not perfect, but today's technology is useful enough to warrant a space in your cockpit if you keep its use in perspective. I've come to think of mine as a handy assistant who is always on duty and right more often than wrong. I reserve the right to make the final call whether the route it suggests is efficient or whether the indicated turn is correct.

The biggest benefit a GPS offers is that you never have to ask for directions unless you want to make conversation. You have the freedom to explore any side road or series of roads with the peace of mind that you'll always be able to get to your end destination without getting turned around. With navigator duties handed off, you and your co-rider can enjoy your journey without having to be absorbed in directional details. If you slip up and make a wrong turn, the GPS announces you're off course. The biggest benefit may be this—a GPS won't get mad at you. It continues to patiently recalculate your route and put you back on course regardless of how many bone-headed wrong turns you make. If a gadget like that can eliminate that source of tension between rider and co-rider on a long trip, that's a good investment.

Important Capabilities

Route planning and monitoring. A GPS will help you choose a route and guide you along it. You'll find a number of ways to use this feature to increase your ability to explore new roads and routes with impunity. For one, you can create an entirely pre-planned route on your personal computer and upload it to the GPS unit. Or, with map detail loaded, enter your current location and the street address of your desired destination and let the GPS map a route for you. (I find the latter method more appealing. I'll ride where I like until I'm ready to call it a day, then enter either the town or hotel address I'm heading toward.) Turn-by-turn directions keep you on course. As you approach a turn, the routing function will audibly advise you of the turn and display it on the screen. Very handy when you're in unfamiliar, congested urban areas.

▶ **HOW GPS WORKS**

Triangulation. That's the operational theory behind GPS. A constellation of twenty-four satellites circle the Earth twice a day, each emitting a time signal. A GPS receives these signals and calculates the difference in time it took to receive them. This allows the GPS to calculate the distance between it and a satellite.

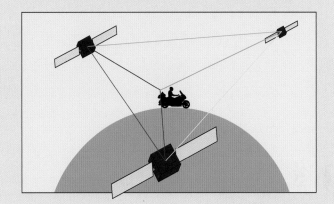

A GPS has to lock onto at least three satellite signals to calculate your latitude and longitude (location). If the unit detects four or more satellites, it also calculates altitude. As you move, the GPS continuously calculates the time difference between your last position and current position, telling you how fast you're moving. Knowing the location of your end point and your speed, the GPS can figure out how long it will take you to arrive at your destination. ■

Mount your GPS should be mounted in a location where you can easily glance at it.

Map data built into a GPS will point you to the closest services. No guessing which way to turn to find gas.

Key stats. If you're a numbers person or you plan to campaign your bike in an endurance rally you'll benefit from the stats a GPS provides. It will tell you things like riding time, time stopped, average speed, top speed, current heading and coordinates, odometer, current speed, and mileage log.

Speed. This is displayed on the main screen along with your route. Your GPS speed is more accurate than your speedometer and it's handy to be able to glance at the screen to see exactly how fast you're going.

Time and distance to turn. As part of the routing function, a GPS will display how far and how long until your next turn. After you've made a turn, a quick glance at the updated directions will give you a sense of how far you'll travel on the next segment of your trip.

ETA. In the car, knowing the estimated time of arrival eliminates those endless "Are we there yet?" questions from the kids. On the bike, the ETA function helps you plan on-the-fly. If you're not sure whether you should stop in Beckley or Charleston, calculate both and compare the ETA. This will assist you in deciding where you should plan to stop for the night.

Services. Shops, restaurants, and gas stations open and close all the time so the services data built into the map database won't always be accurate. When I use this feature to look ahead at

what travel services are available, I'm looking f or locations that have several entries. If my search turns up a town that lists several gas stations, I figure at least one of them will be open.

Waypoints. When I was out riding with my new acquaintance, we crossed a low water bridge over the Shenandoah River I'd never seen. Using the waypoint feature of the GPS, I was able to quickly mark that spot so I could find it again later on my maps. On the StreetPilot you hold one button for a couple of seconds and the spot is marked.

THE DO-IT-ALL GPS

As GPS units continue to evolve, they're jockeying for a central role on your bike and your car. The latest Garmin units include GPS, XM radio, traffic information, weather data and advisories and an MP3 player. Where previous GPSs would announce generic turns, e.g., "In 400 feet, turn right," the new Garmin units will announce the actual street name. I wonder how well it will pronounce "Zzyzx Road?" ∎

GPS Types and Features

There are dozens of GPS units on the market today but they boil down to three broad categories: basic handheld units for hiking, geocaching, etc.; extended handhelds with navigational, routing, and tracking functions; and marine/vehicle-based units with navigation, routing, tracking, and even satellite radio, traffic, and weather functions.

Handheld units are designed to be used on and off the bike. Basic ones like the Garmin eTrex (garmin.com) is used as a navigational aid for activities like hiking and geocaching. The eTrex and other simple GPS units display coordinates which you then correlate to a map.

For motorcycling, we're interested in the class of GPS-enabled navigation computers that come in handheld or vehicle form. Detailed maps are loaded or built into the unit and as coordinates are received, your location on the map is updated automatically. You are always in the middle of the screen and the map scrolls automatically as you travel. (If you always thought the world revolved around you, this device proves it.)

Your choice of product will hinge on two important considerations. Will you use this product more off the bike or on? Will you be averaging high or low mileage on a daily basis?

If your answer is "off bike, low average daily mileage" you're in the market for a product like the Garmin GPSMAP 60C. The 60C uses batteries or takes power from an external supply. On the bike, you'll want to wire it for power to save the batteries. It performs all the basic routing and tracking functions you'd want in a navigation computer, including turn-by-turn directions. The trade-off with a unit like this is the amount of map detail you can load. With no facility for auxiliary storage, you're limited to uploading 24 MB of maps. That's fine for a day of riding, but you'll find yourself updating maps every day or two.

Vehicle-based systems such as the Garmin StreetPilot or 376C series are a better choice if you're planning to cover a lot of territory. You lose portability, but you get massive storage in return. The StreetPilot is pre-loaded with the

The Garmin GPSMap60 is best for those who want a portable unit.

entire North American database, eliminating the need to supplement your maps as you go. Both feature larger displays that are easy to glance at while moving. Routing and planning functions are extensive. Aftermarket accessories will allow you to fully integrate one of these into your bike for improved reliability, security, performance, and a looks-like-stock fit.

▶ BUYER BEWARE

You can find good deals on used GPS and satellite radio units on the Internet. However, you must be certain that the unit can be transferred to you and that you have all the unlock codes you need to activate the unit or its software. To tie an XM Radio to your account, you have to call in the ID number on the unit like you would activate a cell phone. If the unit was stolen or can't be activated for some reason, you've bought a useless piece of junk. Likewise, the mapping software that comes with Garmin units has to be unlocked after it is installed. Garmin's software license is non-transferable, meaning you'll have to purchase a new copy with your used GPS. ■

▶ WHAT IS WAAS?

The Wide Area Augmentation System (WAAS) was originally built by the Federal Aviation Administration and Department of Transportation to aid in precision flight approaches. WAAS is now a feature built in to all new GPS devices. WAAS is a collection of satellites and twenty-five ground stations around North America that provide error-correction for GPS satellite signals, meaning you get increased location accuracy.

Under normal conditions, WAAS-enabled GPSs are position accurate to within three meters. Other regions of the world have augmentation services using different standards and protocols, so while your GPS might work in Europe, it will be less accurate. If worldwide compatibility is important, check to see if the model you are evaluating supports other correction standards. ∎

GPS Characteristics

Besides *portability*, several other factors will help you narrow your choices when choosing a GPS for your bike.

Weather resistance is imperative on a motorcycle. Some units designed exclusively for vehicle use aren't suitable for applications outside the cabin. Make sure the model you choose is rated for outdoor use.

Shock resistance is another important factor. Choose a GPS that stores its data on solid-state storage devices like Compact Flash or SD RAM cards. I would not recommend a unit that uses a hard drive for storage. Hard drives are sensitive to vibration and even the smoothest bike will transmit a lot of vibration to a GPS.

Capacity is becoming less of an issue because new models feature the maps already integrated into the unit. If you're considering a model that uses removable media, buy the biggest media card without resorting to a Microdrive (that's a hard disk drive packaged in Compact Flash form). One thing I dislike about the Garmin 376C is the continued use of proprietary data cards. The 256 MB supplementary card (purchased separately) will hold a lot of maps, but this unit would be even better if it supported an industry standard.

Adequate daytime visibility is another desirable characteristic. This can be difficult to assess, especially if you purchase by mail order, so you may need to purchase or improvise a sunshade if the screen is washed out in daylight.

Easy operation is important. Your interaction with the unit should be very limited while you're moving, so touchscreen operation is an important feature. Your gloved hand will make some tasks difficult to perform so save those for when you're stopped.

Mounting options. The mounts that come with GPSs aren't suitable for motorcycle applications. Forget the stick-on adhesives, magnetic mounts, beanbags, etc. I like the RAM systems device holders that are specific to a particular model of device. If you really like a particular GPS, RAM makes generic holders that will secure it, and possibly one for your specific model.

Integration options. You can tell which product models are best sellers based on the availability of modular wiring kits. This should not be the primary driver of your purchasing decision, but it makes the installation process easier, cleaner, and more functional. A wiring harness from Garmin and an integration module from Kennedy Technologies allowed me to both power my StreetPilot and integrate it into the audio system on my Gold Wing so I could hear the directional prompts.

GPS Installation

Circuit considerations. GPS units draw two amps or less and can be powered from an accessory circuit if your bike is so equipped. For occasional use, the cigarette lighter adapter included with the GPS works well enough. If you plan to wire a permanent power connection for your GPS, this is a good application for a fuse block (see Chapter 5). You can decide whether the GPS should be wired to the battery or to the relay side of the block. Wiring to the relay side means the unit will only work when the ignition switch is on. Wiring to the battery side means it can be used any time, whether the bike is running or not.

Mounting. A GPS needs to be mounted where you can easily glance at it and reach it. On most bikes, a location on the right handlebar or between the handlebars are popular locations. If you choose the RAM mounting system, the model B-309 brake mount is a good base mount. From there, a 3-inch arm (B-201) will elevate the GPS to a comfortable viewing position. You just need a device mount and ball to complete the mounting.

Antenna location. GPS units have a self-contained antenna. In my experience this works fine everywhere except heavily forested locations like the redwood forests along the Pacific coast. Units that include XM radio, traffic, and weather functions will include an additional antenna. For best performance this antenna needs to be mounted where it can have the clearest view of the sky. The GX-30 antenna from Garmin is designed to receive XM weather and traffic info as well as music from the satellite, so its form factor is larger than radio-only micro antennas. A shelf mounted to your tail trunk is a good location for this.

Audio integration. Models with voice navigation can be wired into your bike's sound system to announce turns. Optionally, you can direct that audio to a helmet headset if your bike doesn't have an audio system. An FM transmitter is included on some GPS models to send audio through your bike's onboard radio. This works okay but if you pass through an urban area, you may encounter a local radio station using that frequency. In that case, you'll have to change the setting on the unit.

The best solution is to wire the audio directly into your bike. If a plug-compatible harness is not available, you'll need to purchase a harness with bare wire ends, find a diagram that details the wires in the harness, then consult your bike's wiring diagram to find a convenient insertion point.

SATELLITE TRACKING

When you're planning a trip into the unknown, your route, or lack of it, will be of interest to your spouse, your children, and anyone else concerned about your welfare.

Sometimes, it's that factor of simply knowing where you are, that influences how or where a trip is planned. GPS systems tell you where you are but they can't inform anyone else. That's why I like the idea of satellite tracking systems.

Star-Traxx (star-traxx.com) is a proven vehicle tracking system suitable for motorcycles and

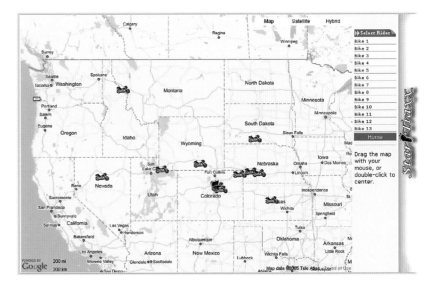

A rider's family can easily keep tabs on his or her location through the StarTraxx website.

used by competitors in the Iron Butt Rally. The basic unit is a sealed Skywave satellite communications terminal that combines GPS and a transmitter. The GPS tracks position and feeds these coordinates to the transmitter. When you are moving, the transmitter fires off your current location every thirty minutes to the satellite, which sends the data back to servers that collect, process, and display the data. To cut down on redundant data, the system doesn't transmit your location when you are not moving.

Those who want to find your location use a web browser to query the Star-Traxx site. As long as your position continues to change, your at-home contacts will know you're okay. If your position remains stationary and you don't check in as expected, your satellite transponder will give responders some idea where to look for you.

Although the capability is limited, it is possible for others to send you a message. From the Star-Traxx site, a user can enter a request to page a particular transponder unit. This page can take several minutes to make it to the transponder. When activated, the transponder blinks a small LED light. You would have to prearrange what action is required when activated, but most users take that as a signal to "call home."

Mounting location is important for a transponder. It needs a flat, horizontal surface with a

► GPS USAGE TIPS

► *Don't abandon your maps.* Paper maps are still the best resource for planning. If your GPS fails, you'll want a ready backup.

► *Believe your eyes.* The road sign says your hotel is at the next exit. The GPS says your turn is three exits ahead. Trust your common sense and the road sign. Navigators are only as good as the maps they're based on and GPS maps definitely contain mistakes.

► *Learn as you go.* GPSs and accompanying software contain many features. Master the basic routing functions of the GPS, then start to explore the more esoteric features. You don't have to master it all at once.

► *Watch the road!* I'm telling you from experience that it's addictive to watch the map moving under you on a GPS screen. Condition yourself to glance only briefly at the screen. If you need to reprogram your route or perform other functions, pull over. ■

clear view of the sky. Some users have found it can interfere with other satellite devices like your sat radio or GPS. Helge Pedersen, an accomplished world traveler, mounts his transponder to the top of his right-rear pannier. Another possibility would be a shelf extension mounted to a rear top bag or rack.

RADAR DETECTORS

One of the mantras of long-distance riders is "slow down to go faster." That seems at odds with the common use of radar detectors by that group, but many riders do use them in the States, purportedly to avoid speed traps and surprises. In the interest of giving you all the facts, here's how the detector may fit into your portfolio of information gathering tools.

Traditional radar uses radio waves to measure speed based on the principle of an effect called Doppler shift. A radar gun emits radio waves that strike an object. As a vehicle moves in relation to the radar source (closer or farther),

those radio waves are modified as they are reflected back to the gun. The radar gun measures those modifications to determine the vehicle's speed.

Since radar guns emit radio waves in specific frequencies, referred to as "X" and "K" bands, a basic radar detector is little more than a radio tuned to the frequencies that radar guns use. When a radar detector encounters a signal in that range, an audible and visible alarm are activated.

Older radar transmitters took time to warm up before they could be used so they were left "on." This gave detector users a decided advantage. Technology continues to escalate the battle on both sides of the ticket. X and K band radars are now portable and instant-on. Laser-based detection systems (LIDAR) use a pinpoint light beam to measure speed and are almost undetectable, until that beam hits you. LIDAR systems must be stationary and have a clear line of sight to be effective.

Detector Installation

Radar detectors require a clear view of the road ahead and are typically mounted at the base of the fairing. Among mounting solutions, the Techmount product line offers a better range of options for detectors. The fairing mount lets you put the detector right up front where it has the best unobstructed view of the road ahead. The Valentine 1 (valentine1.com), a popular model with riders, also detects signals from the rear and requires visibility in that direction. You can accommodate this with the Techmount.

Most detectors are designed for operation inside a vehicle and can't tolerate exposure to weather. You'll need to devise a cover for yours or remove the radar detector when it rains.

Power required by detectors is small. Detectors can easily be powered by an accessory circuit, if you have one, or a dedicated circuit taken from a fuse block.

What about the audio alert your detector sounds? If you're behind a bike with a large fairing like a Wing or Harley, you might be able to hear your detector. Kennedy Technologies RadRide (cellset.com) is a trick solution for riders with a headset. Attach one plug to your MP3 or satellite radio, another plug to a GPS or radar

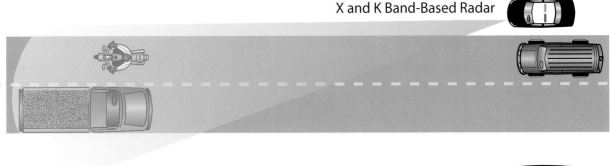

X and K Band-Based Radar

Laser-Based Radar or LIDAR

X or K band radio-based radar has been around for many years. It is inexpensive and easy to operate, but at a quarter-mile, the radar image is very wide, possibly indicating the speed of several vehicles. Radar requires the operator to be able to distinguish which among the vehicles was moving at improper speed.

By contrast, laser-based radar projects a much narrower beam. A traffic officer can measure speed very precisely with a laser-based unit. However, unlike radar, laser requires a line-of-sight contact with the target vehicle. This requires more targeting expertise on the part of the user.

detector. Finally, plug your headset into the jack. By default, you'll hear audio from your music source until an alarm from the detector overrides the signal. This also works with voice navigation on GPS devices. The Kennedy product is a passive device that draws no power and will easily fit in your tank bag. Kennedy also manufactures similar interfaces for bikes with built-in audio systems.

SUMMARY

In this chapter, we took a look at technologies that can provide you or others with more information about your travels.

Navigation systems using global positioning satellites are becoming more popular with motorcyclists. They aren't an outright necessity, but a navigation system can be a real boon to navigationally-impaired riders or those who just want the freedom to explore side roads knowing they will always be able to get to their end-of-day destination.

For riders traveling into difficult terrain where help may be limited or slow in coming, a satellite transponder system could add an important level of security. When everything is going well, family and friends can enjoy tracking your location on a website. When things go wrong, help can arrive a lot faster if your general location is known.

Finally, radar detectors should never be relied upon as a way to avoid a speeding ticket because we already know that you should "slow down to go faster." However, a radar detector can be an effective reminder to check your speed, particularly when entering lower speed zones or approaching town limits.

Entertainment and Communication

Entertainment and communication accessories aren't the highest priority for making your bike safer, but they add enjoyment to any ride. Personal satisfaction is one of the important reasons why we ride, isn't it?

I make no apologies for the fact that I like to carry a few accessories along with me when I travel. Music is important to me. Some times a song underscores the ride so perfectly I feel like I'm in a movie. At other times, music or talk radio keeps me company on a long, lonely stretch of road.

When you're riding with a companion or other riders, communication by a means more efficient than hand signals makes it easy to coordinate your actions and be aware of who is where, especially if you're in a larger group.

Even when you're riding alone, knowing what's going on around you is good, too. A stray conversation on the CB once saved my butt. I'll save that story for later.

PRODUCT LIFECYCLES

One of the drawbacks of rapid innovation is short product lifecycles. Nowhere is this more true than in consumer electronics. Honda's Gold Wing, introduced in 1975 has been revamped four times. By contrast, Apple's iPod is reinvented every single year.

It's good that we have so many choices, but it seems that by the time you've decided on a particular product, it's discontinued. Keep that in mind as you read this chapter. Product names and models change often.

ON-BIKE AUDIO OPTIONS

Clarion claims the title for producing the first motorcycle radio set for Honda in the early 1980s. Since then any touring bike aspiring to be top of the line has included some type of integrated audio system. Even if your bike doesn't have factory audio, you can add it to your bike. There are so many small, well-designed audio products for motorcycles, it's easy to bolt on nearly anything you want and swap out for the latest and greatest whenever you want!

The first step is to decide what types of audio devices you want to add to your bike. Options include:

▶ *AM/FM/weather radio* For local music, weather, news, and sports

▶ *Satellite radio* Nationwide, commercial-free broadcasts

This bike is loaded with more entertainment options than some cars.

▶ *MP3 player* Music, podcasts and audiobooks

▶ *GPS* Some models announce turn-by-turn directions

▶ *Radar* Audible alerts when radar signals detected

▶ *Cell phone* Telephone conversations

▶ *Rider-passenger intercom* Conversations with your co-rider

▶ *CB radio* Coordination with other riders, road/traffic updates from truckers

▶ *Bike-to-bike intercom* For conversation and coordination with riders on other bikes

▶ *Family Radio Service radio* Same as above

▶ *Onboard fridge* Low beverage alert. (Just kidding)

AUDIO INTEGRATION

As you can see there are lots of options, but if you're willing to pay a premium, the trend of device consolidation can help you get everything you want. As I mentioned in the previous chapter GPS devices such as the StreetPilot are taking on multiple functions, including turn announcements, satellite radio, and MP3 audio. Motorcycle electronics manufacturers are building consolidated products, too.

J&M's JMCB-2003 (jmcorp.com) is a handlebar-mounted audio system that includes a CB

This J&M product combines CB, rider-passenger intercom, weather-band radio and amp for an MP3 or similar audio device.

radio, weather band, rider/passenger intercom and amplification for any plug-compatible audio device. Plug your GPS into the J&M unit to route all the audio output from that device into the J&M and you've covered nearly every audio application on this list with just two devices.

If you already have several audio gadgets and need an interface to bring them all together, consider a product like the Autocom Active-7 or Pro-7 audio system (autocomamerica.com). This product acts like a mini audio switcher and amplifier. The main unit can be mounted out of the way and wired for direct power from the bike. Inputs can then be connected to all your audio devices, including your telephone. Music is the default audio but GPS or radar signals will automatically override music. For a phone call, music is muted completely. With a dual headset unit, a rider/co-rider intercom is added. The co-rider can also participate in phone calls.

A third and less expensive option is a mixer/ amplifier like the MixIt M2 (mixitproducts. com). This is good for solo riders who need to tie together a few devices. The portable, battery-operated MixIt contains inputs for up to four devices. It doesn't have an audio override feature like the J&M or Autocom so if you wire in a GPS, its announcements will compete with any other audio source. This may not be a big deal to you because you can always glance at the GPS to see what the next turn is.

The Mixit mixer/amp is perfect for riders who want a solution they can carry in their pocket.

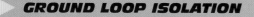

► GROUND LOOP ISOLATION

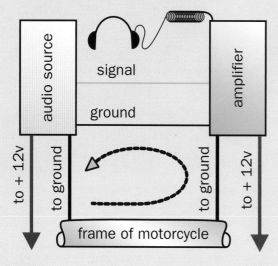

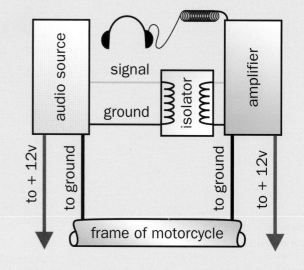

You know you've wired everything properly on your bike but when you connect your GPS into your audio system, there is a noticeable buzzing sound that is not present otherwise. The sound doesn't change when you start or rev the bike. This is symptomatic of a "ground loop." It's really annoying but easy to fix.

Every electronic device wired to your bike uses a shared "ground," the bike's chassis. When you connect two devices together, it's possible that you'll create a loop consisting of the wire that connects the two devices, and a path through the bike's frame between the two points where the devices attach to the frame. Unintended currents can pass through the loop, some of which you may be able to hear.

A ground loop isolation transformer is a simple device that allows the intended signal to pass

between the devices but breaks the ground loop. This eliminates the undesired noise. Products that say they are "ground loop isolated" in their specs will not suffer from ground loop buzzing.

An infrequent problem these days is a variable pitch whine that changes according to your engine speed. This interference is generated by your alternator. If everything on your bike has been working normally and you've just started hearing it, that may indicate a diode in the alternator is failing. If you've never heard it before until you added a new device, check all the grounds on your installation. If the grounds are secure, the whine may be due to inferior circuit design in the device you bought (sorry). A filter capacitor can help alleviate the problem. So can a good return policy at the location where you bought the product. ■

HEADSET OPTIONS

Before you purchase a headset, make sure it's compatible with your audio system or can be adapted for your application. The more functions an integration device performs, the more likely you'll be limited to that brand's headset. If you purchase an Autocom system, your best bet is an Autocom headset. J&M makes a universal headset that is designed to work with other audio systems including integrated systems from the bike manufacturers as well as add-ons like the Autocom. But before you decide to mix brands, make sure you have an opportunity to test the headset and audio system together to be sure everything works.

Headsets boil down to two options: ear buds and helmet speakers. If you're planning on any type of talk-back application (intercom, CB, phone), your headset will be permanently mounted in your helmet with speakers and microphone. Both helmet and headset design have

IMC's Multi-Channel Communications Center kit includes everything you need to add a complete audio management system to your bike and your helmet.

evolved over time so it is now much easier to install a headset. Years ago I had to practically disassemble my Shoei and I felt uncomfortable cutting into the foam insert, but many of today's helmets are designed to accommodate headsets. In addition, headsets have gotten smaller and easier to install. In fact, if you're shopping for a new helmet, you might as well purchase one with the headset already built in. J&M sells their adaptable headset pre-installed in Arai and Nolan helmets.

If you're in the market for a headset with microphone, get a premium quality set. You can purchase the best bike intercom or phone interface made, but if the microphone attached to it is cheap, your expensive audio solution will sound like junk. Premium quality sets have better noise reduction characteristics, are easier to install, have better quality connectors and a wider range of connectors to fit more devices.

For simpler applications, especially if you're just adding an audio source like an MP3 player, your options are wider. IMC's helmet speaker kit is an inexpensive (but good quality) solution that uses hook and loop material (Velcro) to attach inside the helmet. The extra thin speakers stay out of your way and are easy to move from one helmet to another.

▶ BLUETOOTH FOR ALL

If you've heard of Bluetooth technology, it has been in conjunction with cell phones and computers. Bluetooth is a short-range communication technology that makes it possible for devices to communicate with one another without interconnecting wires. Have you seen those guys standing in line at 7-11 wearing an earpiece that looks like a bionic ear attachment? That's Bluetooth.

New Bluetooth kits allow you to bring that same functionality to your helmet, and that opens up a whole new range of possibilities. Beyond the cell phone, look for Bluetooth to become available on other devices and adaptors. This will allow you to dispense with wires altogether when you use your intercom, CB, FRS radio, GPS and MP3 player. ■

BLUETOOTH HEADSETS

"Bluetooth" is a low-power, close-range communication technology that allows compatible devices to connect and work together. A common application is a Bluetooth-compatible phone and headset. Bluetooth devices must be "paired" before they can work together. Pairing is done by activating the cell phone to find

Bluetooth headsets in range (about thirty feet). Bluetooth operates on 2.5 GHz, a frequency also used for wireless computer networks. Entering a PIN code (supplied in documentation for the headset) ensures that you're connecting to your headset and not someone else's.

When using a Bluetooth headset with a cell phone, you can accept and terminate phone calls with the headset alone. Your phone can be packed away in a saddlebag and you can still accept calls or use voice dialing to place outgoing calls. Bluetooth compatibility between your cell phone and computer can save you money on the road, allowing your cell phone to act as a dial-up modem for your computer.

By their very nature as fully wireless devices, Bluetooth headsets are battery-powered. Helmet headsets like the Cardio Scala Rider and the Motorola HS830 use rechargable batteries that last for about seven hours of talk time and up to one week on standby. That kind of battery life is fine when using the headset occasionally throughout the day, but you will need access to overnight power during your trip to recharge the headset.

Emerging standard Bluetooth 2.0 promises to make this technology even more practical while doubling battery life. The new standard will transmit data at 3 mbps, about three times faster than the current Bluetooth 1.2 standard. Since more data can be transmitted in a shorter time, this will require less radio transmission between devices, subsequently lowering battery drain. Before long, Bluetooth-enabled MP3 players, GPS navigation systems, intercoms, and more will enable you to add audio-generating devices to your bike almost instantly with no integration, and best of all—no wires!

CANALPHONES

In a motorcycle application, forget the earphones and headphones that come with portable players. Those tiny devices of torture won't stay positioned well in your ears and they can't achieve a seal. As a result, their sound quality is poor and, if you're like me, the screens on these little buggers catch the hairs (that should be growing on my head, but aren't) every time they come loose.

The better solution is a set of canalphones. Rather than sitting just outside your ear like buds or earphones, canalphones have an earplug-like shape that is designed to be inserted into your ear. When properly situated, you get two benefits from canalphones. First, like earplugs, you can expect ambient noise (like wind) to be reduced substantially. This is particularly true if you use the foam covers that come with plugs rather than the silicone inserts. With less ambient noise to compete with, canalphones deliver higher fidelity sound at a lower volume level than other options. Canalphones range from $20 all the way up to a stunning $500 for a set of high fidelity plugs. You'll find them available from Shure, Sony, Panasonic, Koss, and Etymotic Research.

Laws in some states may limit the use of helmet speakers, headphones, or in-ear devices that may impair your ability to hear another vehicle's horn or emergency vehicles.

DEVICES À LA CARTE

All-in-one integrated solutions aren't the best choice if you already have some of those functions covered on your bike. I'd like to take a few minutes to examine products at a more individual level to give you some idea what to look for if you're shopping for just one feature to add to your bike.

Etymotic ER-4S earphones

SATELLITE RADIO

Let's start with an option that is fast becoming a standard. Harley-Davidson now features satellite radio integrated into its heavyweight cruiser product line. Expect other top shelf touring bikes to offer the same in the next few years.

Yes, you have to pay for satellite radio, but you definitely get value in exchange for a small monthly sum. Buy it one year at a time and you'll pay less than $10 a month for programming. With a portable receiver or a computer and internet connection, you can get sat radio on your bike, in your car, and anywhere you have Internet access. Many channels are talk-free and commercial-free. With over 150 channels, you can find any style of music that suits the moment. What's just as important is the fact that you can stay tuned to the same station as long as you like.

Mounting and Integration

Satellite radios are small and don't draw much power. Delphi's Roady2 for XM Radio (xmradio.com) is a popular choice with riders. It is inexpensive and easy to mount. RAM makes a device holder compatible with the Roady. After mounting, there are three connection points to make: power, audio, and antenna. The Roady requires a six-volt power source. You can use the supplied cigarette adaptor which converts the voltage, or purchase a wiring harness from a specialty retailer like CycleGadgets.com that will allow you to tap your bike's power and convert it to the six-volt source the Roady needs.

The Roady and many other satellite radios intended for car use contain a low-power FM transmitter. This is convenient when you already have an FM radio on-board your bike. The Roady's transmitter broadcasts on frequencies the bike's FM radio can receive, so you don't have to wire it in. This works best in rural areas. In urban areas with many FM stations, interference from a strong station on an adjacent frequency will override the Roady's small transmitter. Your better option is to tap into the 3.5mm (1/8-inch) headphone output jack and put the receiver's audio directly into your audio system or headphones.

My favorite entertainment addition in recent years is satellite radio.

The final connection is the antenna. I've experimented with satellite antennas all over the bike, sometimes exposed and sometimes covered by plastic bodywork. The best and most consistent result I've found so far is with the antenna equipped with a short 12-inch lead. The antenna has a strong magnetic base that clamps firmly to the clutch adjustment knob on the Gold Wing. This position gives the antenna a good view of the sky and the shortened antenna lead should mean less signal loss. Some mounting brackets thoughtfully include a metal plate that the antenna will attach to. Despite the mounting position you choose, you will experience some signal loss when you travel through heavily wooded areas and at the bottom of some gorges that have a limited sky view. All in all, performance of these systems is pretty impressive.

Final note. Satellite radios are not waterproof. You'll need to purchase or devise a cover for yours in case you get caught in the rain.

MP3 PLAYERS

The MP3 player has displaced portable CD players as the preferred container for portable music libraries. Why carry a few dozen songs on CDs you have to swap every forty-five minutes when you can have an entire music library—thousands of songs—at your fingertips?

Everyone knows about the Apple iPod (apple.com/ipod). With 70% of the MP3 player market share in the U.S., just about everyone who buys an MP3 player owns an iPod. Adding an MP3 player to your bike requires no installation when it's the only device you're adding. Throw it in the top of your tank bag and use a set of canalphones and you're good to go. To mount the player on your bike, consult the RAM catalog for a specific holder. As mentioned before, MP3 playback capability is being built into other devices. Your recent model smartphone, PDA, or GPS may already have this capability.

Mounting your MP3 to the bike is optional but doing so makes it easier to get to the player's controls when riding. And like satellite radios, MP3 players need to be protected from the weather. A good mounting solution that also protects is the RAM Aqua Box, which offers several advantages. First, it's weatherproof. If your player's controls are all front-mounted like the iPod, you can operate them through the flexible cover. Second, the box can be locked with a small padlock. This won't prevent serious thieves from grabbing your player but you can feel more secure about walking away from the bike for short periods of time at gas stops. Finally, the interior of the Aqua box is designed to accommodate different device sizes. If you change your MP3 player, you won't have to change mounts.

Autocom makes on-bike audio solutions for integrated audio just like you'd find on touring bikes.

A Smartphone combines multiple functions so you can take fewer gadgets with you on the road.

CELL PHONES

I don't care for phones of any type, so it has taken me a long time to warm up to the idea of cell phones. Even so, I recognize the value of having a cell phone along when riding. It's convenient to be able to check in from anywhere and it's a lot less expensive than using the long-distance service in hotels. For emergency use, it's a vital tool to let you raise help more quickly.

Cell phone technology and rate plans change every day, so I'll share just a couple of general thoughts. I replaced my old cell phone with a "smart phone," that is, a phone that contains software similar to a computer and merges multiple functions into one device. I can use the smart phone for calls, e-mail, web browsing, and for listening to music. On the road, this is a real space saver. I no longer have to carry my laptop to keep up with e-mail when I am traveling through major cities. Data service for the phone works only in metro areas; therefore, services such as e-mail and browsing won't work in rural areas. So when I'm farther out, I look for an

Internet café or use the business center computer at the hotel I'm staying in to connect to the Internet.

Second, motorcycle touring by definition almost guarantees you'll be traveling outside your home cell area. On a standard plan, you may rack up substantial roaming charges. Check with your carrier to see if they offer a fixed-fee roaming plan. It may be well worth the few extra dollars to avoid a big bill.

Mounting and Integration

The trend now seems to be to not only carry your phone with you but to also integrate it into your audio system. The simplest integration is to add a Bluetooth headset to your helmet. With Bluetooth, you don't even have to mount the phone anywhere on the bike. You can answer any incoming calls from the headset and you can initiate outbound calls with voice dialing.

If your bike already has an integrated audio system, you can find a manufacturer who has developed an interface to add a cell phone. Kennedy Technologies (cellset.com) offers a whole series of interfaces for cell phones and other devices. An interface that integrates your cell phone with an override to mute incoming audio is the cleanest solution. Kennedy's Ultra Classic interface performs just this function for Harleys while the CellSet is designed for Gold Wings. Autocom and J&M have integration solutions for bikes without built-in audio systems.

RIDER-PASSENGER INTERCOMS

A rider-passenger intercom allows you to have a conversation with your co-rider without shouting or straining to hear that you were supposed to turn two hundred yards earlier. Built-in systems aside, you would be better off avoiding single-purpose intercoms. Low-end, intercom-only systems have a reputation for low component quality, which means you'll spend more time fiddling with the unit or replacing defective parts than getting good use out of the system.

You'll also find that after you have a headset mounted in your helmet, you'll want to use it for other applications. You're better off springing for a basic audio system like the IMC MIT 10 (whitehorsegear.com). If you think a rider-

Equip your passenger with a headset and mic so you can talk without having to shout at one another. I'm not aware of a current headset solution for pets.

FULL- VS. HALF-DUPLEX

When evaluating an intercom/cell phone interface, make sure it supports full-duplex communication. Like traffic on a two-way street or an ordinary telephone, full-duplex communication allows conversation to flow both ways at the same time. By contrast, half-duplex allows communication to flow both ways between parties, but only in one direction at a time. With intercoms and telephones, this is awkward. CBs and other radio systems are half-duplex, but based on the way they are used for short conversation, riders seem comfortable with a half-duplex solution. ∎

WHY CHANNEL 19?

Every wonder how truckers settled on Channel 19 as their preferred channel? CB radios use a range of frequencies to communicate and the antenna mounted on a vehicle is tuned to receive that range of frequencies. Truckers soon discovered that antennas were most sensitive to Channel 19's frequencies, giving them a longer transmission range than other channels. ∎

passenger intercom is really all you need, I recommend a portable intercom that you can use on any bike. In that case, a basic unit like the IMC MIT 15 makes sense.

RADIO COMMUNICATION SOLUTIONS

Communicating with riding buddies becomes more important as the number of people or length of trip increases. You need a convenient method of staying in touch with everyone on your ride without having to constantly monitor your mirrors. Being in radio contact allows everyone to ride within their limits and ensures everyone is having a good time. It's easier to coordinate stops with inter-bike communication and it adds that layer of give-and-take conversational BS that makes riding with friends so much fun.

CB Radio

Citizens Band or CB radio was an early participant in the development of the consumer electronics craze in America. CB burst onto the scene in the mid-70s and quickly became a phenomenon, foreshadowing our culture's taste for other instant communication devices like the cell

FRS radios transmit greater distances and with much greater clarity than CB radios

phone. The CB fad subsided about the same time that disco died, but CBs still have a role in the rider's communication arsenal. I'm certain that a CB radio conversation I caught by accident saved me from causing one.

Some years ago I was riding a bike back from Dallas for a friend, towing an enormous trailer that weighed more than the bike. Somewhere around Little Rock, Arkansas, construction had rendered the road a mess with countless jolts, jars, edge traps and potholes. The condition of the road didn't slow down anyone else. Traffic was moving at a good clip and I had little choice but to move with it or create an even more dangerous situation by riding too slow. I was getting weary and needed a diversion so I snapped on the CB for a bit. When I heard one trucker's transmission end with "yeah, that bike is throwing out some big sparks," that caught my attention pretty quick. Another trucker, probably the one on my tail said "Looks like he's dragging something along pretty big under that trailer." I made quick work of finding a safe place to pull over where I discovered that one of the trailer's jack stands had jarred loose and was dragging along behind me.

Until another standard communication channel evolves where truckers congregate, there will always be a good reason to tune into Channel 19 on a CB radio. Truckers observing highway conditions, radar setups, and accidents relay that information to one another as they pass along the road. That info is usually accurate and timely although it comes interspersed with a healthy dose of inane and salty conversation.

A CB makes sense for your bike if you're interested in hearing that highway info or if you're riding with other riders who are similarly equipped. Gold Wing riders have a long time tradition of using CB Channel 1 for communication. When you meet a CB-equipped Wing along the road, that's where their radio is likely to be set.

Family Radio Service

Not so long ago, the only realistic option for bike-to-bike communication was CB radio. Some manufacturers made cheap communication systems that operated on 49 MHz, the same frequency used by cordless phones, baby monitors, and other home radio applications. These sets transmitted using amplitude modulation technology (AM radio) and they were terrible for a number of reasons: atmospheric interference, limited range, and too many devices using the same set of frequencies.

Family Radio Service (FRS) solves many of those problems and makes it a superior alternative to CB. FRS uses a set of frequencies in the UHF range. FRS radios are allowed to transmit at 500 milliwatts of power on fourteen channels using frequency modulation (FM), rather than AM. Within each channel, you can choose one of thirty-eight privacy codes, giving you effectively 532 "talk groups." Even at just half a watt, transmission range is up to two miles. Transmissions within range are static-free and clear. Plus, with so many channels, you won't have a hard time finding a clear one. FRS radios require no license to operate and you are free to use them for both private and commercial use. They are available from any electronics retailer, sold in pairs for prices ranging from $20 to $40. Motorola and Uniden are the most commonly found and popular units.

FRS Mounting and Integration

FRS radios are only available as handheld units with integrated antennas. That's because FCC regulations require FRS radios to have non-detachable antennas. For this reason, you won't find FRS integrated into your bike. However, interfaces for FRS radios are found on many of the audio systems we've already discussed.

For radio-only applications, I like the IMC HS110 that was built specifically for use with FRS and GMRS radios. Compared to others, it's an inexpensive but well-built solution that includes a push-to-talk button. This is just my opinion, but I prefer using a PTT button to chat rather than relying on voice activation (VOX). VOX settings can be difficult to get just right but you always know whether your speaking or not when you push the PTT button.

FRS radios run on AA or AAA batteries and will accept rechargeables. There are a few helmet-mounted FRS radios now, but given the choice, I'd stick with adding a handheld to the bike via a RAM mount. You can use these radios

► NOISE REDUCTION

The motorcycle cockpit is a noisy place. Wind buffeting, road noise, and the whine of that big motor you're sitting on all generate sound that makes it difficult to hear conversation through a headset. Noise reducing headsets can eliminate ambient noise, making conversations clearer. Noise reduction works on the principle of sound wave phases.

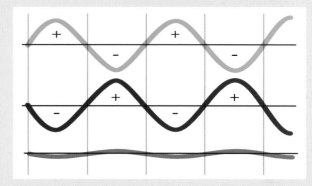

Blue - Original sound wave
Red - Same wave 180º out of phase
Purple - The two combined

All audio waves have peaks and valleys. If a second sound wave of the same size is mixed with an original wave, but the peaks of the second wave correspond with the valleys of the original wave and vice versa, the waves are 180 degrees "out of phase." When two identical waves are mixed together but are out of phase with one another, they cancel each other out. In an audio application, the result is silence.

In noise canceling headsets, a microphone near the headset samples the ambient noise in your environment and converts this to an electrical signal. A circuit in the headset "flips" the sound signal so it is out of phase with the surrounding noise and pumps this alternate signal into the headphones. This "flipped" sound, combined with the environmental noise reaching your ears around the headset, cancel each other. ■

in so many ways off the bike, it makes sense to just stick with handheld units.

I also prefer radios that use replaceable batteries rather than built-in rechargeables. If you're on a long trip, you'll use up the battery in the first day or two and will have yet another power adaptor to lug along to recharge the radio. I'd favor using alkalines when on the road, then switch back to rechargeables for around town and day ride use.

General Mobile Radio Service

Like FRS, General Mobile Radio Service (GMRS) is designed primarily for family use. GMRS radios transmit using FM on fifteen UHF channels, seven of which they share with FRS. There are a few characteristics that distinguish GMRS from FRS, but the most important for you to consider are power output and licensing.

GMRS radios can generate as much as 50 watts of power output and can use detachable antennas. So, like a CB, you could attach an antenna somewhere on the bike and integrate a GMRS radio into your bike. In practical terms, mobile GMRS units deliver one to five watts of power output, making them effective at two to ten miles. Like FRS radios, GMRS radios are

GMRS - Motorola FV200R

typically sold in pairs and are available for $30 to $60 at electronics retailers and mass merchandisers.

The FCC requires that GMRS uers purchase a license, good for five years. In practical terms, enforcement has been a bit lacking. Combination radios that transmit on both FRS and GMRS frequencies are sold in blister packs at mass retailers. I'm willing to bet that it won't be long before licensing on GMRS frequencies will go the same way CB licensing went: out the door.

BATTERY TECHNOLOGIES

You probably have a drawer in your house like mine that holds a dozen or more different types of battery chargers for those devices that inform and entertain us in modern life. Aren't they a pain? They're doubly so when you have to deal with rechargeable adaptors on the road. If a harness is available to wire a device like an MP3 player to your bike, you'll enjoy it more and worry less because you don't have to lug a charger with you. If I'm looking at two different models of product and they work equally well, I'll purchase the one that uses disposable batteries to avoid having to add yet another charger to my pile at home (or on the bike). When you do choose a product that has a built in rechargeable battery, there are three types.

Nickel-Cadmium (NiCad) was the first popular rechargeable technology and is still used in less expensive products. Among rechargeables, NiCad batteries can sustain a high drain and can handle over 1,000 recharge cycles, but they have one irritating characteristic—an effect called "memory." If you don't fully drain a nickel cadmium battery at least once a month, it begins to hold less charge with each recharge cycle. NiCad batteries contain toxic materials and should be properly recycled.

Nickel-Metal Hydride (NiMH) is an advance over nickel-cadmium for its ability to hold 30 to 40% more charge in a cell (it will last longer) and requires a deep discharge about once every three months to avoid developing capacity-robbing "memory." However, NiMH batteries can sustain fewer recharge cycles, about 300 to 500. Heavy use applications result in a lower number of recharge cycles.

Lithium-Ion (LI) is a newer technology found in batteries like your laptop. LI is working its way into other applications due to its ability to hold more power at a comparable size than either type of nickel battery. LI batteries can be recharged at any time with no regard for the dreaded memory effect. LI technology is still new compared to nickel technologies, so we can expect continued increases in storage capacity and longevity. LI batteries do have two drawbacks. They are more expensive to manufacture and, more significantly, are subject to an aging effect that causes them to lose capacity and fail, often within two to three years.

Despite this limitation, I'd choose a product equipped with a LI battery over one using NiCad. The extra battery life is significant and not having to purposely run down a battery so it will charge properly makes the LI battery more user-friendly.

SUMMARY

Is your head spinning yet? Even though these devices may not be your first priority, the number and variety of entertainment and communication options show that this is a popular and important category of products for riders.

Products that add music, sports, and news programming to your bike will help you when you're trying to make time or when you're traveling through uninspiring terrain. Just as cassette tape players gave way to CDs, those players are now disappearing in favor of MP3 players that can hold volumes of music in a very small package. You have many choices for fully integrating audio into your bike, or just adding it into your helmet for a truly portable solution.

Communication products are valuable for coordinating a ride with others, but CBs in particular can be a good source of information about road conditions, and entertaining too. Radios using FRS and GMRS frequencies are being adopted by riders for bike-to-bike communication because they have superior range and clarity over older CB technology.

An MP3 player with four gigs of memory can hold about a thousand songs, the eqivalent of about 100 CDs.

9

Cameras and Camcorders

As Robert Fulton, Jr. prepared for his incredible intercontinental motorcycle tour in 1932, he strapped to his bike a motion picture camera and canisters containing 4,000 feet of 35 mm camera film.

Can you imagine what effort was required, not only to carry that equipment, but to protect it, set up and capture a scene and then preserve the film? Fulton's riding accomplishments, recounted in his book *One Man Carava*n are a fascinating read, but carrying that camera and film, capturing images of cultures and vistas from his time is, to me, one of the most important achievements of his journey.

Whether you plan to record some of the same scenic and cultural time capsules as Mr. Fulton or get a few good shots of your trip to share with friends, the equipment choices are dazzling. And in either case, your camera equipment is an important touring accessory because it's the primary means you will use to communicate your adventures with others. Classic images of *you*r time and place are just waiting to be found.

Have your camera handy for those improbable shots like zebras by the road, UFOs, that sort of thing.

FILM OR DIGITAL?

Had this book been written just a couple of years ago, we would have debated at length the merits of digital photography versus film. Not today. Digital photography is the predominant choice of amateur and professional photographers for all but specialized applications.

If you already have a film camera and you're pleased with the results you get, don't throw it out. After all, film cameras do have a few lasting advantages over digital images. Film resolution

Good pictures will let you relive those great tours over and over.

and dynamic range are superior to digital images. This means that you can print larger pictures with excellent results using a film negative than a digital image. Film is future-proof. An image taken with my thirty-year-old Canon body and lenses is still superior to the Nikon D100 that just a few years ago was the height of digital technology.

Both CompactFlash (CF) and Secure Digital (SD) cards are small. A one gigabyte card will hold over 300 pictures shot at 6 megapixels

That said, I know a lot of riders aren't thinking about dynamic range or the merits of Kodak Ektachrome versus Fujichrome. What they're after is an easy way to take consistently good pictures that are easy to share with others. Digital cameras fit this application very nicely.

Digital cameras take better pictures across a wider range of conditions than film. You can purchase very small digital cameras that require practically no space to carry, yet take excellent pictures. A large capacity storage card will hold hundreds of high-resolution pictures that are easy to load onto your computer. Previews are instant so you can make sure you got that group shot in front of the Corn Palace just the way you wanted it. If there is any significant drawback to digital cameras for casual use, it may be how you manage all those pictures you took once you get back home.

PURCHASING CONSIDERATIONS

Walk into any electronics store that sells digital cameras and prepare to be overwhelmed. There are so many cameras to choose from they all start to look about the same after a while. I'm going to

This compact camera fits nicely in even an eight-year-old's hand. It would be easy to store in the pocket of your riding suit for quick access.

restrict my purchase recommendations to point-and-shoot style digital cameras for the very first reason on the following list.

Size and shape. Given that actual picture capturing performance among so many cameras is about the same, I think usability becomes an important evaluation factor. You will find more opportunities to use a camera that's easy to grasp and shoot with one hand than one that requires two hands to use. An SLR digital may be the height of technology, but you can't exactly "whip out" an SLR whenever you want. For this reason alone I gravitate toward cameras like the Canon Powershot series with a large right-hand grip.

Ease of use. How quickly can you start up the camera, snap off a couple of pics, and look at the previews? The faster and more intuitive this process is, the happier you'll be with the camera. The first digital camera I bought took at least ten seconds to start up (I suspected it ran on vacuum tubes) and then required eight to ten seconds between shots to store the last picture it took. That's fine for scenic views but entirely unacceptable for fleeting action and candid photos. Ease of use extends to the menu system and navigation controls on the camera. It should be easy to access basic camera controls, especially previewing and deleting images. Those are the two features you'll use all the time.

Resolution. Typically measured in "megapixels" this number gives you an idea of the detail a digital camera is capable of capturing. These numbers continue to escalate as technology advances but even modestly priced cameras are powerful enough for taking travel pictures. For example, a mid-range camera like the Canon Powershot A510 has a maximum resolution of 3.2 megapixels. That's enough resolution for an acceptable 8 x 10 photo print. How many 8 x 10 vacation pictures do you plan to print? The typical 4 x 6 print from a camera with this resolution is indistinguishable from a film 4 x 6 print to all but professionals. For full-size display on computer screens, you'd need less than two megapixels of resolution.

Other considerations. Ignore the claims manufacturers make about digital zooms and pay attention only to what kind of optical zoom a camera has. Do you already have a device using Compact Flash or Secure Digital media? Choose a camera that support a storage format you already own.

The Sportbikecam mount is easily adjustable and holds your camera steady for a great shot.

MOUNTING AND INTEGRATION

I "mount" my camera in my top left Aerostich pocket where I can easily reach it but like anything else, there are some surprisingly innovative solutions available from garage-based entrepreneurs that cause you to start thinking, "you know with that type of mount I could . . ."

The only mounting solutions I can recommend involve platforms that are bolted onto your bike in some fashion. Suction cup solutions might stick to your bike just fine, but you have to be concerned about making sure the surface is clean, otherwise suction cups can scratch your paint.

Tankbag solution. Sometimes the best solution is the least expensive solution. If you have a bike with a high tank relative to the windscreen of the bike (like a sport bike), you can get very satisfactory results with your video camera by modifying a cheap tank bag to hold the camera with a hole in front for the lens. Find a bag sized to hold your camera when you zip the top closed. You might also need to fill the area on each side with something to hold the camera in place. This camcorder-only solution won't work for touring bikes with large consoles.

Sportbike Cam (sportbikecam.com) is a solid, adjustable pivot mount that bolts onto the rim around your flush mount gas tank lid. You can move the camera or camcorder 360 degrees and move it up or down as well. This solution would preclude use of a tank bag, so it is probably best for day trips and track days. The makers of Sportbike Cam also sell a rear-facing mount for taking unobstructed videos of your riding buddies.

This camera is mounted up front where the rider can easily snap off shots along the way.

RAM Mount has a dozen different solutions for mounting cameras. The simplest would involve a RAM clutch mount base, long arm and B-202A camera mount. This solution is flexible for positioning and doesn't steal your tank bag space. If the long arm transmits too much movement to the camera, use a shorter arm.

My favorite design is the *Cammount* solution from Desert Iron Images (cammount.com). This unique mount fixes on your handlebar like the RAM mount but features a grip-and-release mechanism that makes it easy to reposition the camera. Unlike the Sportbike Cam, RAM mount, or tank bag solution, this approach allows you to reposition the camera and change angles as easily as you would adjust a rearview mirror.

CAMCORDERS

These days you are hardly limited to still images and unlike Robert Fulton's equipment, modern cameras allow you to capture your ride in progress. With and image-stabilizing camcorder and a specialty camera or two, you can generate your own sporting reality video with all those crazy camera angles you see on motorcycle racing shows. Or you can create a short highlights video of your trip to share with your favorite Internet discussion group. Here's the short list of must-have features for an onboard camcorder.

Image stabilization is the most important feature for cycle-mounted cameras and it's practically a standard today. There are two methods: optical and electronic image stabilization. Optical is the preferred method because it does nothing to compromise image quality.

Video and microphone inputs are important for producing a watchable video. We'll talk about external lipstick cams in just a minute, but your camcorder will need to be able to accommodate external video via a composite video or S-video connection. S-video is sharper and takes better advantage of your camera. The built-in mic on the camcorder is poorly situated to pick up your voice. An external mic wired to your helmet will let you add audio commentary that you'll be able to hear and understand later.

Firewire video transfer makes it easy to move video from your camcorder to computer. Add an

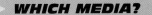

WHICH MEDIA?

Camcorders on today's market support a handful of media types. Which is best for you? Here's a snapshot review of each.

Smaller media sizes lead to smaller devices. miniDV tapes are half the size of the previous popular format, Hi8mm.

miniDV is a compact, high-resolution tape format that is supported by the widest range of cameras and is recognized by all video editing software. Among tape-based systems, this is a best choice for a first-time buyer and works just fine on a bike.

Digital8 is a competing high-resolution tape format supported by Sony. The form factor is a little larger than miniDV. This format is also widely recognized by video editing software. Good choice if you have an extensive 8mm library. Digital8 cams will play back analog 8mm and Hi8mm tapes.

MicroMV is a tiny tape format from Sony that allows for even smaller camera designs yet it can still hold high-resolution video. Good choice if you want high-quality tape video in the smallest available package.

Mini DVD-R and *DVD-RAM* are disk formats. An okay choice if you don't want to futz with computer editing and just want to pop your disks right into a DVD player. If you want editing flexibility, choose another format.

CompactFlash and *SD-RAM* are solid-state formats (no moving parts) that allow for pocket-size recorder designs. These are a good choice for high-vibration environments where you would be concerned about the longevity of a hard-disk or tape-based system. With a reader-equipped PC, you can pop the card directly into the computer for transfer. The primary limitation with RAM cards are the short recording time at tape-equivalent quality settings. ∎

inexpensive Firewire interface (also known as IEEE 1394) to your computer and you can capture high quality video directly to disk. Camcorders with Firewire can be controlled by your computer's capture software.

Extended battery life is a significant convenience feature. It's a pain to go through a nice set of curves only to find your camera's battery has crapped out half-way through the run. If you're planning extensive filming, look for a car adaptor for your model and you can avoid battery concerns altogether.

A flip-out, rotating LCD screen gives you the best view of what you're taping without having to peek through the viewfinder. Once you get your view set though, flip that screen closed for actual taping. You'll be able to tape for a longer time (the LCD screen uses a lot of power) and you won't be tempted to watch your ride through the video camera.

LIPSTICK CAMERAS

With today's compact video camera designs, you can mount your video camera in a lot of places on your bike to get cool camera angles. However, as you see your camera hanging out there in

This lipstick camera lets you capture movies that look like made-for-television viewing.

the wind, you may not be so crazy about putting that high-priced gadget into harm's way. The better solution is to capture those radical angles with a lipstick camera.

Lipstick cameras brought an entirely new dimension to motorcycle racing a few years ago, bringing viewers on-board with riders during the intense competition of a race. Yes, as a motorcycle touring accessory, a lipstick cam is definitely a luxury. But lipstick cams have declined in price so they're affordable for consumers and if you really want to capture impressive footage of your trip, this is a great add-on.

Bullet, lipstick, cigar—all are different sizes of portable camera but refer to the same basic concept; a tiny color camera mounted inside a tube that can be placed nearly anywhere on your bike with lipsticks being the most popular in motorcycle applications. Lipsticks are designed to work in rough environments. A good lipstick is housed in a heavy metal casing and is sealed against all forms of moisture. Some makers like Helmetcamera.com advertise you can run over their cam with a truck and it won't break. If yours is ever run over by a truck while it's mounted on your helmet, well, you've got bigger problems.

Mounting and Integration

Lipstick cams are usually packaged with their own mounting solution. Often they are fixed in a certain location, but manufacturers like Peter Lisand Machine Corporation (peterlisand.com) also sell pan/tilt mounts.

Lipsticks will send video on either a composite video connection (a yellow "RCA" type plug) or a four-pin S-video connection. Whenever possible, use the S-video output to connect to your camera. These cameras are often shipped with a battery pack and that's fine for applications where you want to move the camera among bikes. For permanent installations, look for a 12-volt camera (many are) that you can wire directly into your bike's power grid.

Where should you mount your lipstick camera? Anywhere you want. That's what they're designed for.

▶ TAKING BETTER PICTURES

Digital cameras take all the guess work out of exposure, letting you focus more on the composition of photos. Here are a few simple tips I've picked up that have served me well.

▶ Add people in your pics. After I shot several rolls of test pics for my first book project, Whitehorse publisher Dan Kennedy said, "Your pictures are fine technically but where are the people?" He was right. People like looking at people.

▶ Morning and late afternoon are the best times for outdoor picture taking. The sun's low position in the sky makes for more dramatic shadows and richer colors.

▶ Use your flash outdoors. Faces are easy to lose in the shadows under brightly lit conditions. Experiment with your camera settings to generate a flash when shooting people, even in full daylight.

▶ Speaking of people, don't be afraid to get in close. In photos where people are the subject, a person's face is the money shot. That's what you want to see and remember. Don't feel like you have to stand far enough back to get everything in the shot from head to foot. Striking portraits and candid shots capture faces up close.

▶ In scenic vistas, move the main subject from the middle of the picture. Imagine a tic-tac-toe grid on your camera and position your subject into one third of that grid. (This guideline is also referred to

Shoot a lot of pictures and a few will turn out like this great shot. Glyde Hannah looks like he's ready to find out what lies ahead.

as the "rule of thirds.") For example, the monument you're photographing might occupy the right third of the frame, allowing you to capture more of its surroundings to give the picture better context. When a landscape is the subject, position it to consume the bottom two-thirds of the picture. When sky is the feature, position it to take the top two-thirds.

▶ Learn to crop. You took a picture for a reason. Use your photo editing software to crop out everything else. Good cropping will turn an ordinary photo into a great one. I especially like to crop the top and bottom of photos to create a panoramic effect. ■

SUMMARY

A camera is one of the few pieces of travel gear everyone packs. We're a visual society and seeing where others have been is exciting because it fuels our own imagination.

Film systems are still the best choice for capturing the highest-resolution images, but the market is quickly shifting to digital-based systems for the majority of people who just want to take good pictures of their travels.

Camcorders add a new dimension to travel documentaries. Digital camcorders, lipstick cameras, and special camera mounts allow any rider to capture stunning on-the-road travel footage. Your bigger challenge will be figuring out how to manage the volumes of good stuff you capture on the trip.

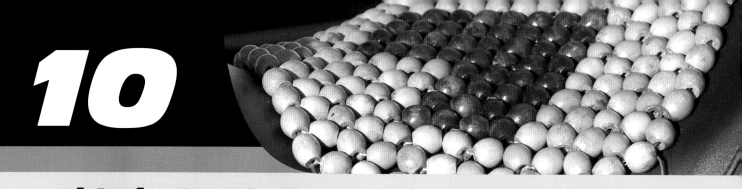

Ride in Comfort

Motorcyclists put up with a lot of grief beyond clueless four-wheelers and kamikaze wildlife. Survey riders at any gathering spot and you'll discover a catalog of aches and pains your great aunt could only dream of. Tightness between the shoulders, aching wrists, chafed thighs, sore bum, tension headache, stiff back and legs—these are all common complaints of riders. Someone not familiar with the overwhelming joys of motorcycling might wonder why we put up with it at all.

A bike's overall ergonomic design is the biggest determinant of comfort, or lack of it. The quality of the seat makes a major difference. Wind pressure, where it comes from, and how much, is a factor. Engine noise and vibration contribute. All these factors and others either add to or subtract from what I'll call your bike's overall "comfort account." You as the primary rider are the only person who can tabulate the balance of this account for any particular bike you own.

Dan Bard poses beside his Gold Wing. The Wing and bikes like the BMW K1200LT and Harley Electra Glide Classic are designed to be comfortable for rider and co-rider over long distances.

I'll bet you can think of one bike you've ridden with a "large negative comfort balance," a bike so uncomfortable it would take wholesale changes to make it rideable over any distance. Off the showroom floor, I believe most bikes have a slightly negative balance in the comfort account. They look good, but like any relationship, you have to ride the bike for varying distances and in different conditions to get a sense of the bike's strong and weak points. Your objective should be to make changes that add to the bike's comfort account until you bring the balance into positive territory. You don't have to do everything at once. For many riders, adjusting their bike for greater comfort is a continuing pursuit.

Years ago, along the Blue Ridge Parkway, I fell into a conversation about touring accessories with a fellow rider at one of the overlooks. I could tell this guy was a serious rider because his changes were all about rider and passenger comfort. They looked like they were well used. As we talked, he related each change as the outcome of a particular trip he'd taken. The highway pegs corresponded with a long trip out West a few years before, the arm rests for his passenger after a couple of weeks riding two-up through Canada. "But this is the most important thing I added to my bike," he said pointing in the area of the seat. "The saddle?" I asked. It looked stock to me. "No this," he said as he picked up a simple beaded mat that covered the seat. "Best $30 I've ever spent in my life."

I took away two lessons from that conversation. First, you're better off making modifications to your bike as you put the miles on it and discover what really needs improvement. The best time to document ideas for changes comes at the end of a long day of riding when you can easily recall the discomforts you experienced during the day. Second, modifications like that beaded seat cover might make a big deposit in the comfort account for a smaller cash outlay than bigger changes.

LISTEN TO YOUR BODY

The human body is a funny and wondrous contraption. We get so much feedback from our body, we focus on fixing the bigger issues and ignore the smaller things. Think about how often you have pulled back from the handlebars during a ride to relieve the ache in your wrists and let the numbness in your palms dissipate. You've done it so often, you don't think about it any more. These minor aches and pains indicate problems that, if not addressed, become chronic issues over time, that will bug you whether you're on the bike or off.

Sometime when you have a few quiet minutes, put your riding gear on, lift your bike up on the centerstand and put yourself into riding position. Hold yourself like that for a while and concentrate on different areas of your body. Ask yourself, "Am I comfortable in this position? Where do I feel the pressure of my body coming into contact with the bike? Which areas feel like they are stressed?" Close your eyes if that helps you focus. If you keep still long enough, you will begin to clearly "hear" what your body is telling you. Those knees sure would enjoy a stretch. There's that tightness in the shoulders you've felt before. It's been just a few minutes and already your palms are numb.

In this section we examine long-term solutions for your list of gripes in order to build up the balance in that comfort account for you and your co-rider. You can make a few small investments along the way to make your bike enjoyable over the long haul, or you can clip off $50 bills three times a week to your chiropractor every time you ride a thousand miles. He's going to use that extra cash to buy this stuff for his bike.

IMPROVING THE BOTTOM LINE

Comfort starts by keeping your butt happy. A large measure of the punishment you take on the road is absorbed by your rear end. After a couple

Early motorcycles were hardly comfortable and yet people made trips on them anyway.

hundred miles, your stock seat may begin to feel more like a vinyl-covered plank designed to spank you continuously through your day's ride. Or perhaps you have the opposite problem: your vinyl seat is so soft that you achieve a near hermetic seal on long runs that prevents sweat from escaping. Both situations will lead to trouble.

The last time I checked eBay, there were over 1,300 motorcycle seating items for sale. Many of those were stock seats listed by owners trying to pawn them off to someone else like a rejected Christmas gift. When designing new bikes, I think engineers must save seat design for last. This is the only thing that could explain why stock motorcycle seats are so poor, compared to the other marvels of material and fabrication found all over the bike. "Yeah, I had thirty-seven days to design the headlight reflectors and saddle. By the time I got done with the reflectors, I had thirty-seven minutes to design the seat."

Actually, I think it's a sales technique. Soft seats are more appealing on the showroom floor. More than that, each person's unique body shape will determine how comfortable the stock seat feels. The largest contact area and feedback point is the seat. You need to achieve a fit with your seat that gives you long-term comfort without isolating you from the road, preventing you from feeling what the bike is doing. If you are big around the posterior region you'll need a

► NAMING THAT PAIN IN THE BUTT

No, I'm not talking about your co-rider. You'll have to look elsewhere for solutions to that issue, but I'm still talking about butts. Rear-end discomforts stemming from poor seat design manifest themselves in three primary ways: pressure points, chafing, and moisture build-up. All can be eliminated when you identify the source of the problem.

Pressure points produce pain or numbness in your buttocks as a result of uneven weight distribution and a drop in blood flow. Thin riders often experience sharp pain when the ischium (lower rear section of the pelvis) tries to push through the buttocks. Bigger riders often experience numbness rather than pain. Either can be eliminated with increased blood flow that results from more uniform distribution of weight and pressure from a better saddle or saddle pad.

Chafing is that painful skin irritation that occurs when friction between your clothing and skin rubs you raw. This seems to occur particularly on the inside of the thighs where you straddle the tank and can also happen when the seams in your clothing (underwear in particular) rub against the skin. Bicycle pants, the kind with a padded chamois crotch, are a great solution to this problem. The padding, flat seams and diamond gusset construction make them very comfortable for long rides.

Moisture management is another seat-related issue. Moisture build-up, combined with concentrated pressure, is like straddling a rolling pressure cooker. Steamed butt. Bike pants and other breathable fabrics that remove and disperse moisture are a big improvement over cotton briefs. Seat covers of velour, sheepskin, even wooden beads are a major improvement over stock vinyl coverings. ■

saddle configuration may work fine. On longer journeys, that stock seat will be exposed as the butt killer it really is, when the light-density OEM padding begins to compress.

There are several ways to address problematic bun support. The least expensive is an overlay solution constructed of sheepskin, air cells, beads, or gel, all of which are designed to fit over your OEM seat. A custom-made saddle is an expensive fix, but it's preferred by many riders as the best long term solution. Let's look at each of these solutions.

CUSTOM SADDLES

The superior performance of a custom saddle begins with premium materials. High-density foam is a feature of aftermarket saddles. High-density foam doesn't compress easily and won't break down as quickly over time. Because it doesn't compress, this distributes your weight more evenly across the seat, resulting in reduced pressure points. This foam feels hard at first, but breaks in over time to give you a better fit.

Most stock seats I've experienced are either flat as a board or rounded down at the edges, the latter feeling like sitting on a sawhorse. Neither of these designs is comfortable. Custom seats offer a wider, contoured seating area. Regardless of butt size, when you settle into a seat, your butt spreads to accommodate pressure from the upper body. A contoured seat provides extra support area from the sides. This too helps even out the pressure you apply to the seat.

Vinyl is a good material for shower curtains but not for seat covers. Vinyl is used for seat covers because it is waterproof, but that also means it traps moisture between you and the seat. You'll see a range of coverings used in custom seats, including vinyl, but leather is a better choice. Leather is breathable and stretches in concert with the underlying foam to create a personal fit. Look for a saddle that uses real, untreated cowhide rather than treated leather. The rubberized coating on treated leather creates a blemish-free look with no color variance but it doesn't breathe any better than vinyl.

One alternative to leather is the velour-covered seat. Velour fabric feels soft to the touch but its more important function is to provide some

wider-than-stock seat so you can get the benefit of support from the sides of the saddle. If you spread over the edges of the saddle, you quickly feel uncomfortable pressure around the perimeter of your bottom where it presses against the firm edge of the saddle. Riders with shorter legs often prefer a seat that is narrower to make it easier for them to get their feet comfortably on the ground at stops. One universal saddle design for a bike won't fit everyone.

How frequently and how far you ride can magnify discomfort. If you ride your bike infrequently or only for short distances, the OEM

air space between you and the bike seat. This air space provides some circulation which gives moisture a means of escape. The biggest downside to velour is the wear factor. As you move back and forth, on and off the seat, wear is inevitable. You'll crush the fibers, resulting in less loft.

The custom seat you're considering may include other options you can't get in a stock seat. Well-known Corbin Seats (corbin.com) makes some models that include storage compartments. If you ride solo more of the time, Corbin makes a "Smuggler" design that converts your two-up seating arrangement to a trick café racer look with a flip-up storage compartment. Travelcade, makers of the Road Sofa, specialize in seats for large touring bikes that include lumbar support, side support adjustments, even heated seats.

The most important seating extra is a good backrest. Some saddles use a stepped design between the rider and passenger to add back support. These are okay, but a higher backrest that reaches the middle of the back lets you fully unload the tension required to hold yourself straight.

ORDERING A CUSTOM SEAT

If you own a popular touring bike and are happy with an in-stock seat from a large maker, you can get a custom seat as quickly as any other product. When a manufacturer doesn't stock seats for your model of bike, you can send in your stock seat. The seat maker will strip off the old material and recover the pan using their foam, cover, and other components. I sent my crappy old Yamaha seat with quarter-inch padding and got a great-looking and great-fitting saddle in return six weeks later. You may prefer to keep your stock seat, particularly if you're ordering a solo seat that converts co-rider space into storage. eBay is a good source for original seats, in case you need an extra seat pan for rebuilding. As long as the pan is okay, condition of the seating materials doesn't matter.

Some seat builders, like Russell Day-Long (day-long.com), makes your seat from pictures of you and your co-rider seated on the bike in riding position. The pictures, along with other height and weight information, allow Russell to

Seat upgrades are one of the first comfort improvements many riders make.

create a very personalized saddle. A Russell seat takes about three weeks to complete once it is scheduled for production. Many long-distance riders I've spoken with have mentioned the comfort of their Russell saddle.

A custom seat is definitely something you want to order and break in well before you head out for a long trip. Saddle makers recommend you put at least a thousand miles on the seat before making any final judgments about its comfort. High-density foam is stiff and takes a little time and mileage to break in. As you ride, the foam and leather will begin to take on and retain your shape; support will improve as the saddle ages.

SEAT PADS

A custom seat isn't the only answer to improved comfort. Seat pads are appreciated by owners of multiple bikes who like the flexibility to move a pad quickly from one seat to another. And what if you're not really in pain, just a little uncomfortable? Should you spend a lot on a custom seat? Try an inexpensive solution like a beaded mat, then decide if you need to step up.

Comfort is a subjective measure and that subjectivity is fully apparent when discussing seating solutions. There are at least a half dozen approaches to seat enhancements and countless opinions about their utility. Sheepskin saves the day for one rider but gel is favored by another. Air cushions are used by many, but another large contingent of riders is satisfied with a beaded mat.

► RAIN PROTECTION

Saddles and seat pads alike need to be protected from the rain. The stitching in seats creates small holes that water can penetrate if left standing. And you can just imagine the amount of water a sheepskin cover can hold. (Answer: a lot.) Leather waterproofing can be used to improve water resistance on saddles, but too much will compromise the leather's breathability.

Your best bet is simply to make sure the seat is covered when rain threatens. When you stop for the night, make sure the seat is covered (preferably, the whole bike), regardless of weather conditions, to protect it from rain and morning dew. Some saddles, like the Travelcade, come with a built-in cover.

If your seat does get caught in the rain, some manufacturers advise that you remove the seat from the bike and stand it on one end. The theory is, this will cause the moisture to work toward one end and will speed the drying process. Drying should occur at a slow but measured pace, especially if your seat cover is leather. Drying leather too quickly will cause it to crack. ■

Low-density foam pads are one solution you can ignore. You're already sitting on a low-density foam pad in your stock seat. More of it won't help. Don't be suckered by how soft it feels when you're trying a foam pad at a rally. Low-density pads, regardless of the thickness or price, will increase your comfort factor marginally at best and even then only when your OEM seat is a splintered wooden plank.

Gel pads get the thumbs-up from some riders. Gel pads like those from Travelcade are filled with high-density foam injected with a viscoelastic goo similar to the glop in therapy pads you can throw in the microwave or freezer. Other pads consist entirely of gel in a fabric cover. A gel pad by itself is worth a try if you experience minimal discomfort from your stock saddle and you're looking for a little extra comfort. The close fit of gel pads doesn't allow as much air to circulate as other solutions, unless the gel pad is combined with something like sheepskin, an option you can get with the Travelcade product (saddlemen.com).

Sheepskin pads look so plush and inviting, you just can't help reaching out to stroke them. Ahhh, that feels good to the touch. And for many riders, it feels good on the seat too. Sheepskin absorbs some road vibration, but not as well as other pads. It does a great job of helping keep moisture and temperature at comfortable levels. As advertised, sheepskin really does keep you cooler in the summer and warmer in the winter. Sheepskin covers are the easiest to clean and refresh. Just toss them in the washer. If your primary discomfort is skin irritation from moisture, give the sheepskin a try.

Cheap foam pads feel like they should work but they don't do squat. *Cheap wooden beaded seat covers* look like the worst idea in the world for a seat. Beads rock. When you move around on a beaded seat, the beads move, massaging your lower quarters. This action not only feels good, it restores blood flow and reduces soreness. Beaded seats are well ventilated so moisture build-up is never a problem. Veteran bead riders note that on those occasions when you're caught by a surprise shower, wooden beads keep you above the seat and don't absorb water; true to the old cliché, you are kept "high and dry." A bike-specific product like the BeadRider (beadrider.com) is an inexpensive experiment and might provide all the comfort you need.

The comfort of beads isn't instantly apparent, but the idea of an *air cushion seat pad* makes intuitive sense. Select Comfort built a business out of air mattresses for sleeping, so it follows

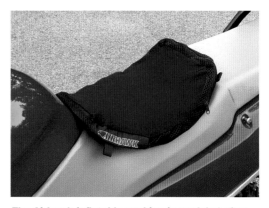

The Airhawk inflatable cushion is modeled after versions used in hospitals and rehab centers. Many riders report these cushions work exceptionally well.

that sitting on an air mattresses should work pretty well. It does. In fact, of all the recommended strategies for bolstering seat comfort, an air pad, particularly the motorcycle-specific Roho Airhawk, is a frequently-cited seat-topping favorite. The Airhawk pad (rohoinc.com) consists of a series of interconnected air cells. The neoprene top is molded into ice-cube-size squares with channels, promoting air flow. The air cell system is self-equalizing. When you sit on the cushion, force is applied to the center of the pad. That force pushes air out to the sides of the pad, providing more support which, in turn, helps distribute your load more evenly. As you move around in the seat, the air cells adjust immediately.

HANDLEBAR IMPROVEMENTS

With tush issues are resolved, other pains become more evident. Numbness and pain in wrists, hands, shoulders, and neck are symptoms reported almost as widely as saddlesoreness. These upper body issues are caused by excessive lean angles and can be lessened or solved by changing your body's position on the bike.

Sport bike riders with lean-forward seating positions are not the only riders who experience this problem. Even a small amount of excess pressure on your hands can lead to reduced circulation and accompanying numbness. Leaning forward puts pressure on your shoulders, and that causes a pinching, burning sensation between your shoulder blades. Your head and neck are cocked upward at a more extreme angle, contributing to muscle tension.

Handlebar Risers

A popular solution for this is a set of handlebar risers. Risers are an easy modification available for many bike models, particularly sport and sport touring bikes. Handlebar risers change the position and angle of your handlebars from a crouched, racing position to something a bit more practical for long distances.

Depending on their design, risers can elevate your handgrips, move them closer to you, and change the downward angle of the grip to something less radical. As you approach a more upright riding position, the reduction in arm

Changing the location of hand grips by even an inch or two can make a huge difference in comfort by relieving pressure on your palms. This riser kit from Heli Modified offers adjustability in several dimensions, making it adaptable to personal preferences.

pressure will lessen your upper body aches. Risers are also a great modification for riders with shorter arms who find themselves leaning forward to reach the handlebars on otherwise straight-up bikes.

When researching handlebar risers, look carefully at the installation notes and sample installation photos. You want to pay attention to whether the riser will require longer cables or if you need to make any other modifications to your handlebars for installation. Some risers include adjustments that allow you to change the handlebar position from "touring rider" back to "full sporty mode" if you desire.

Throttle Accessories

Your throttle hand is particularly susceptible to stiffness because it spends so much time in the same position. Two inexpensive items can give you some relief here.

A throttle lock is a friction ring that fits on your throttle between the handgrip and the switch housing. Pressing on the lock with your thumb closes the ring, clamping the throttle into position. When properly adjusted, you can make small changes in your throttle position without resetting the clamp. These work surprisingly well.

Even if your bike is equipped with cruise control, you can't use that all the time. You'll have to operate the throttle the old fashioned way. You can still provide relief for your hand by adding a wrist rest like the Throttle Rocker (throttlerocker.com). This molded plastic paddle clamps to the throttle grip with a Velcro wrap. With a Throttle Rocker installed, you don't have to fully grip the throttle to operate it. You can relax your fingers a bit and allow the palm of your hand to help you maintain throttle position.

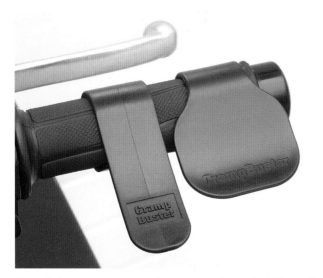

Throttle levers are available in several styles and widths to fit almost any bike. On long trips they relieve fatigue by allowing you to control throttle position with the palm of your hand, rather then by gripping the handlebar.

Grips and Weights

Motorcycles of all sizes generate vibrations that are transmitted throughout the bike. Engines, transmissions, drive belts, chains—in short, anything that moves on a bike—generates vibration. Big-bore American twins, British triples, Japanese four-bangers—doesn't matter. Some vibrations match a resonant frequency that will be picked up and amplified by the bars like a giant tuning fork. In addition to irritating the crap out of you, that constant buzz will generate numbness in your hands and wrists.

Foam replacement grips are a solution many riders try as a first step. Foam grips are helpful in cases where you're experiencing just a little vibration. I've always liked the feel of these grips, even on bikes that didn't have a vibration problem.

Foam grips won't solve significant, persistent vibration problems. A better approach is to attack the problem closer to the source: your handlebars. Bikes today have a wide assortment of handlebar arrangements. Fewer have a continuous tube handlebar, but regardless of the shape, all handlebars have hollow components that are subject to vibration. Anything you do to change the composition of those bars can change their resonant frequency. This may reduce your vibration problem, eliminate it, or shift the vibration to a different speed band, preferably one where you don't spend a lot of time.

Bar-end weights are another simple first-step solution. These weights replace or supplement the caps on the end of your handlebars. The extra weight changes the resonant frequency of the handlebar. More serious vibration problems can be addressed with products like the Bar Snake (barsnake.com). This length of rubber tube slides into the entire length of the handlebar assembly. Filling the whole handlebar will significantly reduce vibration. If you don't have traditional handlebars, Bar Snake sells a liquid that pours and sets, turning into a similar vibration absorbing material.

Heated Grips

Let's finish off the subject of handlebars with a brief look at heated grips. Heated grips by themselves aren't a complete cold-weather riding solution. If, like me, you dislike thick, heavy winter gloves, heated grips may be attractive to you. With the heat generated by grips, you can forgo the heaviest gloves except on the coldest days.

Heated grip solutions are made with heat generating wire encased in mylar sheets that mount under your grips. Installing grips sounds easy, but requires patience. The thin mylar sheets are easily damaged and epoxy is involved. Whenever epoxy is part of the installation procedure, that's a cue to lay out every thing and rehearse your installation before taking the plunge. Once it has been mixed and set, epoxy is a permanent bonding solution. The left hand grip is straightforward because it doesn't move. Installing the throttle grip is dicier. Above all, make sure you remove any excess epoxy as you install the handgrips.

WINDSCREENS AND FAIRINGS

Some riders insist that motorcycling lost its uniqueness the day the fairing was invented. I would argue that's the day the motorcycle became a viable machine for touring. A motorcycle with a partial or full fairing is no less romantic than a naked bike. Putting a windscreen or fairing on your bike will hardly isolate you from the environment, it just gives you a little more control over the elements. You can drop a lot of cash on a great custom seat and get your handlebars positioned just so, but if you're fighting the wind from the front or behind, you will still find yourself miserable at the end of the day.

Being fully exposed to wind isn't bad for you, it just creates fatigue, which means you'll cover fewer miles in a day than a similarly equipped rider who uses some protection. Holding on to the bike in a 65 mile per hour wind, more if you're riding into a strong headwind, will wear you out. You may discover that the "motorcycling experience" is about more than having all the wind in your face.

I believe a fairing improves your motorcycling experience, it doesn't compromise it. A fairing refers to protective bodywork mounted to the front of your bike. Understand that windscreens and fairings refer to two separate items though you'll usually see them together. The windscreen is mounted on top of the fairing. So when I refer to a fairing, I am implying that a windscreen is part of the package.

Fairing Configurations

Fairings are designed as either partial or full fairings and are usually attached rigidly to the bike's frame. A partial fairing like that found on a sport bike isn't designed to protect you from the rain. Its primary purpose is to shape the wind flowing over the front of the bike to reduce wind buffeting and improve your aerodynamic profile.

Full dress bikes like the BMW K1200LT and Honda Gold Wing are built with a fully integrated fairing as big as the bow of a small ocean-going vessel. Even full coverage fairings like these won't keep you dry, but will afford you significant protection from wind and rain.

Heated grips can be a blessing in cold, wet weather. Some of the newer deluxe touring bikes are delivered from the factory with heated grips. Kits, such as this one, are available for many older motorcycles.

Cruisers occupy a middle ground on the use of fairings. Many cruisers don't have a fairing but they have a removable windscreen. Harley's Road King is a good example. Its windscreen can be quickly attached or removed, allowing you to change from touring posture to cruise mode.

Windscreen Positioning

You can't change the position of a fairing; they're fixed onto the bike in a certain way. But you can and should pay particular attention to the height of the windscreen. When you're riding at typical highway speeds, you want the air blowing off the top of the windscreen to hit you in one of two places: the middle portion of your chest or over the top of your helmet.

When air strikes you in the middle of your chest, this positive pressure air flow gives you a bit of support and helps relieve pressure from your wrists and forearms, especially if you're riding a lean-forward sport bike. The effect is a little like leaning on a tank bag. If the windscreen is taller, air should flow over the top of your helmet for a smooth air flow. If air hits you square on the helmet, your head will dance in all directions as wind turbulence blows over the top of the windscreen. You'll be miserable.

► CO-RIDER COMFORT

Do everything you can to make your passenger's accommodations as comfortable as your own. A co-rider who feels secure on the back seat will have more fun and will ride with you more often than one who feels like they're barely hanging on as you blast down the highway.

If you really want to serve your passenger effectively, ask them what they like and don't like about riding on your bike. You may be able to make a few small changes that will improve their comfort immensely. A backrest will ease any concern they may have about sliding off the back of the bike. Passenger footpegs are often mounted too high. Relocating them will help the passenger feel more at ease. Do you use an aftermarket seat product? Provide one for your co-rider as well. ■

Experiment with different height windscreens to find one that puts air in the right place for you. Replacement windscreens are available in different heights for many bikes. If you find your stock screen to be just a little too tall, check with a glass shop in your town. Many will cut down a stock Plexiglas windscreen for a nominal fee. Then purchase a second, taller-than-stock screen for long-distance touring or colder weather.

Sometimes it isn't the height of the screen but its shape that contributes to air turbulence. Aftermarket deflectors like Saeng Wing-Tips (saeng.com) give you better control of air flow over your wind screen. Wing-Tips stick to the top of your windscreen and pivot to let you decide where you want air to flow.

It's also possible to have too much protection. In the summer, it's not uncommon for me to be out riding on the Gold Wing and spot a flying insect circling around the cockpit between me and the windshield, seemingly indifferent to the

hurricane force winds blowing by the bike. The Wing's air displacement is so significant that a small pocket of low pressure air is created behind the windshield. The pressure of the air flowing over the top of your windshield and helmet is greater than the air between you and the windshield, creating a forward-pulling effect that will wear you down over the miles. A popular remedy is an aftermarket windscreen with a small vent near its base. Opening this vent allows a small amount of air to flow into the cockpit, equalizing the pressure. It's also nice to have that extra air flow on hot days.

Speaking of air flow, another popular product for bikes with big fairings are Baker Built Air Wings (bakerbuilt.com). These air deflectors are designed to mount to the fairing on the side of the bike. In warm weather, you tilt the wings in to bring more air into the cockpit. In cold weather, turn them out to deflect air away.

HIGHWAY PEGS

If it weren't for highway pegs, we wouldn't have the phrase "laid-back." Word historians trace the initial use of that phrase, describing a person who is "relaxed," to around 1973 and they believe it originally described a person riding a motorcycle. That rider had to be using highway pegs.

Highway pegs are an extra set of footpegs mounted near the front of the motorcycle on an engine guard or frame member. Highway pegs give you that cool "laid back" look," but their more practical purpose is to give you an optional place to move your feet. Move your feet and you automatically shift seating position. This change helps smooth out pressure points. I've found that highway pegs provide particular relief to tired knees.

Highway pegs should always be used in conjunction with some form of lower back support, preferably a backrest. When you put up your feet and shift weight, it puts pressure on your back. To give your back support, you need something to lean against.

Highway pegs are easy to install but there are a few things you should keep in mind. The pegs you purchase should be designed to bolt to a substantial location on your bike. When you ease on and off the pegs, you'll put extra stress on them and the location where they are mounted should be able to handle it. So too should the pegs. The clamp and mounting hardware are particularly important. When pressure is applied, your highway pegs should be rock solid with no shift in alignment. I know it sounds trivial, but a highway peg that shifts out of place during a ride is a big disappointment—and distraction.

Before you permanently bolt down your pegs, you'll want to check the position for two factors: leg comfort and ground clearance. Mount the footpegs close enough to you that you have a slight bend in your knee when your foot is resting on the footpeg. This gives you the option of later resting the heel of your boot on top of the footpeg, giving you an extra foot location. Check your ground clearance to make sure you can still lean the bike as you like without grinding down the ends of the footpegs.

FOOTPEGS AND FLOORBOARDS

Your lean angle is significantly influenced by the position of your footpegs. When you add handlebar risers to straighten your upper body, you may also need to reposition the footpegs. Footpeg relocators are brackets that bolt into the original footpeg location on the frame, then provide a mounting point in a new location for the original footpeg. Depending on the shape of the bracket and the area where the peg is mounted, you may have some flexibility to move the peg around.

Floorboards are bolt-on replacements for footpegs on touring bikes. Floorboards give you a little more room to move your feet around in the lower position. If you add floorboards then you'll need to replace the toe shifter with a heel/toe shifter. To shift up in gears, you press down with your heel on the back of the lever. To downshift, you press on the front of the lever with your toe.

BACK SUPPORT

Your co-rider only has to put up with you some of the time, but your back never gets a break. We've talked about the utility of back rests, but it's possible that your bike won't accommodate a back rest or the options available don't appeal to you. In that case, the guys and gals down at the

This kidney belt features a built-in lumbar support to help you maintain good spine posture. Many riders with back problems say these belts allow them to ride long distances in relative comfort.

loading dock have a solution for you, a Back-A-Line belt (backaline.com). The Back-A-Line wraps around your waist and can be worn over or under your clothes. The Back-A-Line incorporates a built-in lumbar support that promotes good posture and reduces back fatigue.

SUMMARY

A modern motorcycle is a comfortable place to sit compared to older machines, but there are many things you can do to make your bike more comfortable to ride for many miles.

The first priority for comfort is to pamper your butt. Your rear end is in contact with the bike longer than any other part of your body and absorbs the greatest portion of the punishment the road dishes out. There are several approaches to seat comfort. Some riders prefer a wholesale seat swap, trading out the stock seat for a custom-made saddle with improved support and materials. Other riders find that the stock seat, enhanced with a beaded mat or inflatable cover are just fine.

Comfort can also be enhanced by a range of products that tailor the motorcycle's ergonomics to your unique requirements. The position of your hands and feet, the height and attitude (or absence) of your fairing, use of highway pegs, and a half-dozen other accessories can all improve your comfort over the long haul.

Underpinnings

We're going to cover motorcycle luggage in the next chapter, but before we do, it is important to first discuss the major systems that will bear that load: your bike's tires and suspension. You may already be happy with your bike's tires and suspension, so why consider changes? Good question. You may need to do nothing. The answer depends on how your riding habits change as a result of long-distance touring.

As you increase the frequency and distance of your journeys, tire wear will become more important to you. You'd never think about tire wear if you put only a couple thousand miles a year on

This tire shows the effects of many miles ridden in a straight line. The center of the tread is worn flat.

your bike, but cover a few thousand per trip and you'll start looking for longer-wearing shoes. You may even need to arrange for a mid-tour tire change on long journeys.

An average size rider, traveling solo with a modest amount of luggage, won't need to give the suspension any special attention except to make sure it's working properly and perhaps to adjust it to handle a little extra load. Suspension mods will become more important when you add a co-rider or need to carry more equipment.

TIRES

Motorcycle tires deserve more respect and attention than they receive from most of us. Bike tires carry up to a half ton in weight over crappy pavement and debris, at lower than recommended pressure toward the upper end of highway speeds, on a contact patch about the size of your palm. And then the best we often say of them is "This set is okay," followed by, "I think I'll try a set of X next time." No respect.

When you're pulling a load like this camper, you need to consider its effect on your bike's basic systems—tires, suspension and brakes.

Engineers may not spend a lot of time on seat design, but they do expend considerable effort to match your bike's design with proper tires. If you're happy with the tread life, grip, load capacity, speed rating, and weather performance of your tires, stick with the tires your manufacturer put on the bike, and then give them frequent inspections and pressure checks, of course.

Many design choices and materials affect the performance of your tires. The number of plys, ply weight and angle, tire type (bias or radial), tire profile, tread design, and rubber compound are a few. Touring riders should focus on profiles and compounds because they have the greatest impact on tire performance and longevity.

This tire is literally screwed, but given the placement and angle of the screw, it can be safely repaired with a plug kit.

A portable air pump is preferable to throw-away CO_2 cannisters for inflating tires. You can use it for inflating other things and you won't be filling a landfill with throwaway cartridges.

Radial vs. Bias

Bias and radial tires are markedly different in construction and performance, enough so that manufacturers design a bike with a particular tire type in mind. The trend among manufacturers is to transition new bikes to radials because they do have significant performance advantages. If your bike came with bias-ply tires, stick with that tire type unless your bike's manufacturer explicitly approves the use of radial tires.

Compounds: Stickiness vs. Wear

When you start racking up even ten or fifteen thousand miles a year, the financial controller in your household will begin to start asking questions about the motorcycle tire line item in your budget. When the average set of tires is good for seven thousand miles, you'll be looking at up to two sets of tires per year. You may need to re-evaluatte the balance your current tires offer between grip versus wear.

How well your tire grabs the pavement (stickiness) and how long it lasts (wear) are inversely related. A tire made from soft rubber compounds is super sticky and gives you great cornering performance, but wears quickly. Hard rubber compounds don't have as much grab, but last considerably longer. Stock tires are chosen to give you the best performing compromise between these two factors.

Compounding is the science of developing rubber formulations and applying them to tire design. The continuing goal of the compounder is to challenge that inverse relationship, to make tires that are stickier *and* last longer. Recent advances in compounding and manufacturing have led to multi-compound tires that can be both sticky and longer-lasting.

When you're riding on a straight stretch of road, the middle third of your tire (the crown) makes contact with the road. On corners, either the left or right third are used. Multi-compound tires put a harder, longer wearing rubber in the

► TIRE PRESSURE POLICE

Tire engineers attending rallies have found a large percentage of bikes with underinflated tires. Some have been off the recommended air pressure by more than half!

I know, it's easy to ignore tires. Even when a tire is significantly down on air pressure, it "looks" okay. It's a pain to get down on your hands and knees to check pressures. On the other hand, an underinflated tire is able to carry significantly less load. According to Dunlop, every four psi of air pressure equals eighty pounds of cargo capacity.

Check your tire pressure before every day's ride. Once I was leading a group ride when we stopped for lunch. One member of the group noticed that my tires looked a little soft, so during lunch he measured them. As we were getting ready to leave, he said, "Dale, there is a problem with your motorcycle. Your tires are severely underinflated." I was embarrassed by that, but I deserved it. I'm glad he called me out on it. Since then I've kept a portable air compressor on the bike and check my tire pressures regularly. ∎

Have you checked your tire pressure lately? Tire engineers routinely find tires that are half inflated or less.

On the left is the profile of a touring tire and on the right a tire designed for sport riding. They create very different handling response when entering a turn.

Tire Profiles

The shape of a tire affects how quickly or smoothly a bike will roll into and out of curves. Look at the curve of the tread across the tire from sidewall to sidewall and you'll see what I mean.

Sport tires have an angular profile. There is a sharper transition from side to side. When you lean the bike, the tire rolls quickly from one side to the other. This gives you the ability to attack curves and makes the bike "flickable." On straights, it makes the bike less stable and more susceptible to pavement tracking, that is, following contours in the pavement rather than your steering input.

Tires designed for long-distance touring have a flatter profile. Your bike will steer a little slower or require more steering input as you roll through the twisties, but you'll gain greater straight-line stability. Your bike will respond less to rain grooves and wander less over steel gratings. Which profile you choose is your preference but if you plan on pulling a trailer, I would recommend tires with a flatter profile.

What about those crazy fat tires you've seen on custom bikes? Flatter is better, right? It's my opinion that extra wide tires are not your best choice for touring. Super-wide tires have an even flatter profile which will substantially change the handling characteristics of your bike. At the edges, super-wides have a significant roll-off in the last inch or so of tread, which feels really unsettling as you lean the bike. Entering a corner, you're on the flat portion of the tread for a long time, you have to really work to lean the bike, then you hit that angled corner and zzzzip! Over you go. I don't mean you'll drop the bike, but the transition is so sudden, you won't want to do it again.

middle third of the tire and a softer, stickier compound on the sides.

Properly inflated and under normal use, today's high-performance, multi-compound tires will last up to fifteen thousand miles. That's an increase of fifty to a hundred percent over stock tires. The rider covering fifteen thousand miles in a year can eliminate a tire change. Or, you may still change tires twice a year, but now you can ride twice as far.

▶ TIRE MARKINGS DECODED

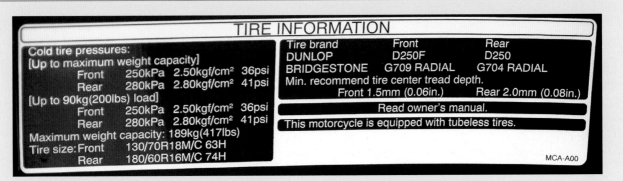

TIRE INFORMATION		
Cold tire pressures: [Up to maximum weight capacity]	Tire brand Front Rear	
Front 250kPa 2.50kgf/cm² 36psi	DUNLOP D250F D250	
Rear 280kPa 2.80kgf/cm² 41psi	BRIDGESTONE G709 RADIAL G704 RADIAL	
[Up to 90kg(200lbs) load]	Min. recommend tire center tread depth.	
Front 250kPa 2.50kgf/cm² 36psi	Front 1.5mm (0.06in.) Rear 2.0mm (0.08in.)	
Rear 280kPa 2.80kgf/cm² 41psi	Read owner's manual.	
Maximum weight capacity: 189kg(417lbs)	This motorcycle is equipped with tubeless tires.	
Tire size: Front 130/70R18M/C 63H		
Rear 180/60R16M/C 74H	MCA-A00	

OEM tire information and recommended tire pressures can be found on a sticker on your bike.

All the info you need to shop for replacement tires is molded on the side of your tire. In particular, look at the model number of your stock tire. If it contains a letter designation at the end, this indicates a special OEM configuration of that model tire. For example, the Bridgestone Battlax BT-010 found on the CBR600 is an OEM variant because the marking on the tire indicates it is a BT-010"F", a version with a slightly different bias-ply configuration. A manufacturer might request a slightly different configuration from the mass market tire, such as lighter weight, higher mileage, or perhaps a different tread pattern. Look for OEM tires at your dealer to ensure that you get the same performance when you replace your tires.

Take a look too at the date code. This number, found near the DOT mark, indicates the week and year of the tire's manufacture. For example, 2604 would mean the tire was made on the 26th week of 2004. Tire compounds harden with age. Check the date code to make sure you aren't getting a tire that's been sitting in a warehouse for several years. ■

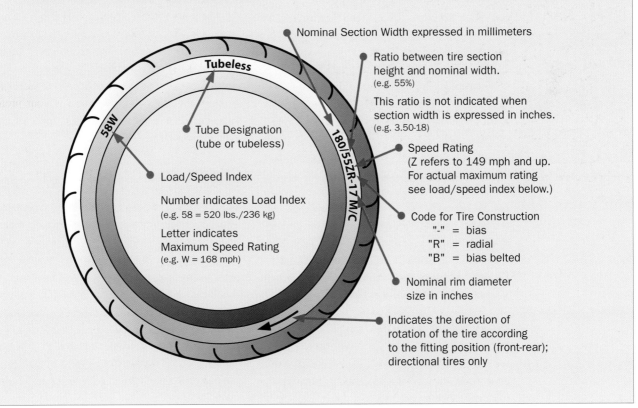

Nominal Section Width expressed in millimeters

Ratio between tire section height and nominal width. (e.g. 55%)

This ratio is not indicated when section width is expressed in inches. (e.g. 3.50-18)

Tubeless

Tube Designation (tube or tubeless)

Load/Speed Index

Number indicates Load Index (e.g. 58 = 520 lbs./236 kg)

Letter indicates Maximum Speed Rating (e.g. W = 168 mph)

58W

180/55ZR-17 M/C

Speed Rating (Z refers to 149 mph and up. For actual maximum rating see load/speed index below.)

Code for Tire Construction
"-" = bias
"R" = radial
"B" = bias belted

Nominal rim diameter size in inches

Indicates the direction of rotation of the tire according to the fitting position (front-rear); directional tires only

119

Reading Tire Condition

What's your tire trying to tell you? Look across the breadth of the tread. You should see even wear from side to side. Here are some other conditions you might see.

Cupping will make you think something is drastically wrong with your bike. It's a wear pattern characterized by shallow depressions around the circumference of the crown that looks as if someone scalloped your tire. Cupping affects tires on all vehicles but rotating the tires virtually eliminates the effect on four-wheelers. Since you don't rotate tires on a bike, it's more noticeable. Cupping can be reduced on your bike by eliminating hard braking habits, keeping tires properly inflated, and making sure your front forks and suspension are well maintained.

A *flattened crown on the rear tire* is frequently seen on heavy touring bikes that spend a lot of time on high speed Interstates, and bikes that pull trailers. A flattened crown isn't dangerous per se, but it affects how the bike responds when you tip it into the corners. Best solution: Lighten your load and ride curvier roads.

Wear concentrated in the center of the tire may also be an indication your tires are carrying too much pressure. Tires should be inflated to maximum pressures when you're carrying extra gear or a passenger. If you're riding solo on a lightly loaded bike, the best tire pressure is somewhat less than maximum. Check your owners manual or visit your tire maker's website for recommended pressures with varying amounts of load.

Sidewall cracks are the result of exposure to environmental conditions like ozone, ultraviolet radiation from the sun, and weather. Sidewalls that show severe cracks should be replaced. Aftermarket dressings and sealants hasten the destructive process by removing protective compounds added to the rubber during its manufacture. Stick with a mild soap solution and clear water rinse when washing your bike.

SUSPENSION BASICS

For purposes of this book it is useful to have a basic understanding of how your suspension operates and, as it relates to touring, how heavy loads affect your bike.

Your bike's suspension has two important jobs to perform. Its primary task is to keep your bike's wheels firmly planted on the pavement, especially when those wheels encounter surface imperfections. Its second job is to isolate the rest of the bike from those same imperfections to help you maintain control of the machine.

Front and rear suspensions are composed of many components, but the two "active ingredients" are the same: springs and dampers. The front of most bikes carry these springs and dampers in the front forks. On the back, the springs and dampers are packaged together in one unit, a shock absorber.

Spring Compression and Rebound

When your wheel encounters a bump, the wheel is displaced upward, generating an upward force that causes the spring to compress. A compressed spring stores the energy of that movement, and as I'm sure you remember from high school physics, that energy has to go somewhere. After you pass over the bump, the spring has an opportunity to unload that energy, so it pushes the wheel back to the ground. This downward return is called "rebound."

If no other forces acted on that sprung wheel to control its motion, it would bounce several times before returning to steady contact with the pavement. With the wheel bouncing on the ground, that energy would be transmitted through the rest of the bike to you. You'd feel like you were riding a pogo stick. Or a vintage motorcycle.

Damping

That's where damping comes in to play. Damping is the process of restraining the wheel's up and down motion by applying friction whenever it tries to change its vertical position. Designs vary, but the inside of a basic shock absorber contains a piston encased in fluid. The piston has a valve that allows the fluid to pass through in both directions. If you've ever drawn medicine out of a bottle with a syringe, it's the same effect. If you pull the liquid out of the bottle very slowly, it doesn't require much effort, but it takes much greater force to pull liquid quickly.

Now let's add that to our wheel-spring application. When the bike's wheel hits a bump, the spring compresses. With our damper added, that motion also pushes the piston through the fluid. This resistant action absorbs some of the mechanical energy of the spring, converting that action to heat and slowing the action of the spring. As the spring rebounds and releases energy, the damping mechanism absorbs some of that energy so the spring will return to its normal state without bouncing.

Effects of Heavy Loading

With all those factors involved, you can better appreciate the work a suspension does and it's easier to understand why the suspension's work gets harder as you begin to load up the bike. As you add weight, you compress the springs. A spring has a finite load capacity and as you add weight to the bike, you are using up some of that capacity.

Out on the road, a heavily loaded bike has less capacity for absorbing energy transmitted by bumps. When you hit a bump that compresses the front spring to its limit, you'll feel it in the handlebars as a jolt. Hit that bump with the rear of the bike and that excess energy is transmitted right to the business end of you and your co-rider. That's what is known as "bottoming out" your suspension.

Every bike bottoms out once in a while, but if it happens to you regularly and you are still within the gross vehicle weight limit for your vehicle (weight fully loaded including passengers), you'll need to make some suspension adjustments or lighten your load.

What You Can Control

If you ride a sport bike, you have several adjustments for tuning your suspension setup, including damping and load settings. Touring bikes have fewer controls; some, like the GL-1800, have only a pre-load adjustment. (People who ride big bikes desire the ease of use that comes with fewer controls more than the ability to fine tune a bike's suspension for track day.)

To account for the extra weight the bike will carry, adjusting the rear spring pre-load is usually the only accommodation you need to make

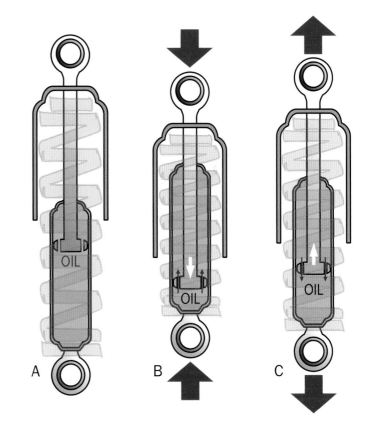

Your bike's suspension is designed to keep your tire planted when it meets irregularities in road surface. We'll focus on the rear suspension that typically uses a spring and shock absorber combined (A).

Compression Damping (B) When your tire encounters an irregularity in the road— such as a rock—this causes the tire to move upward. Energy is stored by the spring as it compresses. Oil is forced through small holes in the damper piston, slowing the rate of compression.

Rebound Damping (C) After passing over the irregularity the wheel is pushed back to its normal position by the spring as it releases the energy it stored. The rate at which the spring releases its energy is also controlled by oil flowing through small holes in the damper piston.

for a trip. Setting the rear shock pre-load adjusts your ride height so you will be less likely to bottom out when you encounter a bump. On sport bikes, this is done by rotating a collar on the shock that compresses the spring. On luxury bikes, it's done by pressing a button.

Compression damping is an adjustment frequently found on sportier bikes. When you modify compression damping you are affecting the restraining force applied when the spring is absorbing a bump. Too much compression damping will prevent the spring from compressing

Preload adjustment is handled with the push of a button on big touring bikes.

fast enough and will make your ride harsh; too little will allow the spring to compress too quickly and it will bottom out.

Rebound damping is the opposite. When you adjust rebound damping, you're affecting how quickly the spring is allowed to release the energy it stored and how fast it will return to its original pre-bump state. Too much rebound damping (not letting the spring rebound fast enough) results in a condition called "packing." When you ride over a series of bumps, the spring can't return fast enough between bumps and it compresses smaller and smaller until the bike bottoms out. Too little rebound damping results in a pogo-stick action. Your bike will hop up and down like a '69 Lincoln with bad shocks.

Suspension Adjustment Tips

Suspension adjustments are most effective if you take a methodical approach to changes, rather than randomly tweaking things.

Load your bike as you would for your trip so you're getting an accurate feel for the suspension's behavior. Pick out a circuit of roads you can easily repeat that contains pavement flaws like patches, bumps, and potholes.

Write down the initial settings of anything you plan to change. These are your "baseline settings." Any changes you make should be compared to the way these settings feel.

Make one change at a time. Suspension tuning is a science experiment. You want to change just one variable at a time in your experiment so that when you feel a difference in your suspension, you can attribute it to that change.

Document every change you make. Okay, if you're only adjusting pre-load on the rear shock, there's no need to do this. But if you are adjusting front and rear suspension settings, changing damping rates, etc., you'd better write down those changes as you make them. You say you'll remember, then a buddy will come over, you'll have a couple of beers and then . . . "Did I change that adjusting screw by a half turn or a full turn?"

If all else fails, you can find your manufacturer's recommended default settings in your owner's manual. This will let you reset everything to factory defaults and start the process all over again.

BIKE PROTECTION

In previous chapters we focused on gear to protect you from the hazards of traveling in an open environment. What about your bike? It deserves some protection, too. Hazards come in more

A skid plate is added to bikes expected to cover rough roads. The extra protection prevents rocks and other obstacles from punching holes in the crankcase or radiator.

forms than laying your bike down and scraping off a layer of plastic. Protective gear is available to take the brunt of low speed drops and prevent flying debris from damaging your bike's drive train, controls, and expensive body panels. Stuff happens. Following are a few ideas to help protect you and your bike against that stuff.

Light Guards

Pop! That's the sound of two hundred bucks fleeing from your pocket when your bike's headlight and a piece of flying gravel meet in the space-time continuum. Headlight reflector housings are expensive, and on modern bikes they must be replaced as a complete unit. Light guards—clear, form-fitting sheets of Plexiglas—were developed to stand between those chance encounters and your expensive lights. Makers like Ventura (ventura-bike.com) and Cee Bailey's (ceebaileys.com) sell versions to match headlight shapes for many bikes. You'd have to go through three or four sets of light guards to match the cost of a single reflector housing.

Kickstand Plate

Heavy, gear-laden bikes put a lot of force on the foot of the kickstand. When a bike is parked on warm pavement (especially new surfaces) or soft ground, it's just a matter of time before the kickstand digs in and gravity takes over. A

A piece of plastic or a flattened can will prevent your bike from sinking into soft asphalt on hot days.

Expecting to encounter flying boulders? This light guard is equal to the task.

kickstand plate slides under the foot of the kickstand to spread the pressure and prevent your bike from toppling over.

You can make a kickstand plate out of any solid flat material that will support the weight of your bike. A flattened aluminum can is popular, although something like a Kickstand Critter (kickstandcritters.mrbun.com) will generate a few laughs at your next rest stop. Either way, this is another cheap fix to prevent greater damage to your bike, or the one parked next to yours.

Tipover Guards

I'll group engine and saddlebag guards together because they serve the same purpose. If your bike does happen to tip over or drop at parking lot speeds, tip-over guards are designed to catch your bike before it hits the expensive chrome or plastic bodywork.

I've seen an increase in the number of OEM guards built onto bikes in the last few years. If your bike doesn't have guards factory installed, check to see if OEM units are available. A factory product will be guaranteed to fit but better units might be available with a little searching. For example, Lindby makes good looking guards for cruisers that include integrated highway pegs.

This engine guard also provides a convenient mounting point for highway pegs.

Skid Plates and Assorted Armor

Skid plates, pump guards, and other undercarriage guards are designed to prevent damage in extreme riding conditions. Skid plates are built for adventure touring bikes like the Kawasaki KLR-650 and BMW GS bikes, both designed for handling street duties and riding paths that are "roads" in name only. These should be on the list for every North American traveler who is thinking about including remote highways in their travel plans.

FUEL CELLS

There are two types of riders who add auxiliary fuel tanks or fuel storage to their bikes: long-distance riders who plan to campaign their bikes in endurance rallies, and touring riders who aim to travel into remote areas where gas stations aren't located at every exit—in fact, there aren't any exits.

How much fuel capacity do you want to add to your bike? Where is your tank located now? It's getting harder to find the gas tanks on some bikes, especially big bikes. For years, Honda has buried the Gold Wing's gas tank beneath the seat to move the weight down low and improve handling. If you're thinking about adding capacity to

a Wing, you'll be looking at some type of external device.

Bikes with traditional gas tanks at the front of the bike have a few more options. It's fairly easy to find larger-than-stock fuel tanks for popular adventure bikes such as the Kawasaki KLR and BMW GS series. These are mostly bolt-on products that add one to two gallons of capacity. Another option is to have your existing gas tank modified to accommodate extra fuel. An automotive shop or machine shop should be able to help you if you decide to take that path. Mounted up high this extra capacity will make your bike a little top heavier (about six pounds per gallon)

Riders have mounted auxiliary fuel tanks just about everywhere you can imagine. There is no shortage of companies who make auxiliary tanks that fit in your co-rider's pillion seat, mount on a luggage rack, behind your license plate, or even in your saddlebags. While you're considering those options you can decide if you want a cell that's permanently mounted or one that's removable. Removable units are designed for the pillion or a saddlebag. Chances are pretty good that you'll be riding alone when using an auxiliary tank, so the pillion seems a good choice for a temporary tank.

Can't find a tank designed to fit your bike? Sampson, makers of fuel tanks for popular long-distance bikes, will gladly give you a quote for a custom tank design if you don't find a model specifically for your bike or if you want to mount your tank in a different place.

SUMMARY

There are two important systems you need to look at before loading up your bike with luggage and trailers. The load you carry will affect tire wear and your bike's handling. You need to make sure that your tires and suspension are equipped to handle what you will ask of them.

Tire design and compounding have led to a revolution in tire wear for motorcycles. Even though bikes carry more weight per square inch on their tires than cars, tire wear is beginning to approach car-like standards with an acceptable level of grip. Tire profiles impact bike handling by affecting how quickly the bike can lean into curves.

Fuel cells are most often used by endurance riders to eliminate fuel stops but some touring riders use them to relieve anxiety about running out of fuel.

The suspension that keeps your tires glued to the road also helps you maintain control of the bike and gives you a comfortable ride. Suspension components can be adjusted to manage different loads, but you need to take a methodical approach when you experiment.

We also looked at other basic components you might consider adding to protect your bike. Light guards, kickstand plates, and engine guards will eliminate some on-the-road headaches and expensive repair bills.

Last, we looked at auxiliary fuel cells. These devices are favored primarily by riders who plan to travel very long distances without stopping, but they may also serve the purpose of someone who pulls a heavy load and wants to preserve their original mileage range.

12

Storage Solutions

Fifteen years ago I learned an expensive lesson about motorcycle travel. Back then it was harder to find bags that would fit my little 600 and my budget. Bungee cords, on the other hand, were cheap. I had developed something of a system for packing the bike that made extensive use of bungee cords and cargo nets and though it seemed to work pretty well, the bike resembled Santa's sleigh piled high with goodies.

That's how it looked one bright weekend when I rode away from the house for a motorcycle campout. Rather than blast down the Interstate, I followed the call of the back roads, tracing a zigzag route through the valley toward

The perfect example of how not to load your bike. Weight placed high on the bike changes the center of gravity, making the bike feel like it is about to flop over when leaned into a curve. Cargo stacked on the rear affects weight distribution between front and rear tire. The front of the bike will feel light and hard to steer, possibly leading to loss of control.

the campground. Just before I pulled into the campground, I stopped for gas and realized something was wrong when I tilted the bike to drop it on the kickstand. It felt light. Too light. Surprise. Shock. Disbelief. All I found of my gear was a shredded bungee net hanging loosely off the back of the bike.

My gear was spread out over the last 150 miles like a trail of breadcrumbs. I retraced my route for a few miles to a section of road that had been particularly bumpy and found the tent in the road. A tire mark ran the length of the carrying bag. The sleeping bag, cooking gear, ground cover, and everything else had disappeared earlier. Those were expensive breadcrumbs.

You can find cargo systems for bikes across the price spectrum. There are practical limits to the quantity of gear you can carry on a motorcycle, but with so many different luggage systems to choose from, your limitation won't be a lack of space, it will be your bike's weight capacity.

Luggage systems specifically adapted for use on motorcycles have several advantages over strapping your gear to the bike. From my tale of woe, you can appreciate that one obvious advantage to having a reliable way to carry your gear is safety; it's reassuring to know that your gear will stay on the bike and won't shift or fall off. Had my stuff gotten tangled up in the rear wheel, the outcome might have been a lot worse than lost gear.

Luggage provides some extra level of security. A determined thief can open anything, but keeping valuables out of sight and tethered will deter someone from just walking away with your expensive helmet and jacket or snagging the radio off your bike.

Large top cases are convenient but you should use them only for light objects.

Finally, luggage protects your belongings from the harsh environment and road conditions you can experience on a bike. This is of special interest if you're bringing along sensitive gear like a laptop. You would never lash that to the back of a bike without some way to protect it—unless you were looking for an excuse to get a new laptop.

Motorcycles are sensitive to where they carry weight. Put too much weight in the wrong place and your bike's handling will become unpredictable and ill-mannered. A well thought-out luggage system allows you to distribute that weight as evenly and low as possible to preserve your bike's handling.

Finally there are matters of efficiency and convenience. Good luggage allows you to pack more gear and makes it easier to access when you need it. At the end of a hard day's ride, it's a welcome relief to unburden your bike with a few quick flips, toss your gear into your room, and be done with it.

The information in this chapter is organized from the ground up, the same way you would build up a luggage system for your bike. Popular luggage systems are discussed first, hard cases used as saddlebags and trunks, then softbag alternatives. After that, we'll discuss other types of luggage, particularly tankbags and tailbags. Finally we'll review luggage that fits on top of your base luggage such as "expedition bags," seat bags, stuff stacks, dry bags, and more.

LUGGAGE SYSTEMS

Luggage systems offer the largest cargo carrying capability on a motorcycle and are a necessity if you spend a lot of time on the road. Luggage systems are best suited for carrying your clothing, overnight gear, and items you need at the end of the day, not the things you need throughout a day's ride.

There are three types of luggage systems: integrated luggage, removable hard luggage, and soft bag systems. Depending on your bike and the style of luggage it may already have, some choices may already have been made for you. To some extent you can mix and match luggage systems and, as we'll soon see, it's particularly easy to supplement your hard luggage system with soft components.

Integrated Luggage

Integrated luggage is found on big touring bikes like the Honda Gold Wing, Kawasaki Voyager and BMW K1200LT. These bikes are "turnkey" touring machines because they roll off the showroom floor with storage compartments that are a permanent part of the bike. Integrated luggage is fully lockable and uses the same key as your bike's ignition. Unlike soft luggage systems, you

This cruiser has a nice-looking set of integrated saddlebags. They are designed to hold a lot of gear, are lockable, and will keep contents dry.

don't need to take any weather precautions because integrated luggage is waterproof. Integrated saddlebags pop open to let you store and retrieve items easily. The trunks of many bikes are large enough to swallow two full-face helmets.

Integrated luggage can hold a lot of gear, but not necessarily heavy stuff. For example, the Wing's saddlebags and trunk can accommodate up to 147 liters of storage space yet the recommended weight limits are fifteen pounds for the trunk and twenty pounds for each saddlebag. Clearly the Wing's luggage was designed for hauling clothing and other lightweight materials. Systems like this are at the biggest disadvantage when you want to lighten your bike's load for a sportier ride or you need to cover some tough terrain. I've ridden a fully loaded Wing over some rough back roads and as I feel the rear luggage assembly shudder, I keep expecting the back end to snap off like the stern of the Titanic. On the positive side, if that ever does happen, I'm likely to notice it more quickly than when the tent slipped off the back of my Radian.

These simulated leather bags match the style of this bike while offering the improved performance of hard luggage.

Removable Hard Luggage

Just as the Gold Wing redefined touring in early part of the '70s, Kawasaki introduced a new bike that redefined it again in the mid-80s. The Kawasaki Concours was a sporty bike powered by the company's legendary Ninja engine, but the Concours fairing and ergonomics were designed for long-distance touring. It featured factory-mounted hard saddlebags that could be removed quickly, converting the Concours from touring mount to a sportier configuration in just a few seconds. A new class of motorcycle, the "sport-tourer" was born. (Purists might argue that a bike like the BMW R90S was the first sport-touring bike, but they didn't call it sport-touring back then.)

Like integrated luggage, hard bags are more secure and waterproof than soft bags. Removable bags not only allowed the bike to be transformed, but made it a cinch to unpack. Pop off the bags, drop them in your hotel room. Done.

Success of the Concours led to the introduction of other sport-touring bikes with removable hard luggage, notably the Honda ST1100 (now the ST1300) and the Yamaha FJR1300. Both the Honda and Yamaha feature hard saddlebags with mounting brackets that disappear when the luggage is removed from the bike. The result is a bike with clean lines whether the bags are mounted or not.

Removable hard luggage systems are also available as aftermarket add-ons for many bikes. For example, the Honda VFR, a bike biased toward the sport end of sport-touring, comes out of

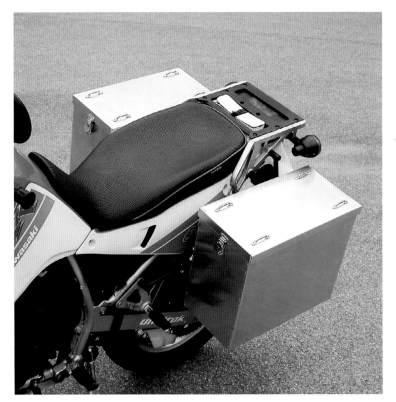

Aluminum panniers are built to take a lot of punishment while protecting your cargo.

the crate with no factory luggage attached. Italian hard luggage maker Givi (giviusa.com) sells a set of brackets that mount Givi's luggage system to the VFR for a nice look that carries a lot of gear. Corbin, the seat maker, sells a hard luggage system for the VFR called "Beetle Bags." Corbin's bags are designed to match the lines of the VFR so closely that the bike looks like it came from the factory equipped with them.

Removable hard luggage is made from either high impact ABS plastics or aluminum. For touring conditions you expect to find in North America, hard plastic cases work fine. They are durable, waterproof, and less expensive than metal. World travelers, or those who anticipate rugged conditions, will opt for the sturdiness that aluminum cases provide. Aluminum cases like those made by Jesse (jesseluggage.com) are particularly adept at surviving harsh conditions and frequent drops that occur when you are venturing along paths unbeaten or thoroughfares so battered they're roads in name only.

That's all great, but what if you own a cruiser? Black plastic bags just don't look right on a laid back ride like that. Many leather bags are now built over plastic forms or contain plastic inserts. These forms allow the bag to hold its shape even when it's empty and they won't sag over time. You won't find top cases on cruisers unless you're talking about a full dress touring bike. There are plenty of other options for adding storage to cruisers and we'll touch on those when we get to soft luggage.

Cases with a matte finish won't show scuffs like polished surfaces.

Buying a Luggage System

Regardless of which system you choose, you'll want answers to a few questions before you spring for any luggage. In particular, you'll want to examine which bags fit your bike best, how the bags will mount and how they'll function once they're put to work.

Hard luggage is available in two forms: saddlebags (also called side cases) that attach to the sides of the bike, and top cases which mount behind the pillion and function like a trunk. Saddlebags have the advantage of putting the added weight down low, preserving your bike's handling. Saddlebags make your bike wider; for that reason top cases are preferred by those who don't want to compromise their bike's narrow profile. Top cases carrying excessive weight will make your bike feel top-heavy but if you don't overload them, you probably won't feel any ill effects. Some models feature a backrest pad for your co-rider, a nice plus. Many riders who want the greatest carrying capacity add both to their bikes.

Before you buy a set of hard luggage, look carefully at how the brackets and bags will fit your bike. If both are custom designed for your bike you should have little trouble mounting them. Several luggage makers use a model-specific mount and universal bags. Have a close look at the final fit. Ask if you have to relocate anything to install the bracket or bags. It's not

Top opening cases allow you to get to your stuff without spilling it on the road. Liners make any saddlebag a breeze to load and unload.

unusual that you might have to move your turn signals. If so, does the bag kit come with the parts to do the relocation? Some bags will block your access to rear components of the bike, meaning you may have to remove a bag and sometimes the bracket to make a shock adjustment or remove a tire. What will the bike look like with the bags off? If you have to remove the brackets to get back to a stock look, how long will that take? If you ride with a passenger, how will the luggage affect their seating position or the amount of space available to them?

Good bags close snugly with ease and are outfitted with high quality hardware. These are signs that you'll be able to make heavy, continued use of the bags. As you look at a particular set, ask yourself how the bags would work on the road. For example, how do they open? Many bags are designed like a clamshell, which can be a bit tricky to load or retrieve items on the road. Other riders favor the top-loading system. They're easier to use because you don't have to worry about spilling the contents when you open the lid. If you use a top-loading system make sure it's either hinged or has some type of tether so you won't lose the lid if you forget to lock it.

Find out if you'll need to relocate your turn signals when you add a bracket for hard luggage.

The finish of the bag is another consideration. Removable bags take more abuse than the finish on other parts of your bike. Think carefully about whether you want painted bags to match your bike or bags with a black matte finish that doesn't show marks as readily. The biggest challenge I ever had with bags on an ST1100 I once owned was preventing them from getting banged up as I took them on and off the bike and moved them around. Bags I had on a later bike showed very little wear because of the matte finish.

SOFT LUGGAGE

The development of advanced lightweight durable fabrics, especially Cordura, opened a world of new possibilities for all outdoor activities, but motorcyclists may be the biggest beneficiaries. Cordura is an important component in nearly every synthetic material garment and the basis for almost all soft luggage applications, except leather and maybe a few other exotic materials.

Soft luggage is available in an amazing variety of shapes and sizes. If you have a little surface area and a place to loop a strap anywhere on your bike, there is probably a piece of soft luggage made to fill the spot. If you already have some hard luggage on your bike, there are numerous soft luggage add-ons that will expand your storage options.

Of equal importance, soft luggage fits any bike. There are mounting considerations we'll discuss, but you don't have to be concerned about finding just the right bracket to fit your bike. Soft luggage can be adjusted to fit your

If you choose your gear carefully, this modest set of soft luggage is all you need to ride for any trip.

particular setup. If you have multiple bikes in the stable, it's easy to move soft luggage from one bike to another. Good quality soft luggage systems are not cheap, but they are significantly less expensive than hard bags, and carry a lot of stuff.

So with all that going for soft bags, why would you travel with anything else? For one thing, soft bags are not waterproof. You can make soft bags water resistant, but they're not entirely waterproof without covers. While soft bags are durable, they won't last as long as a good set of hard cases. I know riders who have worn out bikes and moved their hard bags to the next bike. Soft bags don't provide the same security as hard bags and they have a tendency to lose their shape when heavily loaded.

To sum it up, soft bags are a perfectly good choice as a primary luggage system if hard bags aren't available for your bike or just aren't in your budget. You'll have to be more particular about how you pack so the bags aren't too heavy, but that's better than staying at home.

Saddlebags and Tailbags

When you shop for soft saddlebags and tailbags, the same issues are important as for hard luggage—bag fit, mounting, and features—although the specific details you consider will be a bit different.

This tail pack mounts over a passenger back rest to create extra storage.

What would we do without Cordura? This woven synthetic fabric or its competitors are used in many pieces of riding gear and luggage.

The biggest concern with soft saddlebag fit has to do with exhaust clearance. Bikes with low-swept pipes like the Nighthawk are easier to fit with soft gear than bikes with hi-swept pipes like the VFR. Hard bags avoid this issue because the mounting bracket holds the bag away from the pipe. Your soft bag should be equipped with heat shields on the side of the bag near the exhause pipe. The shield protects the bag's synthetic materials from exhaust heat but this doesn't mean you can rest the bag on the pipe.

Most soft saddlebag systems use two or three straps that connect the two bags. These straps are lined with a hook-and-loop material (Velcro or equivalent) so they can be shortened or lengthened to fit your bike. When you're riding alone you can adjust the straps so you can throw the bags over the bike, connect a couple of bungee hooks, and you're gone. If you're carrying a passenger, you'll want to make sure the straps can work under the seat. Your bags must use some type of soft, foamy material on the surfaces that make contact with your bike's painted parts, to avoid scratching them.

Straps hold the tops of the saddlebags together, but saddlebags need to be secured at the bottom, too. This is tricky since the only thing beneath saddlebags is a muffler or the pavement. Bags use a strap and buckle or some type of bungee cord to attach to other points on the bike. These aren't intended to support weight; their primary purpose is to secure the bags so they don't flop around when you lean the bike. If it is

A simple kit from Powerlet adds power to your tank bag so you can run accessories like an MP3 player from your bag without a permanent mount on the bike.

not immediately obvious where you can attach soft bags, ask your dealer for advice or check into a discussion board online to find out what other riders are using on your model bike.

Better bags have a sturdy inner support system of plastic sleeves. These help the bag retain its shape when it's loaded. Short of adding some type of brackets to the bag, there's nothing you can do to prevent the bags from sagging, but plastic inserts will minimize this. Expandable bags include a zipper that exposes an expansion fold, allowing you to stuff more into the bag. Fully expanded, two large soft saddlebags have more than 60 liters of capacity. That is a lot of space.

Look for a bag that uses a heavy woven nylon exterior and a PVC coating on the inside. This won't make the bag fully waterproof but helps considerably when a rain cover is added. Speaking of rain covers, the better bags stow the cover in their own storage compartment for easy access. Good covers are those that fit well and stay secure when you're traveling at highway speed. You don't want to have to retrace your tracks on a rainy highway to find a lost rain cover. Finally, look for a bag with zippers that are easy to grasp with a gloved hand. Reflective materials are a welcome addition.

TANKBAGS

A tankbag is one of the first luggage accessories many riders purchase. Since it's mounted right in front of you within easy reach, the tankbag is a natural place to keep essentials you need to access throughout the day: medicines, keys, wallet, rain gear, sun screen, ear plugs, MP3 player, maps, and sundry items. If you're traveling light and alone, you might need nothing more than a large tankbag for a trip lasting two or three days.

Tankbags have two basic mounting methods, straps or magnets. Older style tankbags use a series of clips and straps to hold the bag in place. This arrangement works well enough to secure the bag but takes time to remove and replace. In essence you're reinstalling the bag each time you put it back on. More tankbags with strap systems are now designed so the tankbag can be removed while the mount stays in place.

Magnetic bag mounts were developed as an alternative to strap systems. A tankbag with a magnetic mount has a rubberized bottom with six or so powerful magnets (more if the bag is bigger) arranged around the perimeter of the bag. Mounting is as simple as placing the bag on a metal gas tank. A tether wraps around the steering head as a safety restraint in case the bag should work loose. I suppose that's possible but the magnetic bags I've used have all fastened securely to the tank. In theory, you don't want to store magnetic-sensitive products in a magnetic tankbag: digital cameras, MP3 players, credit cards, etc. In practice, many riders I've spoken with have not found this to be an issue. The bigger issue with magnetic tankbags has to do with surface contamination gathering on the underside of the bag. If the bag's mounting surface isn't kept scrupulously clean, it's possible to scratch the tank.

Did I say there were two basic methods for mounting a tankbag? Now there's a third. SW-MOTECH (mo-tech.de) has developed a tankbag mounting system they call "Quick Lock" that features a raised collar fitted to the gas cap. The collar creates a mounting bracket for the bag, which clicks into place, and is easily removed, particularly at fuel stops. The bag never touches the tank surface, eliminating the possibility of scratching the tank.

Tank bags come in as many shapes and sizes as jellybeans have flavors, so one of your primary purchase considerations will be size. Small bags hold around ten to twenty liters. (Divide liters by 3.8 to convert to gallons.) That's enough for all the small convenience items you might care to bring along, and maybe a rain suit, fleece or electric jacket with bags at the large end of this range. Medium bags of twenty-one to thirty liters can handle an extended set of convenience gear and maybe enough to get a light packer through a weekend excursion. Over thirty liters and you start venturing into the carrying capacity of tailbags and saddlebags. One benefit of a large, fully loaded tankbag is the ability to lean forward and use the bag as a temporary cushion to take pressure off your arms for a bit.

Buying a Tankbag

It's easy to buy a tankbag that's too big or one that interferes with the controls on your bike. When you fully load up a tankbag, it can get unwieldy. Either test fit the bag on your bike at the store or make sure the store has an adequate return policy. Compared to the price of other gear, tankbags aren't all that expensive, so you might well end up with two; a small one for day rides and a larger tankbag for extended tours. Buy the smaller one first before you go for a really big tankbag. You may find that a small bag is all you need. Some bags like the FAMSA line are modular. By combining different zip-on modules you

This medium-sized tank bag uses magnets to keep it on the bike.

A mount system with zippers is a valuable feature. You can easily remove your tankbag while leaving the mount in place.

can have anything from a small daytrip bag to a thirty-four liter (nine gallon!) jumbo bag.

Some bags are available in either strap or magnetic mount. If you don't have a steel gas tank, you'll be choosing a strap mount by default. Attachment straps should stay clear of your tank. You should be able to cinch up the bag tightly with nothing contacting the paint except the bag's soft padding on the underside. Another desirable feature is a mount system that stays attached to the bike, like the kind made by SW-MOTECH. If you have a couple of bikes, you can purchase multiple mounts and move your tankbag between bikes. Or you can purchase different size bags and use the same mount.

If you're satisfied with the size and mounting, check out the bag's ease of use. You'll use your tankbag constantly throughout the day, so make sure it is easy to operate with gloved hands. Zippers with large pull tabs are preferable. Many riders feel that a bag can't have too many pockets and I agree with that sentiment. Every pocket seems to call out for a particular type of item. Tank bags include a map pouch on top with a clear plastic cover. Most bags will hold at minimum two panels of a standard size folding map. Pockets that accommodate a wider map are a bonus. Pockets that are too small are a pain because you'll continually be folding your maps to make them fit.

When you've filled up every other space, tank panniers offer yet another place to stuff things.

these bags is close or overlapping, depending on the particular type of bike you're riding. We'll define tailbags as those designed to fit over existing backrest structures on the bike. Rack bags lash to a luggage rack on the rear of the bike. Seat bags mount in the co-rider's position. Both trunk and tailbags can be used with a co-rider on board while the seat bag can only be used on a solo ride. Bags in this category can accommodate as little as twenty liters to fifty liters or more. Some bags include wheel rollers for easy maneuvering off the bike. Other options include insulated bags for carrying hot or (more likely) cold items.

A backpack designed for riding lets you shoulder some of the burden yourself.

MORE SOFT LUGGAGE COMPONENTS

Saddlebags and tank bags are two of the more popular softbag options but there are plenty of other luggage pieces for cargo carrying or special purpose applications. The same general evaluation rules apply for these items as for other soft luggage. Consider what size and shape of gear you need to carry, its weight, and how often you may need to access it when you're on the road. When you look at a particular piece of luggage, think about how and where the luggage will fit your particular bike, how it will be secured, and how it is constructed. Here's a quick look at some common luggage options.

Tail, rack, and seat bags are popular with a lot of riders. There is some mixing of terminology in this category given that the proximity of

If you're purchasing a rack bag for a luggage rack mounted to a trunk like the Gold Wing, be careful how you load it. Trunk racks are rated for just a few pounds of weight. That's because the trunk lid isn't really designed to carry any weight. If you put any substantial weight on the lid, the stress will cause the plastic to crack. Given what those bikes already hold, I would forgo the trunk rack.

Duffel-style bags like the Mag's Bags Grand Touring bag (magsbags.com) or Jo's U-Pac (josupac.com) were created to hold big items for those who camp extensively. Duffel bag designs rest on top of saddlebags and stretch across the co-rider seat. These humongous bags carry from fifty to over eighty liters of stuff. That's enough space for a two-person tent, a pair of camping pads, two sleeping bags and a stove kit. Of course, the second person will need to ride their own bike because a bag this size straddles the passenger area.

Tank panniers are like saddlebags that drape over the front of your tank. They use the same strap system as saddlebags so they can be adjusted to fit many different bikes. Clips on the bottom of each bag secure it to the bike. Panniers are good for carrying heavier items like tools, auxiliary fuel bottles, water—anything that you want to have easy access to and want to keep mounted low. Tank panniers have the same potential for paint abrasion as tankbags and if you have long legs, you'll need to experiment with placement to keep from bumping them with your knees.

Fork bags and windshield bags are often seen on cruisers. Fork bags require exposed forks to mount, a requirement not met with fully-faired bikes. Fork bags are a good spot for a roll of tools. Windshield bags are arranged as a series of small pockets that fit on the inside of the fairing. These are good for convenience items with little value like lip balm, gum, and disposable earplugs.

Don't care about riding with a tank bag? This map pouch keeps your map within easy viewing distance.

Dry bags will positively keep your gear dry. They can be lashed to your bike with bungees or tie-downs.

SPECIAL-PURPOSE SOLUTIONS

We've almost exhausted the options for carrying gear on a bike, but there are a few specialized products worth mentioning before we move on.

One of those items is a *compression sack*, also called a "stuff sack." Items like sleeping bags and fleece clothing contain a lot of air; a compression sack is used to remove that air. You can often reduce the bulk of items by a third or more. When you do use a compression sack on a sleeping bag, take the bag out of the sack well before you plan to use it. Unfold the bag and lay it out to let it regain its loft.

Dry bags are normally associated with outdoor water activities like canoeing. Dry bags are constructed of heavy PVC material and are designed to keep your gear absolutely dry, even if you dump the canoe into the drink. This makes the dry bag an excellent fit for motorcycling applications for withstanding driving rain at 70 m.p.h. Dry bags and compression sacks work well together. After wrapping your sleeping bag with a compression sack and squeezing out the air, your compression sack should drop neatly into the dry bag. Lashing them to the tops of saddlebags or a trunk rack is a popular way to carry these bags.

▶ WHAT WILL MY BIKE CARRY?

A motorcycle's gross vehicle weight rating (GVWR) is the total weight the bike is officially designed to carry, including the bike, fluids, rider, co-rider, and cargo. All bikes have a GVWR value stamped on a tag or sticker somewhere on the bike.

To determine what your bike can actually carry, try to find the bike's "wet weight" in your owners manual. Wet weight is how much the bike weighs unloaded but with fluids (oil, gas, antifreeze). If you can't find a wet weight value, look for the bike's "dry weight" (weight without fluids) and add fifty pounds to this value for a conservative estimate. Subtract the wet weight from the GVWR value to determine what your bike can carry. Here are the GVWR, wet weight and cargo weight for a few popular bikes.

MAKE	MODEL	GVWR	WET	CARGO
Honda	ST1300	1056	727	329
Yamaha	FJR1300	1047	637	410
BMW	K1200GT	1102	681	421
Honda	GL1800	1303	881	422
H-D	VRSCR	1060	636	424
Kawasaki	Concours	1118	671	447
BMW	R1200RT	1091	625	466

Many riders are surprised by those small cargo numbers, especially on "big" bikes like the Gold Wing. With a middle-age rider (like me) and a co-rider (like my twig of a wife) on my bike, it's near the suggested weight limit before we even start adding gear (because of me, I assure you).

When your bike is grossly overloaded, it will handle poorly and your ability to execute emergency avoidance maneuvers or panic stops will be diminished. Worse, you run the risk of snapping a sub-frame or bracket mount that holds your luggage on board. Heavy loads, in combination with low tire pressure, are a frequent cause for rear tire blowouts which can have the most catastrophic consequences of all. Faced with the choice of hauling a passenger or gear, it may be time to outfit your co-rider with their own bike. ■

On some journeys you may have a requirement to carry sensitive gear that requires *special packing*. A typical example might be a camera with a set of lenses or perhaps video equipment. Small items like cell phones and MP3 players

Keep gear secured with products like this bungee net.

need protection from the elements. Delicate items like cigars (for when your journey's destination is achieved) need to be protected from breakage. There are two classes of products that suit these requirements—Pelican Cases (cases bypelican.com) and Otter Boxes (otterbox.com). Pelican specializes in large, waterproof, shock-resistant cases for larger items like cameras. Pelican's interior foam can be removed in sections to create a custom fit for your devices. Otter specializes in smaller boxes for PDAs, handheld computers, cell phones, and other small items. Like Pelican, Otter products are also durable and waterproof. And yes, Otter does make a protective cigar humidor for two to twenty-five of your favorite stogies.

STORAGE ACCESSORIES

There are a few additional items worth mentioning. One of those is *saddlebag liners*. In the earlier discussion about saddlebags, I mentioned that clamshell-style saddlebags can be tricky to load and unload. A saddlebag liner made to fit the shape of the bag makes clamshell bags easier to manage. In fact, with saddlebag liners, you can leave removable luggage attached to the bike at night.

One of the drawbacks of tank bags and tank panniers is their potential for scratching your paint. For some riders, scratches and dings are just part of the motorcycling experience; but for riders traveling on a cherished bike, it's more of an issue—dammit, a scratch is a scratch. Before you slap on a set of bags that have the potential to contact your paint, check out products featuring 3M's *paint protection plastics*. These are thin sheets of clear plastic film treated to resist yellowing. Companies like Invinca Shield (invinca-shield.com) make kits that are pre-cut for many specific bike models. These shields are often marketed as "do it yourself" kits but this is one job you don't want to rush. Either make sure you can do this when you aren't rushed and have plenty of time to study the job beforehand, or consult with your riding peers who can recommend a qualified application specialist in your area.

After you have exhausted the storage options that make sense for your bike, securing that last bit of gear sometimes requires *bungee cords, nets,* and *straps*. What's particularly important about these is having a good place to secure the strap or to hook the end of the bungee cord. Some bikes, racks and saddlebags contain hooks and attachment points for cords and straps. If your bike is deficient in attachment points, a cheap solution is a set of bolt-ons called "Bungee Buddies." These specialized bolts have a large plastic head with an eye for hooking a bungee cord. You have to drill holes to install these, so they won't suit everyone. But if you're more practical-minded than cosmetic-sensitive, you can add these just about anyplace on your bike for extra attachment points.

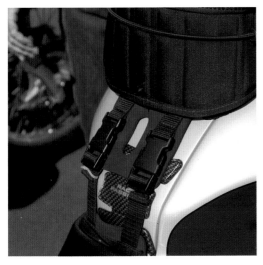

Pads like these protect your paint from the rub of tank bag straps.

Side opening saddlebags are much easier to use with saddlebag liners.

SUMMARY

Luggage systems make it possible for you to carry the things you need with greater security and safety. Large touring bikes feature integrated carrying capacity. With other bikes you can start with some type of basic luggage system, such as a set of hard saddlebags and a top case. If you travel light you may get by with a tank bag and tail bag; this preserves the narrow profile of your bike.

Soft luggage fits any type of standard bike. It is a less expensive alternative but isn't as waterproof and won't handle the same amount of abuse as a hard bag. If you have large cargo requirements, you can supplement a set of base luggage with soft luggage add-ons such as a duffel-style bag for carrying bulky items. Special-purposes cases and bags allow you to pack gear in a smaller space and protect delicate items.

What if you need to carry a lot of gear and a passenger, too? Or golf clubs? What if you like to camp but can't stand sleeping on the ground? What if your journey is a thinly-disguised cross-country shopping expedition? You may be a candidate for a trailer; see the next chapter.

13

Trailer Life

Real motorcycle travelers don't pull trailers, do they? If you think not, mention that thought at a touring rally sometime, where over half the attendees are pulling trailers. Let me know what reaction you get.

In order to understand fully the appeal of trailers you have to adjust your view of motorcycle touring. For many riders, the appeal of motorcycle travel is focused on the riding experience. "The journey is the reward" and all that. Riders who pull trailers enjoy motorcycling like everyone else, but they have a broader definition of the riding experience. What if you want to use the bike to get to a golf resort? Or travel between home and the kids' house for an extended stay? What if you still enjoy camping but can't sleep on the ground?

Early motorcycle trailers were derived from small car trailers. They were heavy, tracked poorly, and were just butt ugly. Today beautifully-designed and manufactured trailers are available from over a dozen makers. These trailers are lighter, carry more cargo, and handle better, thanks to computer-aided design, precision manufacturing, and improved components. Some models are manufactured to match the lines and colors of a particular bike so closely they look like a factory option. For example, both Bushtec (bushtec.com) and Escapade (escapade.com) feature designs that use the same Honda taillights as the GL-1800.

Trailers are also popular because they are easy to use. With a trailer, you don't have to spend time figuring out how to fit camping gear *and your co-rider* on the bike. Within reasonable limits, you can take everything you need to ride two-up and camp for weeks on end. My favorite is the trailer that includes a pop-up camper. I like to camp but don't care for sleeping on the ground or having to pack up a wet tent the next morning. Pop-up campers set up and break down in just a few minutes. Watching the reaction of someone car camping with a ground tent is priceless as you effortlessly open a couple of panels, snap a few arms into place, open the cooler, and pop the top on a cold one. Let the camping begin!

This beautiful Bushtech trailer matches the color and lines of the Gold Wing pulling it.

That said, a trailer certainly isn't for everyone. A trailer is not recommended if you plan to travel roads in poor condition, ride unpaved roads extensively, or if you plan to follow any off-road trails. If your bike has marginal stopping power, you shouldn't pull a trailer. Conventional two-wheel trailers will require you to reduce your speed and lean angle on twisty roads, a facet of riding that many are loathe to surrender simply to haul stuff.

I've pulled both cargo and tent trailers with large touring bikes and while I wouldn't pull one on every trip, I have enjoyed the convenience of a trailer. When I'm riding alone and plan to stay in motels, I'm traveling light so I don't need a trailer. However, when I owned a pop-up camper, I did more motorcycle camping than I do now. I would leave my camping gear in the trailer so there was very little to do but hitch the trailer, go through my pre-ride check, and get on the road.

TRAILER BASICS

Cargo trailers for motorcycles range from very basic self-assembly kits designed for use with any vehicle, to highly-refined color-matched units designed for a specific model of bike. Having pulled a half-dozen different types, my advice is to choose a trailer designed specifically for motorcycle use.

Cars can pull small trailers with impunity. A trailer is a small fraction of the car's weight and unless the trailer whipsaws from side to side, it will have little effect on a stable four-wheel vehicle. Naturally, bikes are sensitive to the handling input and weight added by a trailer. Any misbehavior of the trailer will have an adverse effect on the bike's performance. So what separates a cheap trailer from a good one? There are three important factors: suspension, cargo box design, and styling and features.

Suspension

Each trailer manufacturer has its own idea about what kind of suspension design is best, and this makes it impossible to compare suspensions strictly by their specs. You really need the opportunity to tow a trailer to get a sense of how it feels behind a bike.

Not every trailer hauls golf clubs or lawn chairs. Bill Perry built this custom trailer to carry equipment for his gigs.

A popular suspension design found on low-end trailers is the leaf suspension. It's cheap to build and doesn't require any adjustments. Performance is acceptable if you load it carefully and stick to the Interstate. Modest twisties or bumpy roads will reveal the limitations of this design. Leaf spring suspensions have no damping system. In effect, the weight of the cargo in the cargo box performs this function. Loaded trailers using a leaf spring design stick to the road well enough. However, when you push the leaf springs to their limits, particularly if the trailer is empty or lightly-loaded, the body of the trailer will come unglued from the road and hop across the road surface.

▶ WHAT ABOUT A SIDECAR?

In its day, the sidecar was the preferred method for adding passenger or cargo capacity to a bike. Sidecars are still the only solution when you need to add room for extra passengers. However, for cargo hauling, sidecars have been replaced by trailers. The popularity of trailers can be attributed to their ease of use. Sidecars require modification to a bike. Sidecars add stability to a bike but they require the rider to significantly adjust his or her riding technique. Remember "look right, lean right, go right?" On a sidecar it's "look right, *turn right,* go right." That simple change is tricky for many riders. By contrast, a trailer can be attached or removed quickly. Other than adding a hitch, it requires no special modifications to the bike and adding a trailer doesn't require that a rider learn a new riding technique. ■

compresses the rubber cords wedged between the torsion bar and the outer shell of the axle. Energy from the movement is absorbed and stored briefly by the rubber cords. After the bump is passed over, the compressed rubber cords release their stored energy, applying counter-force to the torsion bar which, in turn, keeps the wheel planted on the road.

Trailers allow you to carry cargo safely without loading down your bike.

Not only is this system more responsive than leaf springs, it is also very compact. Rubber torsion suspensions do not need a solid axle that runs the width of the trailer. Instead, they are packaged as self-contained units with wheel, hub, axle and suspension together. This gives even small trailers the dual benefits of lower empty weight and an independent suspension. Rubber torsion designs have essentially no damping and are therefore subject to bouncing across bumpy surfaces, especially when empty.

A third suspension design involves some variation of shocks or air suspensions. These designs work like the shock suspension on a motorcycle and yield the smoothest ride and most predictable performance over the widest range of pavement surfaces. Shock-based systems ride smoothly whether a trailer is empty or loaded. Unlike a torsion bar system, an air shock requires you to keep a check on air pressure to maintain best performance. This is a factor some owners ignore, just like tire pressure, which leads to uneven tire wear and poor handling.

A better performing suspension is the rubber torsion suspension. Rubber torsion systems are based on a time-tested setup borrowed from automobile designs. In cars, the torsion bar works by converting wheel movement into a twisting motion applied to a steel bar. Damping in automotive systems is usually provided by a separate shock absorber. In trailers, this design is modified to save weight and space. Torsion suspensions on trailers commonly use a series of rubber cords that run parallel to a torsion bar mounted in a hollow axle tube. (Dexter Axle, a major supplier of axles to trailer makers calls their version the TorFlex system.) When a bump or pothole moves the trailer wheel, the torsion arm rotates the torsion bar inside the axle tube. This rotation

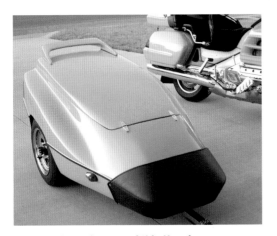

The aerodynamic nose of this Hannigan ensures that exhaust gases will flow away from the rider compartment.

Cargo Box Design

The cargo box on inexpensive trailers is a plastic compound, while better quality trailers use hand-laminated fiberglass that is tough, light, and built to resist cracking. Fiberglass can be molded into sleek contours, sanded, and painted to match any color bike. Diamond-plate aluminum is the material of choice for some trailers. While aluminum is undoubtedly durable, its biggest drawback is weight. Aluminum trailers are as much as fifty percent heavier than their fiberglass counterparts.

A good trailer design is one that provides maximum cargo space relative to their weight and overall size. Novelty trailers shaped like miniature cars and other fun designs are cute and they're great conversation starters, but don't expect them to hold as much of gear as a cargo trailer. If you want maximum cargo hauling, look for a design that loses the minimum about of space to odd angles, wheel wells, and suspension components.

The shape and width of the trailer box is important. You don't want a box that's much wider than your bike. When you clear an obstacle at the side of your bike, you don't want a wide trailer that will catch it. The front of the trailer should have an aerodynamically smooth design. A boxy front-end design can push exhaust gasses into the cockpit; a smooth design allows gasses to be pulled along the body of the trailer and released behind it.

Style and Features

Style can be an important consideration for a major purchase like a trailer. There are many riders who value function over form, and that's cool. If you understand a basic trailer's limitations and aren't interested in aesthetics, an economy trailer may be a good solution. On the other hand, I know many other riders who, having spent $18,000 for a sleek, full-dress bike, want to pull something that matches the lines and colors of their snappy ride.

Fiberglass trailers offer the best combination of style and color possibilities. Diamond-plate aluminum trailers have a boxier design because it isn't as easy to bend aluminum as it is to mold fiberglass.

Upgrades and options will increase the base price of a trailer significantly. Some upgrades—like a cooler rack, spare tire, and an interior light—are worth having; most of the rest are for show. Check the tire size of the trailer you're considering. You can find 4.80 x 10 and 4.00 x 12 tires just about anywhere, including Wal-Mart. Some trailers use unusual tire sizes that aren't readily available. Tapered roller bearings are preferred over sealed bearings because they are reliable and replacements are easily found.

Premium trailers offers convenience options like this garment bag.

▶ WHAT THE HECK WAS THAT?

Not long ago I was cruising along US 60 in West Virginia at what I thought was a pretty decent clip when a few miles into my run, a single headlight appeared about a half-mile behind me. The light was attached to a mint green BMW R-bike and it didn't take long to catch up. Not surprisingly, the rider took quick advantage of my move to the right to let him pass. What did surprise me was that the bike was pulling a single-wheel trailer attached directly to the frame of the bike. For the short time (and I mean short time) I could see the bike, the mono-wheel trailer leaned along with the bike as the rider entered each curve.

I've since learned that single-wheel trailers are building a fan base among sport riders who seek that perfect balance between a trailer's convenience, preserving their bike's handling, and avoiding the need to load the bike with luggage. They are compact enough to roll right into your motel room and they definitely turn heads. One-wheelers can hold up to 200 liters of cargo, as much or more space than if you decked out your bike with complete hard and soft luggage options. The trailer's wheel aligns with the bike's so you maintain your preferred line; the trailer attaches to the bike using a fixed mount so the trailer will lean with the bike. A universal joint allows the trailer some horizontal and vertical movement to improve tracking. ∎

What the . . . ? This one-wheel trailer tracks and leans with the bike so you can take a normal line through the curves. It's a real head-turner, too.

Here's an up-close shot of Jim Lehr's Unigo trailer. This system uses a fixed hitch so the trailer leans through the turns with the bike.

This Roll A Home camper includes a large cargo area for gear.

POP-UP CAMPERS

Motorcycle campers are cargo trailers with a built-in canvas that opens into a tent. Basic campers give you a covered sleeping space about equal to a standard two or three-person tent, while deluxe models are complete with sleeping quarters and a dressing/living area tall enough to stand up straight.

Campers don't have the same cargo carrying ability as a regular trailer because they are significantly heavier. A basic camper trailer weighs around 250 pounds empty. Even so, the trailer should still have enough capacity to carry your camping gear, cook set, and food.

Campers that can be set up by one person are preferred over designs that require two or more people. A camper I once had needed about three and a half people to set up, though I eventually figured out a way to do it myself. It wasn't easy and I was always envious of those who trailered campers that opened like pop-up greeting cards. The tent should be made of breathable tent material with easy-to-use zippers. Look at the available cargo space. Can you get to it with the tent packed on top? What about after you set up the tent?

Campers are a heavy pull but they make camping so convenient you'll enjoy it more often.

This is a bigger bed than the one I sleep in at home.

HITCHES

You won't find "towing kit" listed as a factory option for any bike because no manufacturer sanctions the use of trailers with their bikes. Small market potential, the possibility of product misuse, and resulting liability are enough to keep deep-pocket manufacturers out of the trailer business, but finding a hitch for many larger tour-oriented bikes is not a problem.

The hitch you install must be made from heavy-gauge materials and have clean, solid welds. Tolerate no flex in the hitch. The attachment points are just as important. Good hitches get their primary pulling strength by bolting to the frame of the bike, with additional attachment points for stability. If you're having a custom hitch made, don't let anyone tell you that you can bolt the hitch to luggage brackets alone. The hitch must attach to the frame.

If you plan to install the hitch yourself, make sure you have plenty of clear space to work and take your time. For a fully-faired bike with integrated luggage, you'll have to remove most of the plastic from the rear of the bike to get to the frame. Be sure to observe good wiring techniques (as we discussed in Chapter 5) as you wire in the trailer harness. You will be tapping into your brake and turn signal wires to drive your trailer lights. You certainly don't want to create a faulty wiring connection that will be buried under all that plastic!

You may not have a lot of choices for hitch design unless you're riding a well-known trailering bike like the Gold Wing. If you do have a choice, consider how the design of the hitch will affect your ability to change the rear tire. You may have to unbolt some part of the hitch to get to the rear tire; a good design will make this job easier.

Hitches come with different types of hitch plates. Some are a flat plate with fixed ball; others use a horizontal receiver that allow you to remove the hitch plate and ball when not in use. An improved design uses a vertical receiver that is hidden behind the bodywork on some models. When you remove the vertical adaptor and ball, the hitch disappears entirely.

Hitches can be used for more than trailers. This hitch-mounted cooler hauls a lot of chilled beverages and food.

In your research you'll come across references to fixed versus swivel hitches. A fixed hitch is a ball and socket joint. The trailer hitch fits over a ball mounted to the hitch plate and a clamp holds the hitch to the ball. Your bike has the freedom to move from side to side with this arrangement as the bike turns, but it has a restricted ability to pitch up and down or lean from side to side.

A swivel hitch is designed to pivot, allowing the bike freedom to lean side to side with no range restriction. While no empirical testing has been done to determine whether this is an advantage at highway speeds, it can be a benefit if you happen to drop the bike at low speeds in a parking lot. A swivel hitch will allow the bike to drop to its side (and onto your crash bars, I hope) without damaging the trailer or hitch assembly on the bike.

By the way, even if you don't plan to pull a trailer, a hitch can come in handy. Bushtec makes coolers of several sizes designed to attach to their hitch. You'll need to be careful about loading the cooler up too heavily because its entire weight would be considered "tongue weight," but this is still a convenient method of adding a little extra storage to your bike.

PROPER TRAILER LOADING

Getting the load properly distributed in your trailer is the key to smooth pulling. An improperly balanced trailer will destroy your bike's handling.

You must stay within the manufacturer's total weight rating for your trailer. This is the weight of the empty trailer plus cargo. If you aren't sure what your cargo weighs, stack everything beside the trailer and go get the bathroom scales. Weigh yourself (I won't look) and then start weighing yourself with each item that goes into the trailer. For each item, subtract your body weight. This isn't very precise, but it's better than guessing. Any trailer that weighs more than 350 pounds loaded is going to be a handful, particularly if you need to come to a sudden stop.

Properly distributing weight in your trailer is absolutely critical to avoid an ill-handling rig. You want to distribute the weight so that it is slightly biased toward the front of the trailer. This creates "tongue weight," downward pressure exerted at the point where the trailer hitches to the bike. Your trailer manufacturer will recommend a specific tongue weight. It's about ten percent of the weight of your trailer so for a trailer that weighs three hundred pounds loaded, tongue weight would be about thirty pounds. Again, you can use bathroom scale to get an estimated weight. Use a short wooden dowel or rod to prop up the tongue on the scale to about the same level as the bike hitch.

Never connect a trailer with negative tongue weight to your bike. Negative tongue weight means the back of the trailer is heavier than the front. This creates a lifting effect which lightens the rear end of your bike.

The easiest way to achieve a balanced load is to center the heaviest items over the axle—tents, liquids, food, golf clubs, whatever. Load medium weight items like clothes toward the front and light items like sleeping bags toward the rear. If your trailer includes a cooler rack and you plan to carry a cooler, you must include a loaded cooler in your tongue weight calculations.

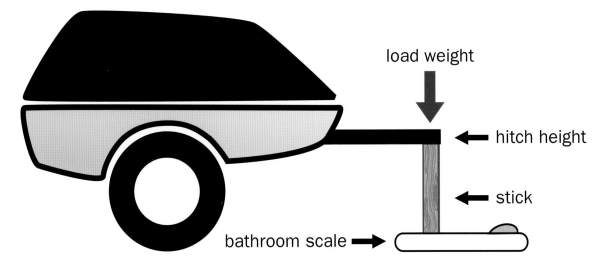

load weight

← hitch height

← stick

bathroom scale →

Tongue weight doesn't have to be exact. A reasonably close estimate will do. The empty weight of your trailer is available from the factory. As you add contents, keep a running total of what they weigh. If your trailer weighs 200 lbs. loaded and the suggested tongue weight is 10% of the total, you need to balance your load to achieve a weight of 20 lbs. at the end of the trailer hitch.

The easiest way to do this is to find a wooden broom handle or other dowel. Cut it to a length so that when you prop up the trailer hitch, it stands at the same height as it would on your bike. Place the stick on a bathroom scale and the hitch on top of the stick. Read the scale to estimate how much downforce the trailer is creating.

PURCHASING A USED TRAILER

New trailers are expensive but a well-maintained used trailer can still provide you with years of service at less cost. You should evaluate a trailer with the same critical eye as you would any other vehicle. Trailers don't have as many moving parts, but there are several areas you can check to determine overall condition. You're going to find some flaws. Some, like worn tires, are expected and easy to repair. Others, like cracks in the cargo box, are serious enough to nix the deal.

Before you visit, ask where the trailer has been kept. Like the best used bikes, the best used trailers are those which were kept in covered storage when they were not in use. I would rule out purchasing a used trailer if it was kept uncovered outdoors. Ask about the trailer's history and paperwork. Is the title clear and does the owner have it in possession? Is the trailer a recent enough model that replacement parts are still available for it? That's a real plus.

On-site, examine the condition of the cargo box and chassis. You're looking for any signs of damage or rust. Look at the point where the cargo box is mounted to the frame. See any stress marks or cracks around the bolts? Any bolts missing? If you find either to be true, let this deal go. Check the condition of the cargo box hinges and locks. They should be tight and rust-free. If the top has a hydraulic assist arm, does it work or is it worn out?

Take a close look at the wheels, bearings, and suspension. Pull a wheel off and check the bearings. They should be well-greased. Dry, ungreased bearings are a sign of neglect. Tires should show an even wear pattern. Do they show any cracks in the sidewalls from dry rot?

Check the condition of the wiring harness and hitch. Is the harness and plug in good condition? Do all the lights work? The hitch should work smoothly and grip firmly on the ball of the hitch plate. A safety chain should be present and of adequate length that the trailer can pivot around the hitch from lock to lock without using up all its slack.

If you're buying a used camper, have the owner set it up for you. As with a new camper, take note of how many people you need to set it up. You might expect a light musty odor from

▶ I ONLY FORGOT ONCE

On a trip into upstate New York, my wife and I were circling a campground looking for a spot to set up for the night. A truck with a boat trailer was having trouble making the turn into his spot and the road was blocked. There was a three-foot gap of open pavement between the truck and a sharp drop-off, an easy obstacle to skirt around on the bike. I forgot, of course, that the trailer I was pulling was a little wider than that.

I realized something was wrong as I powered around the truck and felt the bike lurch to the left and nearly stop. That was the trailer pulling on the bike as one wheel dropped off the pavement. The bike had just cleared the shoulder so I had no room to put down my foot to stabilize the bike. Jack and Jill were headed for a tumble.

Without thinking, I leaned a little to the right and pulled on the throttle to encourage the Wing to respond. A group of stunned campers looked on as the bike grunted and managed to pull us and the trailer away from the brink of disaster. I gave them my "I meant to do that" grin and waved as they watched us ride away. Since that time, I have never forgotten when I am pulling a trailer. ■

being stored in a garage where humidity levels fluctuate, but a heavy musty smell means it has been put away wet without being aired out first. Take a look at each point where the tent attaches to the trailer frame. You're looking for rips and tears or other signs of wear. Check to make sure all the zippers work. If extra hardware is needed to set up the tent or an extra room like an awning, make sure the parts are present and you understand how to set it up.

Finally, hook up the trailer and take it for a test run. Try to load it up if you can so you can get the best idea for how it feels behind your bike. After you've completed your test run, check the wheel hub for excessive heat. Be careful when you do this. If the bearings are too tight, the hub will be hot enough to give you a bad burn. Bearings can be readjusted and replaced if necessary, but that's a point that should be considered when negotiating on price.

SAFE TOWING TIPS

Besides proper cargo loading, there are several other principles and practices you should observe when towing a trailer.

Adding a trailer is like getting a new, heavier bike. Take your bike and loaded trailer to a parking lot and practice maneuvers. Spend a lot of time on braking techniques so you feel really comfortable hauling your rig down to a stop in the shortest distance possible. Your bike is more than twice as long as it was without a trailer. Take this into account and practice making turns around soft obstacles in the lot. Also practice tight radius turns to make sure you have a good feel for how tight you can turn the bike without contacting the trailer. (This is what happens when a trailer "jackknifes.")

Add the trailer to your pre-ride inspection. Before each day's pull, check your trailer's tire pressures, attachment points, safety chains, and lights. A riding buddy or co-rider can give you a quick thumbs up as you cycle through the turn signals and brake lights. Failing that, I've occasionally positioned the trailer's end to face a large section of plate glass where I can see the reflection of the lights with my mirrors.

Increase your following distance on the road. With extra time to identify and respond to road hazards you'll be less likely to find yourself in a panic braking situation. When traveling in a group of bikes, you should run at the back of the pack (the "back door") out of consideration for other riders in the group, in case something should happen to the trailer. A trailer can also hide some road hazards from the view of riders behind you.

Finally, never "forget" you're pulling a trailer. I know that trailer may be smooth, but it makes me shiver when I hear someone say, "Yeah, that trailer pulls so well, I forget it's back there." The problem is, if you forget you're pulling a trailer, you may reassume your normal riding attitude and forget to make the right accommodations for pulling a trailer. You might speed up, follow another vehicle too closely, or make a turn too sharp.

Novelty trailers are fun to pull. Make sure the trailer's design will accommodate the gear you need to carry.

SUMMARY

Motorcycle trailers are for more people than just those who can't travel light. A trailer gives you flexibility in packing and opens up new options for touring when you might otherwise have taken the car.

A light cargo trailer made with a fiberglass body, torsion or air suspension, and standard size trailer tires holds a lot of gear and has less adverse effects on your bike's handling and braking than a super-size trailer.

Even so, there are numerous cautions you should observe when pulling a trailer. It's imperative that you take some time to experiment with loading and towing your trailer, attempting tight turns and fast stops in a safe environment. Never, ever "forget" that you're pulling a trailer.

Many riders enjoy the convenience a trailer provides and I've had fun towing them myself. A trailer isn't for every occasion or every rider, but almost every trailer puller says the same thing. "I can't imagine touring without one."

Section IV

ON THE ROAD

Where are you now? You've researched and planned your trip. You have the right gear. You've outfitted your bike for travel. So what's next? Are you ready to get on the road?

Even grizzled road warriors feel a chill when they hear the bike roar to life, realizing that a new journey is about to unfold. It's a little deflating when you reach the end of the driveway but then have to trudge into the house to pick up your wallet.

To help you avoid that, we'll use Chapter 14 to outline the affairs you need to put into order so you can spend your time on the road with a clear mind. Following the timetable and preparation guides, you won't have to worry about turning around because you forgot to turn off the gas or lock the front door.

In the final Chapter 15, Managing Contingencies, we'll have a look at some of the issues you might encounter on the road and what you can do ahead of time to be prepared for them.

14 Putting It All Together **150**
Six to Twelve Months in Advance . . . 150
Two to Four Months in Advance 152
Four to Six Weeks in Advance 153
One to Two Weeks in Advance 155
Two to Three Days in Advance 156
The Day Before 157
Departure Day. 157
Summary 157

15 Managing Contingencies **158**
Weather 158
Security 160
Handling Breakdowns 161
Night Riding 163
Body Management. 163
Accidents 166
Staying in Touch 166
Food Selections. 167
Sickness. 168
The Final Words. 169

14

Putting It All Together

When I'm ready to head off on a long trip, I want to get up in the morning, look over the bike, and head out. I hate lingering around waiting to get started and I really dislike having to take care of a few last minute to-do's before I leave. Some years ago I started a list of things I might need to do so I could almost roll out of bed and onto the bike.

Your list will not be the same as mine, but mine will give you a sample to build from. Having any kind of checklist with timeframes helps you execute your plan without forgetting something important. With a checklist, you'll be more relaxed and ready to enjoy your trip to the fullest.

When you're planning to visit a popular destination like Glacier, make reservations well in advance then build your trip schedule around them. Glacier's lodge books up a year in advance.

Tasks are arranged in a rough timeframe to reflect what needs to be done and when. Long lead times are important when reservations and paperwork are involved. We'll include a pre-tour inspection that highlights maintenance and repair tasks to perform before you leave. The last section will help you decide how to pack your bike so you can haul everything you need, keeping it safe, secure, and dry.

SIX TO TWELVE MONTHS IN ADVANCE

Map out a route plan, the framework that will help define the rest of your trip. It will help you identify potential overnight areas and give you ideas for things you'd like to see and do along the way. A route plan doesn't have to be super formal; however, I've found that the longer the trip, the more time I spend on planning. When a ride lasts for more than a weekend, I want to do everything I can in advance to allow me to maximize my riding enjoyment. A route plan is essential for that purpose.

After you have some idea of your major destinations, *make reservations for any destinations that are popular with tourists,* particularly if you'll be traveling to the area during popular vacation months. On an around-the-country trip, I booked reservations in January for the Grand Canyon in August. June was already filled and July was nearly so. If you're thinking about doing something like staying at the popular Phantom Ranch (at the bottom of the Canyon), those reservations need to be made even sooner.

Do you have an estate will? Living will? How about a power of attorney? These are *basic legal documents everyone should have, regardless whether you're planning a trip.* Having an estate will isn't for your benefit, you'll be past caring at that point. You need a properly executed will to protect and benefit those you may leave behind. Without a will, your estate will go through probate court in your state. The bottom line is, with a will, you get to call the shots. Without it, someone else makes your final decisions and your assets can be delayed from reaching those who need it most.

A living will expresses your preferences for what should happen if you are severely injured and can't communicate your desires for healthcare. With a living will, you specify what measures you want medical personnel to take in saving or preserving your life, including a "Do Not Resuscitate" order. Like an estate will, a living will benefits your loved ones. A living will won't ease the pain but it will help erase any uncertainty about what to do should the worst happen. While you're at it, have a set of dog tags made, especially if you're traveling alone. A Google search for "dog tags" will identify dozens of suppliers.

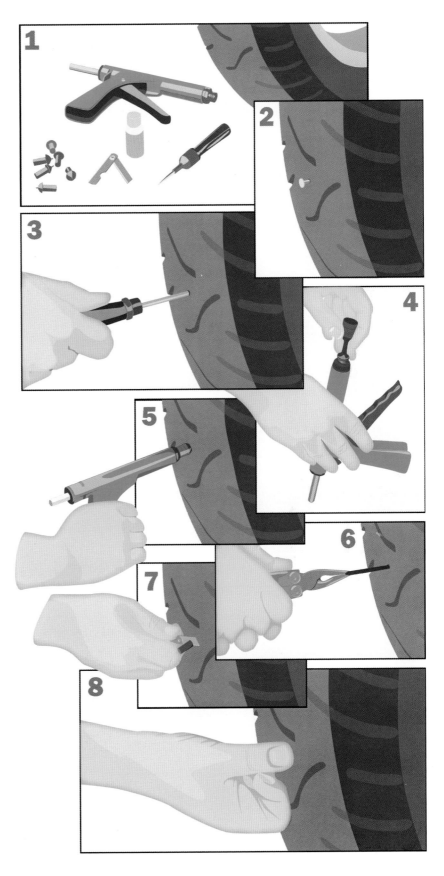

1 Practice using your tire repair kit before you need to use it on the road.

2 To be repairable, the puncture in your tire must be in the tread. If you have something embedded at an angle or in the sidewall, the tire must be replaced.

3 After removing the culprit, ream out the puncture to a size that will accept a plug.

4 Load the tire plugger.

5 Insert the plug.

6 This type of plug has a head on the end that is inserted. Tugging on it will then seat the head of the plug against the inside of the tire.

7 Trim the excess portion of the plug from the exterior of the tire.

8 Inflate with your tire pump and you're good to go.

▶ ## MY SHORT LIST

I don't carry as much gear as I used to. I've found that I enjoy taking pictures and chatting with folks as much as anything. I used to try to "get work done" on the road. Not anymore. I'll make notes and keep up with e-mails, but that's all I can manage. This is my short list of tour gear.

PROTECTIVE GEAR
▶ Flip-up helmet
▶ Riding suit, one- or two-piece
▶ Foam earplugs
▶ Summer-weight riding gloves
▶ Riding boots
  (comfortable enough to wear on and off the bike)
▶ Sunglasses

STREETWEAR AND THERMAL
(INCLUDING WHAT I'M WEARING)
▶ Two pairs of sink-washable socks and underwear
▶ Two pairs of riding shorts
▶ Two T-shirts
▶ One pair of jeans
▶ One pair of sweats
▶ Fleece jacket
▶ Electric vest (September thru May)

OTHER GEAR
▶ Toiletry kit
▶ Camera
▶ Maps
▶ Paperwork kit
▶ Camera
▶ Books (I leave them behind as I finish)

STORED PERMANENTLY IN BIKE
▶ Bike cover
▶ Toolkit
▶ Flat tire repair kit
▶ Air pump
▶ First-aid kit
▶ Hidden spare key

MOUNTED ON BIKE
▶ Satellite radio
▶ GPS ∎

You bought a *flat tire repair kit*, but have you ever used it? This is another task you can perform any time, whether you're planning a big trip or not, but when you have a trip on the horizon, take some time to find an old tire and try out your kit.

You should have your *passport* with you if you venture into Canada or Mexico. If your passport is within a year of expiring, take the time now to get it renewed. A current passport is easier to renew than an expired one.

This is also a good time to *visit discussion boards and resource pages on the Internet* to discuss your travel plans with others who've traveled through the areas you're thinking about. Other riders are a great resource for suggestions of must-ride roads and motorcycle-friendly destinations. Just remember that what others share with you is their opinion.

TWO TO FOUR MONTHS IN ADVANCE
Finalize the purchase and *installation of any major gear or gadgets*. For all the things we talked about earlier, I hope you took away a few ideas for improving your touring experience. If you have a mind to try an item or two, purchase them well in advance of your tour, take the time to install them properly and take them on a shakedown run or two. You need to log a few trips with new equipment or gear (especially if you've purchased a trailer), so you can become accustomed to how it works. You don't want to spend your first day on the road distracted by the new GPS you're trying to figure out, or spend time wondering why your bike isn't tracking as well with that trailer on the back.

Renew your subscription to any *road service or club membership*. If you don't belong to a club with road service, get one. I have a couple of club memberships that include roadside assistance plus a member directory with contact info for every member who cares to be listed. I always carry a membership directory with me on the off chance I'll find myself in a remote area where road service isn't readily available.

Determine whether your travels have any unique insurance or documentation requirements. These records can take some time to obtain. If you're traveling within the states and

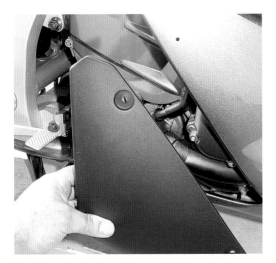

Install gadgets ahead of your big trip and become accustomed to using them. These footguards may offer just the protection this rider wants, or he may find they're an annoyance after using them a few times.

Canada, you only need to make sure your existing medical and vehicle policies will be current (and valid in Canada) through your trip's duration. Travel to other countries will require additional insurance, and possibly visas, medical records, and vehicle documents. Check in with knowledgeable riders on the Horizons Unlimited forum, many of whom have traveled through the area you're considering and can give you authoritative information on current conditions and requirements.

Now is the time to check with your doctor to determine if you need to update your vaccinations since some vaccinations are administered in a series, separated by days or weeks from the first dose. The U.S. Centers for Disease Control divides vaccinations into two major categories—routine and recommended. Routine vaccinations are for diseases that are common in other parts of the world, even though they may be rare in the U.S., such as tetanus, measles and hepatitis. Recommended vaccinations vary by country, time of year, the age of the traveler and other conditions. The CDC website (cdc.gov/travel) maintains an updated list of recommended vaccinations, searchable by the area you plan to visit.

Travel health insurance is worth considering, too. Travel health insurance is purchased in addition to the regular health insurance you may carry, providing benefits that are not part of your regular medical plan including medical, dental and surgical coverage. Separate coverage is also available for medical evacuation back to the U.S., a comforting thought for both you and your family in the event you sustain a life-threatening injury far from home.

FOUR TO SIX WEEKS IN ADVANCE

If your trip will be lengthy, *arrange to have a friend, neighbor, or house sitter around the house* to handle minor tasks like picking up your mail and watering plants. Even a small amount of activity gives the impression someone is around.

Take a look at the mileage on your bike and *determine your next required service event.* If your bike is close, get it on the dealer's schedule to have it serviced now. Will your service event happen somewhere during your trip? If you're going to run over by only a few hundred miles, it won't hurt the bike to hold off until you get home. Maybe you're not comfortable with that idea or you're going to be far from home when the next service is required. Take the time now to locate a dealer along your route and make a service appointment ahead of time. You shouldn't expect to ride into a dealer and have your bike serviced without an appointment. Let them know ahead of time if you'll need any special parts, like tires.

Near your service interval? Have major service performed before you get on the road. If a service event is needed while you're on the road, contact a dealer ahead of time to schedule your maintenance.

▶ TOOLS AND PARTS

I'm an electrical guy, not a mechanic, so I'm biased toward tools that I know how to use: electrical tools and a flat-tire repair kit. Other than light bulbs, I don't carry spare parts. If I blow a gasket or snap a throttle cable, I'll have to rely on road service. Want a more complete toolkit list? The Micapeak website contains a thorough checklist for every kind of kit you can imagine.

MECHANICAL TOOLS

- ▶ Ratcheting metric crescent wrenches
- ▶ "Leatherman" type all-in-one tool
- ▶ Screwdrivers
- ▶ Vise-grip pliers
- ▶ Metric hex wrench set

TIRE TOOLS

- ▶ Air pump
- ▶ Tire pressure gauge
- ▶ Tire repair kit

ELECTRICAL TOOLS AND SPARES

- ▶ One spare of each type of bulb
- ▶ Duct tape
- ▶ Fuses
- ▶ Length 18 gauge stranded wire
- ▶ Assorted crimp connectors
- ▶ Crimp tool
- ▶ Wire cutter
- ▶ Wire stripper
- ▶ Mini voltmeter
- ▶ Electrical tape
- ▶ Zip ties
- ▶ Mini jumper cables ■

Speaking of tires, if yours have significant wear, go ahead and replace them now. You can keep your old tires to reinstall later if they have some life in them, but put fresh shoes on the bike and wear them in a little on your shakedown runs.

Make a list of important phone numbers and contacts. Include contacts like your personal physician, family lawyer, a friend or two, and a relative. If you're visiting friends along the way, add their name and number to the list. Add your medical and vehicle insurance information, including contact names, phone numbers, and policy numbers. Do the same for any club memberships you have; membership number and club or road service phone number. You'll take a copy of this sheet with you and leave a copy with someone at home

Make a separate, short list of credit cards you'll be carrying with you. Include the credit card name, service number, and credit card number. This is to help you in case your cards are lost or stolen. You'll be able to quickly notify the card company to shut down the card and order a replacement. This list should be kept somewhere other than your wallet.

Planning to pick up any *special clothing* before your trip? Do it now while you have the chance to try it for fit and washability before you leave. If an article of clothing doesn't work as well you thought, or shrinks unexpectedly, you'll be able to get a replacement or find a substitute. It's better to break in a new helmet before your trip rather than during. A new helmet will feel a little tight and it will become more comfortable after you've worn it a few times.

Put together a "paperwork kit." This includes a DMV-issued copy of your drivers license along with a photocopy of your bike registration, passport, and personal and vehicle insurance cards. Add your contact list and a small cash reserve to this collection of papers, keep them in a waterproof bag, and find a secure place on your bike to store this collection. My Gold Wing has an empty compartment in the trunk that holds the OEM CD player and CB, but I use it to hold this stash of documents. I attach my credit card list to the underside of the door that covers this area. (Well, I did until now.)

Make a list of gear you're thinking about taking. Everyone's list will be different, but I seem to be traveling lighter with each passing year. Some of that lightening is due to advances in technology. My palm-size MP3 player holds a few hundred CDs worth of music and the smartphone eliminates the need for a laptop to check and send e-mail on the road. But in addition, I just don't carry as much stuff as I used to.

I'm content to bring along a couple of books to read or strike up a conversation with next-door campers.

My must-have gear list is short. It includes my protective outerwear, one set of street clothes that I wear and one change. I have two sets of base layers (sink-washable underwear and socks) and two pairs of riding shorts. I bring along a bike towel that does double duty. If I get caught in the rain I use it to wipe down the seat. When I'm riding in hot weather, I wet it down for cooling. Regardless of where I'm riding, I pack a fleece jacket. Nine months of the year, I'll add my electric gear. That's it for clothing. Ancillary items include toiletry kit, paperwork, maps, camera, and a paperback book or two. The bike cover, tool kit, repair kit, and first-aid kit are always on the bike.

Assemble or check your toolkit. My expertise is in things electrical more than mechanical, so my own toolkit is biased toward correcting electrical problems. I did replace my bike's standard toolkit with a roll-up tool holder. My mechanical tools include a set of GearWrench ratchet wrenches. These operate with just five degrees of movement, great for attacking bolts in tight places. I added a multi-purpose Leatherman-like tool, a couple of fixed-size screwdrivers (I can't stand those multi-tip switchable screwdrivers because the tip I need is usually the one that's missing), vise-grip pliers, and a set of hex-head Allen wrenches. If I'm disabled with something that's really broken, the two tools I'll pull out are my cell phone and my roadside assistance card.

It's a good idea to bring along a spare key. A riding buddy or co-rider can carry it for you when you're traveling with friends. Otherwise, *find a secure spot and secure a spare key with a zip-tie or tape.*

ONE TO TWO WEEKS IN ADVANCE

Pre-treating your gear will enhance its effectiveness at shedding water. If you have a textile suit or boots, apply Scotchguard. Leathers can be treated with a solution like Nikwax Aqueous Wax.

Camping? *Check your camping gear.* Go through a camping gear check. Get out your tent or open your pop-up camper and air them out a

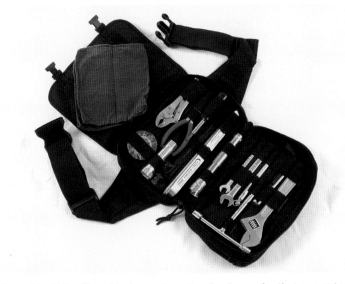

A good toolkit will enable to you to make simple repairs that can get you to a dealer.

bit. While they're open, coat the seams with seam sealer and treat any canvas with Scotchguard. Make sure you have all the hardware you need for your tent. Battery operated items get fresh batteries. Check other gear to make sure it works as expected and replace anything that doesn't.

Check your luggage. If you are using a new luggage system, planning a heavy load, or pulling a trailer, it's imperative that you conduct a couple of test loads before you leave for your trip. If your bike is handling strangely, feels top-heavy, or if the trailer isn't tracking well, you have plenty of time to investigate and correct the problem. Check the tongue weight of the trailer. Make sure your heavy items are distributed evenly on both sides of the bike and are low on the bike in preferred locations like tank panniers or saddlebags. After you've made your run, check the tension on straps and bungees to see if they're holding. How is your gas mileage with a fully loaded bike?

For trips of two weeks or more, *prepay your bills before you leave.* Online bill paying is a convenient method to handle bills on the road, but I like having that stuff done ahead of time. We've also left a few pre-signed checks at home for bills that arrive while we're on the road. My wife's mother fills out the amount and drops them in the mail.

► ## THE EXPRESS PREPARATION PLAN

Everyone goes through some kind of process for planning a ride, whether it's formal or informal. For a day trip or weekend ride, my task list is pretty short.

Glance at a map to get a feel for possible routes. I use anything that's handy when I'm trolling for ideas: Google Maps, CD-ROM maps, DeLorme paper maps, or even travel websites with routes, like MotorcycleVA.com.

Estimate distance and duration based on route ideas. My better half will want to know how long I'm riding, so I come up with a rough number of miles and estimate a return time in the evening.

If routes are new or unfamiliar, make out a tentative route sheet. When I'm riding roads I've covered before or if the route is simple, I don't bother. If I'm riding an entirely new route, I'll jot down a few notes on a piece of paper just to remember the order.

Check the weather forecast and radar to get a sense of weather trends. Online radar maps are a fantastic addition to any planning arsenal. If you have some idea of what weather is coming at you, you can ride around it if you want. I've found the sites with most up-to-date radar images are hosted by local television stations.

Determine a meeting place and time if riding with friends. Breakfast anyone? Have your friends' contact numbers on hand so you'll be able to get in touch with them in case something comes up.

Decide what riding gear is appropriate, based on the forecast. I prepare for dropping temperatures more than rising temperatures. I'd rather bring along a fleece jacket I don't use than get caught after sundown in cooler-than-expected temperatures without one.

Assemble the basic gear and consider what bonus gear may be required. There are a few items I carry on every trip, regardless of length. 1) a charged cell phone, 2) water bottle, 3) a paper-based map or two 4) a first-aid kit and 5) a tool kit. Bonus gear: A camera, National Park passport, and any new touring accessory I want to road test. I get all my gear together and either put it on or near the bike so I don't have to look for it the next morning.

Fill up the tank and complete pre-ride inspection. You can complete all of these steps the night before your ride so you're ready to go in the morning. One exception is tire pressure. You should do this when tires are cold. ■

TWO TO THREE DAYS IN ADVANCE

Top off your rechargeable batteries for anything you'll bring that uses them. Battery chargers are a pain to take on a trip. If I can swing it, I buy an extra rechargeable and take that instead of the charger, to build my inventory of rechargeable batteries. An exception is the auto-adaptor for my cell phone.

Begin assembling the gear on your list. Give some more thought to what you really need to bring and will really use. Before he departs on a new adventure, world traveler Helge Pedersen lays out all his gear on the floor and invites riding companions to ask him to explain why he chooses to bring certain things. As Helge explains, it's easy to justify to yourself why you need certain things, perhaps you think you'll need two extra pairs of shoes, when one extra pair is fine. An extra tent fly makes sense as you stand in your driveway, but when you have to convince someone else of your reasoning, they may either suggest an alternative or help you see that you don't need every thing you've laid out.

Call your credit card company and let them know you're traveling. Card companies closely track usage patterns to reduce their losses from fraud; a change in your spending pattern could lead the company to think your card has been stolen. With you trekking all over the country, you could find your card suddenly turned off. I bring along a couple of credit cards, both of which work with ATMs to get cash. As a backup, I like the American Express Travelers Cheque card, which works like travelers checks but it's in a card form. Rather than an open line of credit, this card is "loaded" with a pre-paid balance. It isn't linked to your bank accounts or credit lines and if it's lost or stolen, you can get a quick replacement.

Purchase any last minute items so you don't have to stop to pick up something within the first ten miles on your way out of town. If you take prescription medication, refill it before you leave town. You might also consider setting aside a couple days of medication and put it with your backup paperwork. In case you lose your meds you'll have a reserve to tap while you seek a replacement.

Give your contact at home a copy of your paperwork. This would include an itinerary with key destinations. (If you make reservations online, it's easy to print two copies of your itinerary.) Include a copy of your "important numbers" sheet.

THE DAY BEFORE

It's almost time to get rolling and if you've worked your plan, you should have very few last-minute trip preparations to make. But there are a few things that are best done the day before your departure.

You'll now have a better idea what weather to expect on your trip in the opening day or two. Unless there is truly threatening weather developing in your path, I wouldn't advise a total rework of your plan. Knowing what to expect for the next day or two will help you adjust your gear, in case you need to move your foul-weather gear closer to the top of your bags, for example.

Before you start loading gear on the bike, find a spot to *hide a little cash for an emergency.* It should be some place you can get to without a key.

Perform your standard pre-ride checklist. You should have had your bike serviced already, but this final check is your opportunity to uncover any hidden problems before they find you during the first or second day of riding. Pay particular attention to your fluid levels and tire pressures.

After your pre-ride check, *fill up your gas tank.* It's a psychological thing. If you are able to run the first hundred or so miles on your trip without worrying about gas, it helps you get off to a better start.

Your bike is ready. Your gear is packed. You might as well get it onto the bike now. After you've packed, maybe you should do another shakedown run around the neighborhood. Just to make sure you have all those straps secured, you know?

Try to sleep. Yeah, that's easier said than done. When you're ready to start an adventure you've been planning for months or years, you can't just curb your enthusiasm. Still, if you can find a way to get a good night's rest, you'll have a better start the next day.

DEPARTURE DAY

Can you believe it? It's time to head out. I'm sure you'll have a few last minute items to attend to, but they should be minimal. Give your bike one last pre-ride check on fluid levels, lights, and tire pressure. Check the load you fastened on last night. Get out your checklist and go over each item to be sure you haven't forgotten anything. That's it!

If you're trying out a new luggage configuration, take your bike on a shakedown run before your real tour. You'll have a chance to identify potential problem areas.

Now you're ready to gear up, hop into the saddle, and thumb that starter.

SUMMARY

There is no reason you should feel rushed in making preparations for a motorcycle tour. Everything you need to do can be accomplished days, weeks, even months in advance of your tour.

As you plan out your trip, make a separate list of things you need to do before you head out. I've given you some suggestions but you will undoubtedly think of others that fit your unique situation. Build a timeline and put your tasks into a time frame that will allow you to get it done without rushing.

Some items on my list are to help head off trouble I might encounter on the road. This is especially true of the paperwork kit. Having copies of important vehicle and insurance documents and a backup list of credit cards is indispensable if trouble finds you. It's also reassuring to those you leave behind if they have some idea of where you're headed.

By the time you're done with your list, you should be ready to get a good night's sleep and do little more than complete a pre-ride check before you begin your journey. And that's where we're headed next.

Managing Contingencies

Read a few "motorcycling around the world" books by folks like Chris Scott and Ted Simon and you'll begin to pick up on a theme. Riders who travel extensively develop a view, often along the road somewhere, that adversity does not equate with failure and obstacles are a gauge to measure the depth of one's desire to succeed.

Neither you nor I may ever document ancient cultures from our bike like Fulton did, or circle the globe more often than Frazier, or outwit a band of guerrillas like Glen Heggstad, but we will face our own challenges that can't be resolved by submitting a credit card number to a website or by calling for road service on a cell phone. Situations arising during your journey will require the same resourcefulness and, perhaps more importantly, the same confidence that world travelers have learned to summon on a regular basis.

This rider is safely dressed, properly packed, and ready to head out for adventure.

That confidence is something you can't obtain from reading a book, it is built exclusively through on-the-road experiences. But I can tell you that you and every other rider who has taken up the challenge to master two-wheel travel already possesses a surprising ability to overcome any adversity you may face.

In the same way, no book will contain answers to every challenge you might meet on the road, but in this final chapter, I'd like to suggest a few guidelines for situations you might encounter in your travels.

WEATHER

Sure, it's possible to travel only on days when skies are clear and temperatures are in the seventy to eight-five degree range but you'll be severely limited in the territory you can cover or it will take you a very long time. It's better just to acknowledge that you will spend some time riding in less than ideal conditions.

In my opinion, heat is an easier challenge to deal with than cold and wet, two conditions that compound the effects of one another and may lead to hypothermia. You will ride though many areas where temperatures drop substantially from daytime highs. For this reason, I have committed a fleece jacket and electric vest to permanent status in my gear for trips of any length at any time of the year.

In North America, "westerlies" describe the prevailing weather patterns that push from west to east across the middle of the continent. This means that weather systems containing rain often arrive along a north-south frontal boundary. Sometimes you can short cut the amount of time you spend in the rain by turning west and riding through the front.

Even in the summer, you need to be aware of weather conditions at high elevations you may be planning to pass through, as changes in conditions there occur fast and with great force. I've experienced this personally on the modest ranges of the Blue Ridge. On one memorable run there, temperatures began in the seventies in Asheville and dropped to the mid-forties less than fifty miles into the trip.

Should lightning strike, motorcyclists do not benefit from the same insulating properties that car drivers enjoy. When it looks like you are riding into a thunderstorm, find covered shelter before the storm hits. This does not include sitting under a highway overpass. Riding out a storm under an overpass makes you a sitting duck for a motorist who slams into your bike because they fixated on it.

Expect quick weather changes. On the eastern side of this ridge it was 87 degrees. On the western side the temperature had dropped to sixty eight.

▶ NOW THAT'S WET

I knew my bike was closer to death with each mile I covered. I was down one cylinder and felt another going. I wasn't exactly sure why, but I suspected the trouble had to do with the torrential rain I was pushing through. I coaxed a few more miles out of the bike and got out of the rain just as the bike quit entirely.

A visual inspection confirmed my suspicions. The rain had met the bike with such force that the ignition was sopping wet, effectively disabling the bike's entire electrical system. I had managed to drown my bike while riding it.

I couldn't fix it. Surprisingly, no one had a blow dryer at the McDonalds where I was stranded. So I took a Big Mac to go and waited overnight for the bike to dry out. The next day when I hit the starter, it sprang to life as if nothing had ever happened. ■

Table 15.1 Wind Chill Equivalence

SPEED IN MPH	AIR TEMPERATURE IN DEGREES FAHRENHEIT						
	70	65	60	55	50	45	40
5	72	66	60	54	48	42	36
10	71	65	58	52	46	40	34
15	70	64	57	51	45	38	32
20	70	63	57	50	44	37	30
25	69	63	56	49	43	36	29
30	69	62	56	49	42	35	28
35	69	62	55	48	41	35	28
40	69	62	55	48	41	34	27
45	69	61	54	47	40	33	26
50	68	61	54	47	40	33	26
55	68	61	54	47	40	32	25
60	68	61	54	46	39	32	25
65	68	61	53	46	39	32	24
70	68	60	53	46	38	31	24
75	68	60	53	46	38	31	23

Use a cover for your bike when you stop for the night. It discourages nosy passersby and keeps morning dew off the seat.

SECURITY

It is a rare thing for a motorcyclist to experience a personal crime on the North American continent. You can do just a few simple things to avoid problems without becoming paranoid.

On the road, your biggest concern will be keeping the stuff on your bike on your bike. An expensive leather jacket or an iPod sticking out of a tankbag are easy targets to be snatched casually when someone walks by. No device can fully protect your property from a determined thief; not locking bags, not tethers, nor cable locks, nor wire mesh. However, used together with good practices, you can create a greater barrier to theft that will discourage casual thieves and at least slow down the ones who really want your stuff.

Riding with friends can make it a bit easier at rest stops or gas stations. One person can watch several bikes while others take care of business, then switch off. At longer stops like restaurants, take a minute to remove your satellite radio and GPS and either bring them with you or pop them into lockable storage. Don't think a "secure" mount will prevent a determined thief from grabbing your gear. They don't care if they break the mount getting something off your bike. If you're not in a position to carry your gear around, a steel cable and lock combo like the Master Lock

Python (masterlock.com) is a convenient way of securing your jacket and helmet to your bike.

At night, bring your gear inside your hotel room and cover your bike. As simple as a cover is, it will keep many people away from your bike and make the nosy ones more obvious to passersby. Fork locks are notoriously weak and easy for a thief to overcome. What's more, after they do, they can wheel the bike anywhere they please. A better solution is to use a wheel lock, a heavy chain and lock that loops through your front or rear wheel. This prevents your bike from being rolled away and is a visible deterrent. You will want to come up with some system for helping you remember you have the lock in place so you don't try to ride away with it in place.

Personal security, for men and women, is built on being aware of your surroundings and removing yourself from an uncomfortable situation. Trust your basic instincts. If you've stopped in an area that doesn't feel right, don't stay. What's the cost of losing one night's room deposit compared to worrying all night or being involved in an incident?

This cable system keeps the tailbag secure from theft and prevents it from flying away if it comes loose.

If someone does challenge you, don't take the bait. Hand over a wallet you've prepared for just this occasion that contains a small amount of cash along with a few expired cards and papers that make the wallet look real. Keep your real wallet somewhere else. What cash you are carrying can be divided between your fake wallet, real wallet and another location on the bike. With debit cards now accepted as widely as credit cards, you don't need to carry much cash anyway.

HANDLING BREAKDOWNS

It is satisfying to take a sputtering bike into your hands and restore it to good running health. If you're traveling in sparsely populated or under-developed areas, it makes sense to enhance your mechanical skills to handle a wider range of problems. For most of us trouble comes in the form of a tire puncture, an electrical problem, or the result of a neglected maintenance task.

Part of your tour planning should include having your bike serviced and purchasing a tire repair kit (and learning to use it before you experience a flat). If you plan to add any electrically-powered accessories, I strongly urge you to consider the fuse block project in Chapter 5. This not only reduces your chances of developing a short in your wiring harness, it also becomes a central point for troubleshooting problems.

Some tour preparation guides contain a laundry list of spare parts you should consider carrying with your bike. That makes a lot of sense if you're crossing the Darien Gap or venturing into the Northwest Territories, but isn't as necessary if you're planning a coast-to-coast run along US-50.

Many national motorcycle clubs and associations—the Gold Wing Road Riders Association, American Motorcyclist Association, and Harley Owners Group, to name just a few—offer a roadside service plan with an 800 number for assistance. AMA's Mo-Tow plan for example is just $25 a year and will get you a tow of up to thirty-five miles. The basic program even includes fuel delivery if you run out of gas. A higher level program covers your bikes and your cars. If you already have a roadside service plan, check to see if your coverage extends to Canada.

The AMA and other groups provide an equally important service: a network of members willing to help out fellow riders. AMA's Help 'n Hands program contains over 8,500 individuals and businesses willing to help out stranded riders. GWRRA, HOG, and many other rider groups publish directories that list members by state and town along with a list of services they are willing or able to provide. Use these in the spirit in which they are intended. Ask for only the help you really need and don't use the directory of a group you don't belong to. Freeloading off of other riders is bad form and will discourage your fellow riders from participating in programs like this.

Jim Breed determines the prognosis for repair following a broken throttle cable. Fellow riders they met at a rally trailered the bike to a repair shop and put up Jim and Patricia for the night.

When you do experience a problem, get the bike as far off the shoulder of the road as possible to avoid being hit by a driver in another vehicle that fixates on your bike. This may be difficult to do on many two-lane rural highways with narrow or non-existent shoulders; if so, find a private driveway or other lane to get the bike safely off the road.

Those who've been through rider training are familiar with this concept. A vehicle goes wherever the driver is looking, and when the driver's attention is drawn to your bike on the side of the road, it becomes a target.

▶ ## MORE TIPS FROM FELLOW RIDERS

I asked a group of riders what tips have made their tours more enjoyable and they had a lot to say. Here are some additional tips that will help you get more out of your next trip.

▶ If your Internet service provider doesn't offer web access to e-mail, get a Hotmail, Yahoo, or Google account. Most public libraries have computers with Internet access you can use for free.

▶ Use a prepaid calling card from locations where you don't have cell service or if you need to dial up to connect to the Internet.

▶ You can use a phone card for dial-up access if you add pauses to the number your computer dials. Each comma you add creates a two second pause. Example: 18005551212,,,,1,356987,7035551212. This includes the phone card number, a long wait followed by entering "1" for English, pause, the phone card number, pause, and the number you're trying to reach.

▶ Pack things you need frequently in a tank bag, top case or at the top of your luggage. This includes items like gloves, rain suit, sun screen, and camera.

▶ If you no longer need certain gear or clothing on a trip, find a packing store in a strip shopping center and ship some stuff home.

▶ If you need to have something mailed to you along the way, have it sent General Delivery to a destination post office a few days ahead of your current location. It will be held at the main post office for up to thirty days.

▶ You'll save time at restaurants if you eat at off times like 10 a.m., 3 p.m. and 8 p.m. when you can get in and out fast. Everyone else wants to eat at 8, noon and 6.

▶ A frequently mentioned alternative to planning each stop along the way is to make reservations at important "anchor points" but leave the rest of the schedule open.

Find a safe spot to work on your bike. Get it well off the road if at all possible. Motorists can become fixated on the bike and crash into you.

▶ Did you make a packing list before you left? Bring it with you and as you think of items you should have brought or things that you'd like to change on your bike, write them down. If you find there are some things you're not using or you could easily do without, cross those off the list for next time.

▶ If you use a compression sack to compress your sleeping bag, take the sleeping bag out when you arrive at your destination so it can regain its loft. When you return home, remove the sleeping bag from the sack. If you keep it compressed for a long time it will lose its lofting ability.

▶ Set up your tent to confirm that you have all the hardware and that none of the poles have split or cracked. Fire up your stove to make sure it lights properly. Inflate your air mattress to ensure it won't go flat on you in camp.

▶ If you participate in Internet forums, drop a line to folks on the list. You may be able to meet up with some of your friends along the way for a ride or a meal.

▶ Pack a roll of toilet paper. You will be really thankful you did when you need it. ■

NIGHT RIDING

Unless you are participating in an endurance rally or driven by necessity, there is more incentive to park your bike than to ride through the night.

The night time road is populated with more critters and impaired drivers (intoxicated and sleepy) than during the day.

Vision on both sides of the highway are challenged at night. You think drivers don't see you during the day? You are even harder to spot at night. Even if you slow down, road hazards are harder to spot and you can't see through curves like you can in the daylight.

Motorcyclists are particularly vulnerable to animal strikes. It's an unpleasant situation to run over any animal with a car, but the animal almost always comes out faring worse than the driver. Bikes can be upset by even small creatures if the bike happens to be cranked over in a corner. Deer are considered the biggest wildlife menace to riders and they are found over nearly all of North America. Collisions involving deer can happen at any time of the year. Many incidents occur in the early and mid evening hours from October through December, the mating season.

If you are forced to ride at night, slow down and increase your following distance. Give yourself more time to react to hazards, animals, and the actions of the car in front of you. Consider

Avoid riding at night if at all possible. You never know what manner of wildlife you'll find on the road.

the recommendations of Chapter 6 for adding more light output to your bike as well as increasing reflective surfaces to improve your conspicuity to others. Make sure your clothing is adequate to keep you warm. Watch oncoming cars with extra suspicion. Most drunk driving accidents occur between midnight and three a.m.

BODY MANAGEMENT

Your bike is designed to operate efficiently when it is properly maintained and working within the range of environmental conditions it was designed to handle. The same is true of your body although, unlike your bike, which can operate reliably for hundreds or thousands of miles between maintenance checks, your body's operating range is limited and requires frequent maintenance. When you are riding, you need to monitor three key body systems to keep your senses operating at peak efficiency: your body temperature, fluids, and fatigue level.

Not Too Hot, Not Too Cold

Your metabolism works within a very narrow temperature range of a few points on either side of 98.6 degrees Fahrenheit. When your core temperature strays too far from this range, metabolism is impaired and your body begins to shut down. In either case, failing to maintain your temperature will shorten your riding day due to exhaustion, make you sick, or lead you to an accident.

On a hot day, heat begins to build up in your body. This in turn triggers mechanisms designed to keep your temperature in check. For example,

If you do ride at night, add reflective tape to your bike and your gear to increase your conspicuity to others.

as your temperature rises, blood vessels near the surface of the skin enlarge, allowing more heat to escape through the skin. This also triggers the sweating process. In effect, your body turns on a built-in swamp cooler. As moisture is released through the skin and evaporates, it takes heat with it, producing a cooling effect.

When heat builds too rapidly for the body to expel, you begin to feel the effects of heat exhaustion. Left unchecked, this may lead to *hyperthermia,* or heat stroke. Have you ever been riding in hot weather and felt a slight out-of-body experience as you're riding? Maybe you've felt a little light-headed or dizzy, or made a simple mental mistake like missing a clearly marked turn. These are symptoms of heat exhaustion. Before you get to this point, take steps to keep your body's temperature in check. In Chapter 4 we discussed several types of gear you can use to prevent overheating even while keeping yourself fully armored. In hot riding weather, use a ventilated "air" jacket in combination with a cooling vest to help your body shed excess heat. Even wetting down your head or wrapping a wet towel around your neck helps draw heat from your body.

Hypothermia is the opposite of hyperthermia. Instead of overheating, your core

Ron Ayres scouts roads through Namibia so this won't happen to guests on his tour. Nevertheless, he demonstrates good hydration practices while waiting for a tow.

temperature drops too low. This occurs when your body can't generate heat fast enough to replace what it is losing. Riders are especially vulnerable to hypothermia because we often encounter conditions that can lead to rapid body cooling. Simple exposure to a cool environment without sufficient protective gear will lead to hypothermia over several hours, but on a motorcycle, this condition can be dramatically accelerated by rain and the effects of wind chill as you ride, wet, through the cool air.

Hypothermia is also potentially more dangerous because onset can be so subtle, you don't really realize you're becoming chilled. This is particularly true when you're pressing to get to a particular destination by day's end. Even though you may feel uncomfortable, it's tempting to ride on. As your core temperature drops, your reflexes slow dramatically and your ability to make decisions is adversely affected. In fact, amnesia is not uncommon. In some cases, people who suffer hypothermia may simply fall off their bike and, presuming they survive the crash, not even realize what happened.

Like hyperthermia, the key to dealing with hypothermia is to guard against it before it begins. Always keep a fleece or electric jacket on your bike, even in summer riding. (For example, if you're riding through an area like Glacier National Park in the summer, it's not unusual to start out in temperatures of ninety degrees outside the park, and find temperature drops of thirty or forty degrees as you climb in elevation.) If your gear allows water to penetrate to your base layers of clothing, you need to stop riding and get dry. If you find you feel cold and can't warm up or you begin to feel even slightly dazed or confused, you need to stop riding and get warmed up right away.

Fluid Management

Water is the main constituent of your body, accounting for 50-60% of your body weight. It plays a key role in nearly every bodily process, maintaining cell structure, transporting oxygen and nutrients to cells as a component of blood, acting as a solvent in the metabolic process, moving waste out of the body, and helping keep body temperature in check. It's no wonder then, with all those duties, that when your fluid levels drop by even as little as 2% below optimal volume, you begin to experience dehydration.

As with hypothermia, motorcyclists are susceptible to dehydration more than other travelers because of our exposure to the elements. As you ride, moving air wicks away moisture from your body like clothes hanging out to dry. When you begin to sweat, dehydration is accelerated. Dehydration compounds the effects of other conditions, like heat fatigue. As your body dries out from producing sweat, it becomes less efficient at cooling, leading to a rise in core temperature.

The most common symptom of dehydration is thirst, but this begins after dehydration is well under way. You may also feel irritable or develop a headache. It's not uncommon to feel depleted, tired, and lose your appetite. You'll also know you're dehydrated if you go long periods of time without needing to pee or if your urine is dark in color.

On an average day, you need to replace about 4% of your body weight due to water loss, roughly 2.5 liters or about four twenty-ounce bottles of water. This doesn't account for riding conditions that include water loss due to wind exposure and the accelerated loss of water due to sweating. To stay properly hydrated, you need to take in water as you lose it. In other words, it won't do you much good to ride all day without drinking, then tip back a large quantity of water at day's end. You need to drink constantly throughout the day as you ride. Some riders mount a bottle holder on their handlebars using a RAM mount or similar device. Others prefer a solution used by hikers such as the Camel-Bak hydration system. This system is like a back pack you can wear with a tube to position within easy reach. Tank bags like the Chicane USA line include a built-in bladder that allow you to drink while you are riding. Whatever the case, keeping yourself hydrated will stave off other potential issues and keep you riding in peak form.

Road Fatigue

Road fatigue or "road hypnosis" is a condition with an onset as subtle as hypothermia and an effect that impairs your driving as much as alcohol. Road fatigue is an accumulation of the stresses you experience as a rider from the environment, your nutritional habits, and mental and physical stresses.

Taken together, many elements contribute to road fatigue. Riding a motorcycle is exhilarating but keeping it upright and pointed in the right direction is taxing. You're not only balancing the forces exerted by and acting on your bike, you're doing that within a complex environment where road conditions are always changing, traffic hazards come and go. Whether or not you realize it, road, wind, and engine noise are mentally fatiguing as well. Environmental conditions like rough pavement, heat, cold, wind buffeting, and long stretches in a seated position take a physical toll. You may be so keyed up about your trip that sleep is difficult or you fall out of your regular sleep habits. Nutrition, which we'll discuss later, plays a significant role.

The onset of road fatigue can happen before you realize it. Fatigue may begin by a recognizable yawn or you'll realize that you can't remember anything about the last few miles you've ridden. Simple decisions become hard to make. Your eyes become sore and you find it harder to focus. When you feel the temptation to close your eyes, even for a second, you're on the verge of becoming another single-rider accident statistic.

There are several techniques you can use to overcome road fatigue:

▶ Take frequent breaks from riding, in addition to stops for gas and food. This should be an encouragement to explore the side roads and take time for pictures along the way.

▶ Improve your bike's ergonomics to make it physically less demanding to ride.

▶ Shift your weight to your footpegs and lift off the seat.

▶ Shrug your shoulders.

▶ Stay hydrated.

▶ Snack lightly.

▶ Suck on sour candies.

▶ Listen to music and sing along.

If you try several things and nothing works, you really need to find a place to rest. During the

Friends quickly came to the aid of the rider who lost the handle on this bike, offering shade and comfort after ensuring he was okay.

day a rest stop is an acceptable spot to check into the Iron Butt motel for a twenty minute nap. ("Iron Butt motel" refers to sleeping on your bike, the grass, or any horizontal surface that's available. This term originated from the Iron Butt endurance rally in which riders cover thousands of miles and have to find a few minutes sleep wherever they can.)

ACCIDENTS

We spend a lot of time not thinking about accidents; happily they are infrequent events. But accidents do happen and you should have a plan of action to follow in the event you, a co-rider, or a member of your group has a medical emergency. Providing first-aid advice is beyond the scope of this book but you should consider first-aid training a basic responsibility like taking a rider safety course.

If you do witness an accident, your first priority is to stabilize anyone who is injured, then seek help. If you're riding in a group and another member is available, one person can be sent for help while the others remain at the scene. If that accident involves another rider, remember that no one should remove the rider's helmet except a medical technician.

Do everything you can to offer assurance and make the victim comfortable. Good Samaritan laws exist in every state in the U.S. to protect you from being sued by a victim for providing assistance at the scene of an accident.

If you have a cell phone dial 911. You will need to be able tell dispatchers where you are, so as you ride, make a mental note of intersections and landmarks you pass, just in case. This practice also benefits you by keeping your head and eyes moving. While you're keeping up with where you are, you can scan for potential hazards.

STAYING IN TOUCH

I found out the painful way how expensive it can be to make a phone call from a hotel room. I'd left my calling card at home, so I thought I was being smart when I called home and had my wife call me back at my room. Later I discovered that each call was $12.50 for the first ten minutes. You can stay in touch more affordably than that. Twenty-five dollars buys a lot of Anti-Monkey Butt powder.

Buy a calling card for cheap long-distance. You pay a fixed fee for a calling card with a predetermined number of minutes. To use the card, you dial a toll-free 800 number on the card, enter a personal ID code from the card, then the number you want to reach. That's a fair amount of dialing, but rates are really cheap. If you are visiting the States from another country, you can find a calling card that includes your country with rates at a fraction of the price you would pay elsewhere. Check the fine print to buy a card that charges for minutes used and doesn't add a per-call fee. I like cards that can be recharged. I also like to buy cards from a reputable retailer like Target or Wal-Mart because I have more recourse if I have a problem.

Check your cell plan to see what it costs to add a fixed roaming fee. My Sprint plan includes a roam-anywhere policy for an extra $5 per month. Traveling back roads and through small towns, my cell phone is frequently in a roaming area, so this is a great deal.

Once in a while I'll bring along the laptop to keep up on e-mail. National chains like Holiday Inn Express and Hampton Inn offer wireless Internet access with your room. I've noticed a growing number of budget motels and private campgrounds have wireless access, too. A smartphone with e-mail capability is a more compact alternative than carrying a laptop, but you have to be on your provider's network. A mobile device like the Blackberry is the ultimate portable e-mail device.

If hauling along your own equipment has no appeal, you can often find a cybercafé by asking around. Remember that a cybercafé computer is a public machine and you have no idea what digital germs might be lurking within. If you're inserting any type of writeable media into the machine, set the erase-lock tab to prevent anything from being written to your media.

FOOD SELECTIONS

A lot of riders, myself included, look on traveling as an excuse to eat what and when we please, and that means hitting the buffet bar early and often. That's a bad idea for a lot of reasons that you already know, but as it relates to motorcycling, heavy meals, particularly those including large amounts of meat, require a lot of energy to digest and have the effect of making you sleepy.

The better strategy for eating on the road is to have several light meals throughout the day. It's better to continually top off your tank, rather than drain it dry and fill it up again. When you go too long without eating, your blood sugar levels

plummet, making you feel drained. By eating numerous light meals, you'll keep your blood sugar at a consistent level. This in turn will keep you alert in the saddle. Fruits are a good choice for snacks, as are nuts and seeds. A light meal at lunch will keep you going without suffering that mid-afternoon slump that comes to many of us after a heavy lunch. Save the steak for your end-of-day meal.

Alcohol in any form is a bad idea when you're riding. Alcohol slows your reflexes dramatically and will also make you very drowsy. Avoid alcohol any time you plan to ride, even the short distance from the restaurant back to your hotel or campsite.

We've already discussed the importance of staying hydrated and now you know that keeping your fluid levels up allows your body to operate efficiently. However, what you drink is as important as how often you drink. In addition to avoiding alcohol during your ride, you should also avoid drinking coffee or soda. The caffeine and sugar contained in these drinks will give you only a temporary boost. After the effects wear off, you'll begin to sag. Stick with regular water

Cold beverages are good, but avoid caffeinated drinks when possible. Water and juice are better choices.

to stay hydrated and avoid the energy swings that other beverages can induce.

Supplemental vitamins can help your body function more efficiently and may help you fight certain types of illness. Like exercise, you only benefit from vitamins if they are part of your daily regimen. You won't derive any benefit from taking vitamins only when you're on the road.

Those parts of your body that aren't covered by protective gear should be treated with sunscreen to prevent skin damage from exposure to ultraviolet radiation. Two forms of sun radiation affect our skin. UVB radiation is absorbed by the outer layers of skin and is responsible for causing sunburns. In recent years, scientists have pinpointed UVA radiation as a more dangerous form. UVA penetrates deeper into the skin. It is the primary cause of wrinkles and plays a larger role in the development of skin melanomas.

The sunscreen you buy is rated at a particular sun protection factor (SPF). This rating tells you what protection you're getting from UVB radiation, but doesn't tell you what protection you're getting from UVA. To make sure you're covered against both types, look for a sunscreen with an SPF rating of fifteen or higher that specifically mentions protection against UVA. Products containing avobenzone (Parsol 1789) are effective at protecting against the full spectrum of UVA radiation.

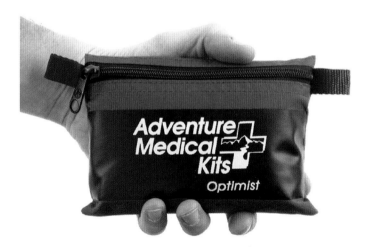

A useful first-aid kit doesn't have to be bulky. It should contain remedies for everyday illnesses, as well as supplies for emergencies.

Long-distance riders often take a low dose of a pain reliever to counter the effects of muscle stiffness over the course of a long day of riding. I can't tell you whether this is a good idea for you, but I have found it helpful on long days of riding. Long-term use of pain relievers will diminish their effectiveness and are tough on your liver, so you won't want to do this every day. You may wish to ask the advice of your doctor before you do this. He or she may advise that you use Tylenol or another form of acetaminophen because this does not thin the blood like aspirin or ibuprofen products.

SICKNESS

I'm not sure there is anything more miserable than trying to manhandle a bunch of gear onto a motorcycle and ride it when you are sick, unless it is doing so in a pouring rain. Somewhere in your travels, you are going to pick up a bug that kicks your butt.

It sounds so simple, but washing your hands often is still the best way to avoid picking up a bug. The trick is, you've got to really wash them. A quick rinse and wipe doesn't give you any substantial protection. The U.S. Centers for Disease Control and Prevention say that effective hand washing means you wet your hands, apply soap and rub your hands together for at least ten seconds. At a minimum, wash up before you take a meal and after you use the bathroom. Hand sanitizers seem like a convenient alternative, but studies have shown that despite their claims, alcohol-based sanitizers are not as effective as the old soap-and-water method of hand washing.

Your first-aid kit should contain a minimum of over-the-counter products to help you deal with illnesses. Make sure your kit contains some form of pain relief medication, a non-drowsy cold remedy, Pepto-Bismol or equivalent stomach upset medicine, and Imodium.

As much as the idea sucks, if you find yourself riding with a fever, you may need to park the bike and find a place to hole up for a day or two to fight off the bug. Safe riding demands all your attention and you can't muster that when you are sick.

THE FINAL WORDS

You want to know the keys to happy touring? I have two for you. Patience and curiosity. Here are a few ways you can put them into practice.

Avoid hurrying through your trip, making every day a high-mileage day to get it all in. Sprinkle in a few days of down time or low-mileage days in your tour. Don't pass up that interesting looking road marker or that great photo opportunity just because it will cost you a few extra minutes. What are the chances you will ever pass that way again?

Linger a little longer on the porch of the general store. Carry on a conversation with the guy in the pickup truck who admired your bike. Even in this age of suspicion, people will lower their guard a little when they find that you're just out to enjoy passing through the part of the country they call home. One of the best on-the-road conversations I've had was with a volunteer fireman standing, literally, in the middle of the road as a work crew scrambled to upright an overturned truck. We chatted about life in eastern Kentucky at some length, oblivious to the time or the line of cars forming behind the wreck. It was half an hour before the road was cleared and we could pass, but to me it seemed like just a few minutes.

Patience abides with change. Somewhere on your week-long trip you may shred a tire and it will take two days to find and mount a replacement. Don't let overblown expectations about schedules and timetables and lost hotel deposits cause you to overlook this detour that may lead you to an unexpected moment of serendipity. *As you ride away from your house,* accept that your plans will change, your schedule may come apart, and you may fall short of riding a particular road or reaching a destination on this journey. Don't give in to frustration. Take comfort in knowing the roads you missed and destinations yet to be attained are where you will find the beginnings of your next great trip.

May you always keep the rubber side down and the shiny side up. I wish you many happy and safe journeys!

Now, when are we going for a ride?

▶ DAILY PRE-RIDE INSPECTIONS

The trouble you experience on the road today is likely an issue that developed earlier. A daily inspection will alert you to many of your problems before they happen.

▶ If you have the capacity to form just one daily pre-ride habit, make it the habit of checking the condition and pressure of your tires. Using your bare hands, run them around the entire outer diameter of the tire, feeling for anything that might be embedded. Afterward, check pressures while your tires are still cold.

▶ Keeping an eye on your fluid levels from one day to the next will keep you informed about the internal condition of your engine. If a fluid level consistently drops from one day to the next or you note an unusual change in color or smell, you should have the bike looked at immediately.

▶ Anyone can maintain lights. Your spares kit should include one of each type of bulb used on your bike. This is a good application for a small Otter box with a foam liner cut to hold each type of bulb.

▶ Check your clutch and brake cables to be sure they work freely without any binding or hanging. While you are at it, spot check a few bolts to be sure they are tight.

▶ Double-check all luggage straps, zippers, buckles, and latches to ensure everything on the bike is lashed correctly and locked down tight. Trailer pullers, check your hitch pin and key and your safety chains.

▶ Last, a trailer puller should check trailer lights and signals. If you're riding alone and can't find someone to spot you, swing around to a building with a glass door or window where you can see the trailer's reflection from your rearview mirror. ∎

The Internet As a Resource

USING GOOGLE

Google and other search engines are valuable tools for the basic research that goes into planning a motorcycle tour. Rather than give you a list of a few hundred helpful website addresses, I'd rather help you learn how to better use these valuable resources to find information for yourself. Websites will come and go, but the fundamentals of searching will remain the same.

Search engines use technology called "spiders" to go through every publicly available website on the Internet and catalog what they find. When you enter a term like *motorcycle luggage* into a search engine, it will compare your term with the content of millions of websites, and in just a few seconds it will send you a list of website pages containing the term you entered.

The usefulness or "relevance" of those results is determined by several factors. Website developers enter hidden codes or "keywords" that help search engines better understand how to categorize what they find on the site. Search engine companies continually tweak the logic of their search programs to return results most relevant to your request. But the two most important factors in getting useful results are a) knowing how to make a good request and b) being a smart consumer of information you find on the Internet.

NARROWING YOUR SEARCH

A good search request is one that will get you reasonably close to the results you seek without being so narrow that your search returns nothing.

Let's say you're interested in luggage options for your Honda VFR800. Enter a broad term like *motorcycle luggage* and Google's search engine will return over 1.9 million references. What these results tell you is that over 1.9 million web pages contain the terms "motorcycle" and "luggage" but not necessarily the phrase "motorcycle luggage." A page containing "motorcycle babes" and "latex luggage" could be part of your results. Interesting, no doubt, but not what you're looking for right now.

One easy way to narrow your search is to use quotes to search for exact phrases. By adding quotes to *"motorcycle luggage"* you'll get results where this exact phrase is used. From 1.9 million, our results are now reduced to about 220,000.

To continue narrowing your search, you can add more qualifiers or keywords to your search term. Adding the bike model *VFR800* to this search gets us down to 737 pages.

A big issue with web searches is that out-of-date information tends to linger on the web. I like to use Google's advanced search page to add a date qualifier to the search. If I limit this example to results created or modified in the last six months, our results are down to 138, a far cry from 1.9 million.

WHAT'S GOOD INFO?

Once you have an acceptable set of results, it's time to decide which will give you the answer you seek. Which sites are credible and which are a waste of time?

Before diving into any specific site, I look at the range of results I've gotten. I'm looking for a website that promises to deliver an answer that is complete and authoritative. Over time I've learned which web sites yield consistently better results. For product reviews, I'll turn to a site like webBikeWorld first if I see it in my list of results. If a site is hosted at a freebie site like members.tripod.com, I don't bother. No disrespect intended if you host web pages there, but I can't stand all the pop-up ads generated in my browser when I visit a free site. (If you care about your site, pay a few measly bucks a month to get a site that won't turn off potential visitors.) If I'm searching on a specific bike model, there's a good chance an owner group site will turn up. The first site on a search for "Kawasaki Concours" lists the excellent Concours Owners Group site.

Wherever you end up, ask yourself a few questions about the site you're visiting. What is the quality of the information contained on the site? Does it appear to be fairly complete or does the content seem to skip around? Is the information structured in a logical format? Does the site contain many categories but little depth? A site with content that is filled with spelling errors or contains a lot of "Coming Soon" sections is probably a site that was hastily constructed by a well-intentioned person who never got back to finishing their project.

You can also make some judgment of the quality of content by the layout of a site. A pretty site doesn't mean you should accept its content without question, but it does mean that its owner cares enough about the topic to invest some time and money to make the site usable.

Regardless of the site's content or layout, I always consider the source of the information when assessing its credibility. If I'm searching on a motorcycle safety question, I'll consider content from a group like the Motorcycle Safety Foundation to be the most authoritative. Discussion forums provide a lot of interesting perspectives on motorcycling questions from forum members, but opinions are usually based on personal experience rather than empirical research. An opinion may be just what you need to help you decide between two sets of bags for the VFR but you won't find many discussion forum members who can correctly cite motorcycle safety statistics.

Online Resources

I said I didn't want to give you a huge list of web addresses, but there are a few I would like to single out that have proven themselves over time as authoritative resources for motorcyclists.

WEBBIKEWORLD

webBikeWorld was created by Rick Korchak to provide information on unique and hard-to-find motorcycle products and accessories so that motorcyclists can make informed purchasing decisions. Since its debut in 2000, Rick's site has grown to include news, how-to's and real-world tests and reviews of over 340 moto-related products. Several hundred thousand riders from around the world find their way to webBikeWorld each month. Visit the site at webBikeWorld.com.

HORIZONS UNLIMITED

Horizons Unlimited is the work of world moto travelers Grant and Susan Johnson and is cited by many as the definitive site for riders planning any type of motorcycle tour. The depth of information is daunting at first glance but you'll soon find yourself lost in a discussion of paperwork requirements for Zambia, even if you have no intention of traveling there. Horizons is particularly helpful for tapping the expertise of riders around the globe who have either successfully ridden anywhere you can put a bike or are in the process of doing so. Horizons Unlimited is at horizonsunlimited.com.

MICAPEAK

Micapeak is a moto resource site operated by H. Marc Lewis and Carl Paukstis. Many riders know Carl as the definitive keeper of the list of motorcycle discussion groups. If you have an interest in a particular bike, a style of riding, or a regional interest, you'll find a resource on Carl's Mailing List Roundup. Micapeak also contains the Motorcycle Registry, a database of over 21,000 entries that document the features, drawbacks and modifications for dozens and dozens of motorcycles. Likewise, the Motorcycle Yellow Pages refers to more than 3,000 motorcycle-related businesses around the world. It is maintained on a regular basis. I also like the section on checklists. You can use Micapeak's tool to create your own custom checklist for touring, camping, first-aid kits and more. You'll find all this and more at micapeak.com.

ROADSIDE AMERICA

I've included this site because I enjoy roadside attractions like the Mothman, the birthplace of Kool Aid, and the world's largest ball of anything. A few thousand excuses for a road trip are just a click away at roadsideamerica.com.

Some Favorite Books

BOOKS FOR RESEARCH

For a well-rounded perspective on motor-cycle touring, here are a few books I'd like to recommend for you to read.

Dig out your dome tent and rinse off your camp cookware. *Motorcycle Camping Made Easy* by Bob Woofter is a concise, practical guide to this perfect pairing of two great outdoor activities. Every time I crack open Bob's book I can almost smell the campfire and hear the laughter of riders gathered around. Is that my imagination or is someone cooking bacon?

Motorcycling Excellence, written by the Motorcycle Safety Foundation, is a great primer on the subject of riding a motorcycle the right way. I also like *Proficient Motorcycling,* by David Hough, as a follow-up on responsible, safe riding because Hough's lessons are delivered in a patient, even tone using simple but vivid descriptions of common situations and hazards we face.

Ron Ayres is a recognized long-distance rider and founder of Ayres Adventures. His book, *Going the Extra Mile* looks at touring from the perspective of riders who cover thousands of miles every time they set off on a tour. That may not be the style of riding you seek, but the long-distance riding community is like a real world R&D lab for the rest of us. Many of the lessons Ron shares in his book are applicable whether you're riding a thousand miles a day or a thousand miles total.

Chris Scott's *Adventure Motorcycling Handbook* began as a thirty page report he wrote in the early 1990's and has since morphed into an important reference work for any rider who contemplates the demanding sport of adventure touring. Even if you don't plan to venture around the world by yourself or would only consider touring with a group, this book will give you some great ideas for traveling beyond the borders of the U.S. And remember too that many of the tips and suggestions for world touring apply to touring in the States.

Any of the books in the *Motorcycle Journeys* series are great resources if you're looking for touring ideas. Several of the Journeys books focus on the U.S. but the series also covers important motorcycling destinations around the world including the biggest riding prize of them all, the European Alps. Closer to home you'll find installments that document the best riding in New England, the Appalachians and mid-Atlantic, the Pacific Northwest, the Rocky Mountains, California, Mexico, the Southwest, and Texas, with more coming all the time.

BOOKS FOR ENTERTAINMENT

I like stories of travel and adventure, risk and reward. Every motorcycle traveler has a few to share, but there are a few whose riding legacy stands above everyone else. Check out these books for chills, thrills, and spills.

The Pan American highway stretches for nearly 30,000 miles from Fairbanks, Alaska to Chile in South America. A fifty-four mile section near the center of the route remains uncompleted. Known as the Darien Gap, few have successfully navigated this difficult terrain on foot, much less by anything motorized. Ed Culberson defied the odds as he attempted to be the first motorcyclist to make successful passage from Panama to Colombia via the Darien. His book, *Obsessions Die Hard* is a thrilling read that documents the successes and failures of this uniquely determined rider.

Ever read the fantastical fictional travel narrative *Around the World in 80 Days* by Jules Verne? Robert Fulton's *One Man Caravan* once again proves that truth is stranger than fiction. Caravan documents Fulton's around the world trip, decided on a whim at a dinner party in England on the eve of Fulton's return to the U.S. Soon after departing London, Fulton began to realize the consequences of his decision. The details of the trip, made in 1932, are fascinating, but what's more striking are Fulton's accounts of the people he met along the way and the aid he received in his journey.

On completing *Jupiter's Travels* by Ted Simon, you'll feel like you've eavesdropped on four years of private counseling sessions. That's meant as a compliment to Ted whose frequent on-the-road introspections demonstrate how motorcycle touring changes the way we perceive our surroundings. After reading his book, you'll realize that motorcycle touring is about more than belt-notching every twisty road you can find.

A

accidents 166
Aerostich 44, 49
air cushion seat pad 110
alcohol consumption 167
Anti Monkey Butt Powder 40
audio headset 90
Autocom 94
Autoswitch 76
Ayres Adventures 25, 28
Ayres, Ron 33, 164, 172

B

back support 115
backpack 134
battery technologies 98
   lithium-ion (LI) 98
   nickel-cadmium (NiCad) 98
   nickel-metal hydride (NiMH) 98
beaded seat covers 106, 110
Beartooth Pass 23
bike protection 122
   kickstand plate 123
   light guards 123
   skid plates and assorted armor 124
   tipover guards 123
Bluetooth headsets 91
body armor 53
body management 163
Bohn's Bodyguard system 53
books, motorcycle adventure 23
boredom 33
breakdowns 161
briefs 39
budgeting worksheet 19
bulbs
   halogen 71–72
   halogen, handling 74
   packaging 72
   technology 72
bungee cord 137
bungee net 136

C

camcorders 100, 103
cameras 100
   digital 101
   film 100
   lipstick 104
   mounting 102
   resolution 102
camping 24
camping gear 155
canalphones 92
Capilene fabric 54
caps 45
CB radio 89, 95–96

cell phones 89, 94
Channel 19 95
clothing, special purpose 154
Code, Keith 34
color (of light) 71
color temperature 71
comfort accessories 106
communication accessories 88
CompactFlash 101, 103
compression sack 135
conspicuity 70
cooling gear 44
cooling vests 45
Coolmax fabric 40, 54
Cordura fabric 54
cotton 39, 54
Culberson, Ed 172

D

damping 120
   compression 121
   rebound 122
Darien Gap 172
Davis, Neal 29
DeLorme state maps 80
DeLorme street atlas 20
device mounts 61
Digital8 103
documentation requirements 152
Draggin' Jeans 51
dry bags 135
duffel-style bags 134

E

ear protection 47
electric gear 43
electrical operating load
   calculating 63
electrical power available
   chart of, for various motorcycles 62
   determining 63
electrical tools and spares 154
electrically-heated clothing 44
E-mail discussion lists 23
endurance riding 33, 125
entertainment accessories 88
essential gear 48
Ex Officio (apparel) 42

F

fabric care 43
fairing configurations 113
fairings 113
Family Radio Service (FRS) 89, 96–97
floorboards 115
fluid management 164
fog lights 75
food 167

footpegs 115
forest roads 22
fork bags 135
Frazier, Gregory 29
fuel cells 124
full- vs. half-duplex 95
Fulton Jr., Robert 29, 172
fuse block 65
   adding 67
fuses 66

G

gel pads 110
General Mobile Radio Service (GMRS) 98
Gerbing, Gordon 44
gloves 51
Google 20, 23, 170
GoreTex 49, 54
GoreTex fabric 54
GPS 80–81, 83–84, 86, 89
   how it works 81
   types 82
GPS mounts 62
grips and weights 112
gross vehicle weight rating (GVWR) 136
ground loop isolation 90

H

handlebar improvements 111
handlebar risers 111
headlight modulators 78
Heat Troller 44
heated grips 112
helmets 46
   flip-up full-face 47
   full-face 47
   half 46
   three-quarter 47
HID lighting 72–73, 76
High Intensity Discharge (HID) systems 71
highway pegs 114
Horizons Unlimited 29, 171
Hough, David 172
hyperthermia 164
hypothermia 164

I

intercom, bike-to-bike 89
intercom, rider-passenger 95
International Brotherhood of Motorcycle
   Campers (IBMC) 25
international touring 27
internet 170
Interstate highways 22
iPod 88
Iron Butt Association 32, 35

J

jacket, fleece 38
jackets 50
   Cordura 50
   leather 50
jeans, denim 42
Joe Rocket 51
Johnson, Grant and Susan 29

K

Kevlar fabric 54
Kevlar inserts 51

L

L.L. Bean 42
layers of gear 39
Leather 54
Lee Parks' Total Control 33
Lewis, H. Marc 171
LIDAR systems 86
Lifa branded fabric 54
light-emitting diodes (LEDs) 72
lighting 70
   auxiliary 75
   modifications 70
   upgrades 73
lights, driving 75
lights, incandescent 71
living will 151
low-density foam pads 110
luggage 155
luggage systems 126–127, 129
luggage, integrated 127
luggage, soft 130, 134
luminance 71
Lycra fabric 40

M

map pouch 135
mapping software 23
mechanical tools 154
media formats for video 103
mental attitude 33
mental preparation 32
Micapeak 171
MicroMV 103
Mini DVD-R 103
miniDV 103
moteling 25
Motorcycle Safety Foundation 170, 172
MP3 player 89, 91, 93, 99

N

night riding 163
Nikwax Tech Wash 49
Nikwax TX-Direct 49
noise reduction 97
nutrition 36

O

Otter Boxes 136
Outlast 52
Outlast fabric 54

P

paint protection plastics 137
panniers
   aluminum 128
   tank 134–135
pants 42
paperwork kit 154
Parks, Lee 34
passengers 27
Paukstis, Carl 171
Pelican cases 136
physical performance 37
physical preparation 36
PIAA lighting products 76
planning 16
   budget 18
   how long? 17
   road types 22
   time of year 23
   where to? 16
Polartec fabric 54
polyester 39–40
Polyester fabric 54
Polypropylene fabric 54
pop-up campers 142
Posi-Lock connectors 66
power consumption
   table of, for various devices 63
power outlets 65
   cigarette lighter 65
   Powerlet 65
   SAE 65
Pratt, Allan 32
preload adjustment 122
prepay your bills 155
pre-ride checklist 157
pre-ride inspections 169
pre-treating your gear 155
Pridmore, Reg 34
proper dress 36

R

rack bags 134
radar 89
radar detectors 86
radial vs. bias tires 117
rain suits 53
RAM Aqua Box 94
RAM mounts 61, 103
Ratay, Chris and Erin 8
really-nice-to-have-gear 48
REI 42

relays 77
removable hard luggage 128
ReviveX 49
rider training 33
riding
   boots 52
   gear 38
   pants 51
   shorts 40
   suits 49
riding range 34–35
road fatigue 165
road service 152
roads
   interstate 22
   state primary 22
   state secondary 22
Roadside Amercia 171
Roberg, Jeff and Anne 25

S

saddlebag liners 136–137
saddlebags 131, 137
saddles, custom 108
Salvadori, Clement 29
satellite radio 88, 92
satellite tracking 85
Scotchguard 49
Scott, Chris 158, 172
SD-RAM 103
seat bags 134
seat pads 109
seat upgrades 109
seating
   chafing 108
   improved 36
   moisture management 108
   pressure points 108
Secure Digital (SD) 101
security 160
service on the road 153
sheepskin pads 110
ShelTex fabric 49
sickness 168
sidecar 140
Simon, Ted 158, 172
Smartphone 94
Smartwool 54
socks 41
soldering and crimping techniques 67
solo or group ride 26
spring compression and rebound 120
staying in touch 166
sunscreen 168
suspension 120
   adjustment 122

T

tailbags 131, 134
tankbags 132–133
tapes
   reflective 79
   retroreflective 79
tee shirts 40
temperature management 36
tethering 62
textile "air" jacket 51
thermal extenders 39, 43
Thinsulate fabric 54
Thomson, Andy 40
throttle accessories 111
Tilley Endurables Quick Dry 40
tire repair kit 152
tires 116
   compounds 117
   pressure 118
   profiles 118
   reading condition of 120
   tools 154

toolkit 155
towing 146
trailers 138
   cargo 139
   cargo box 141
   distributing weight 144
   hitches 143
   leaf suspension 139
   loading 144
   purchasing used 145
   suspension 139
   tent 139
   torsion suspension 140
travel health insurance 153
travelogues 23

U

US highways 22

V

vaccinations 153
vitamins 168
voltage monitor 64

W

waterproofing
   restoring 49
weather 158
weather radio 88
webBikeWorld 171
wicking 41
Widder, George 44
Wide Area Augmentation System (WAAS) 84
windscreen positioning 113
windscreens 113
windshield bags 135
wire gauge 65
wiring tips 65
Woofter, Bob 25, 172
wraps 45
wrist warmers 41

X

XM Radio 93

About the Author

Dale Coyner is the owner of Open Road Outfitters (openroadoutfitters.com), a motorcycle accessory shop in Sterling, Virginia that specializes in the sale and installation of motorcycle trailers, lighting, and electronics. His first book, *Motorcycle Journeys Through the Appalachians*, remains a popular guide for motorcyclists planning trips through the mid-Atlantic.

In 2006, Dale was appointed to the Governor's Motorcycle Advisory Council for the Commonwealth of Virginia to promote motorcycle tourism, safety, and economic development. Dale speaks frequently at rallies and motorcycle club meetings on motorcycle travel, technical topics, and his writing. For more information about his workshops and schedule, or to sign up for his newsletter, visit Dale on the web at dalecoyner.com.

Author Dale Coyner ponders his next photo opportunity along the Blue Ridge Turnpike near home.